Peak
Performance

Peak Performance

Aligning the Hearts and Minds of Your Employees

Jon R. Katzenbach

HARVARD BUSINESS SCHOOL PRESS
Boston, Massachusetts

Library of Congress Cataloging-in-Publication Data

Katzenbach, Jon R., 1932–
    Peak performance : aligning the hearts and minds of your employees /
Jon R. Katzenbach.
        p. cm.
    Includes bibliographical references and index.
    ISBN 0-87584-936-9 (alk. paper)
    1. Employee motivation. 2. Personnel management. I. Title.

HF5549.5.M63 K375 2000
658.3'14—dc21

                                                                99-048878

To my late parents,
Raymond Lowell and Della Bischoff Katzenbach,
who gave me a deep appreciation for honest emotions.

Contents

Preface

We have all been in situations in which our emotions take over—and we simply get "fired up." The adrenaline rushes through our system, and we find the unexpected energy to accomplish the task at hand. Sometimes, of course, emotion can have the opposite effect by paralyzing action (fear) or diverting attention from critical tasks (confusion). In either case, there is little question that our emotions can have powerful effects on our performance.

Emotions can surge through groups of people as well as within individuals, of course. And some well-known institutions—like Marriott International, The Home Depot, Hewlett-Packard, Southwest Airlines, and the U.S. Marine Corps—uniquely and consistently fire up the positive emotions within their workforces and channel the extra energy to higher levels of performance than their competition can. I have long been fascinated by how such organizations capitalize on emotional energy. Since an explanation has never been intuitively obvious to me, I set out on the research that led to this book.

The central topic of this book—energized workforces that deliver higher (peak) performance—can be defined as any group of employees whose emotional commitment enables them to make or deliver products or services that constitute a sustainable competitive advantage for their employer. By *peak performance* we mean better than the norm, better than expected, better than the competition, and better than similar workforces in other places. Such higher-performance groups are usually at or near the front lines of the organization, where they have either important interactions with customers or a direct influence on products and services.

An initial list of companies whose workforce appears to meet this definition was not hard to develop. Many are well-known (often well-researched), highly desired places to work, and their employee programs are widely publicized. To break the list into groups, however, can be a bit confusing, since no two companies seem to achieve higher performance from the key segments of their workforce in the same way. It was this anomaly that led us to the research effort behind this book.

THE RESEARCH EFFORT

Initially, we assumed that digging more deeply into several of these well-known situations would disclose a previously undiscovered pattern that would help any enterprise generate more emotional energy from its people and convert it into higher enterprise performance. We further assumed that the answer would be fairly straightforward—possibly reinforcing a few of the basic principles of good people management and indicating better ways to apply them. Against that assumption, we developed a case methodology based on gaining an in-depth perspective from three different levels of each enterprise (top, middle, and front line). Our methodology proved successful, even though our up-front assumptions did not.

What We Did

Our definition of a fired-up, higher-performing workforce meant we would have to gain in-depth access at several levels of each enterprise. Not only is it difficult to create such a workforce, but identifying, accessing, and evaluating these companies is an equal challenge. We started with an initial list of enterprises whose performance records and reputations establish them as leaders in their field and that strongly believe their competitive advantage is based on a peak-performance workforce. We chose companies that not only espouse such beliefs in their leadership vision and strategy statements, but that also invest heavily in, as well as pay a lot of obvious attention to, those employee segments that differentiate them from the competition. Early on, we probed the available information on the "usual suspects," namely, the companies widely known and well researched for having superior people systems (e.g.,

Hewlett-Packard, Marriott, Southwest Airlines, Toyota, 3M, and The Home Depot).

Although this perusal provided some important clues on how each of these proven performers energize their workers, it still could not readily explain why each workforce situation appeared so different from the others. We also tried, therefore, to go well beyond the usual suspects and seek out companies whose approaches are less well documented in either the public press or other research work. To that end, the research team explored several relatively unknown situations that included enterprises from different industry sectors (i.e., technology, customer service, financial, and industrial), as well as institutions from the public sector. In this respect, we tended to "follow our noses," upon the recommendations of colleagues, clients, and other knowledgeable sources. While our final case sample is neither comprehensive nor representative, we believe it to be credible. It consists of over twenty-five enterprises, most of which have proven their competitive performance superiority (either financially or in the marketplace) over several years. The leaders of these enterprises are convinced that their workforce explains that performance, and case analyses provide reasonable confirming evidence of that claim.

In each case, we applied the criteria implicit in our definition of higher performance, both in selecting the company and the participating employee groups and in evaluating the results of our case study. Sometimes, we looked at the entire enterprise; other times, we sought out the specific parts of the enterprise where a peak-performance workforce was most evident. For all cases, however, we developed information from and about the front line. We also studied middle and upper management levels. Our focus was always on workforce performance, however, not overall company performance.

Probing into three levels of the organization enabled us to triangulate on the probable causes with more certainty. What top management viewed as the primary determinants of workforce performance were not always reflected in the views of middle managers. The information obtained directly from the frontline people was usually the most revealing. Since the interviews covered dozens of people across all three levels of the organization, the research team developed a reasonably thorough picture in each case.

Unfortunately, we could not always differentiate the data on workforce performance clearly from the data on overall enterprise performance, particularly where selected segments of the workforce were the focal point. Hence, we concentrated on enterprises whose success clearly pointed to peak performance by its workforce. Our research includes twenty companies that allowed us to conduct an in-depth case study plus a few other companies for which adequate information was already available from other research and/or client experience to make credible comparisons. Each case study required several days of intensive interviews, surveys, and focus-group discussions. Several hundred people were involved in these interviews, surveys, and discussions across all of the cases, and additional survey data was developed whenever relevant and possible. The insights and conclusions in this book, however, come much more from our direct observations, interviews, and dialogues than from any definitive data analyses. Table A-1 of the appendix lists all the participants and highlights their workforce situation.

We regret that we could not fit descriptions of all the case studies into this book, since each was a rich learning experience for us. In the interest of avoiding reader fatigue, we tried to select those cases that provided the best illustrations of the different paths. As a result, some excellent cases had to be omitted.

WHAT THE BOOK IS ABOUT

This book probes and compares the experiences of many institutions that achieve a significantly "higher" (as defined earlier) level of workforce performance. *Workforce* refers to all employees across the baseline of the organization who either make the products, design the services, or deliver the value to customers. The term does not include upper levels of management or the indirect support people who constitute the rest of the organization.

The diversity among the participating enterprises was much more significant than the similarities. In fact, we undertook the research effort to determine what energizes people in very disparate workforce situations. Despite fairly dramatic differences in business priorities, marketplace dynamics, and leadership philosophies, five distinct patterns, or balanced paths, consistently emerged. The book explores each of these different paths, identifies and clarifies its characteristics, and provides new insights and frameworks for others who wish to significantly improve the performance of their workforce.

Acknowledgments

The writing of a book—particularly one that involves extensive original research—is a story in itself. A great many people contribute in countless ways. The research for this book has extended over three years and required substantial commitments of time from sponsors, participants, researchers, and editors alike. Any effort to name them all results in a lengthy list—and one that I fear would be both incomplete and confusing to the reader. Instead, I have chosen to highlight several very special individuals within five primary categories of contributors.

Two remarkable organizations sponsored the research: McKinsey & Company, Inc., and The Conference Board, and I am indebted to their respective leaders, Rajat Gupta and Richard E. Cavanagh, for their patient support throughout this lengthy project. Without that support, I would have been unable to develop the depth of information required for the case work. Not only would it have been difficult to access the twenty-plus high-performing enterprises that constitute my sample, but it would have been impossible to accomplish the endless hours of interviewing, focus groups, and survey work that each case entailed.

The research itself was led by Quentin Hope, my colleague and friend for many years. Quentin's wisdom, insight, and intelligence is exceeded only by his attention to detail, personal integrity, and dedication to quality work. He not only goes the extra mile to get it right, but is a pleasure to work with and provides a constant source of thought-provoking encouragement. He had the benefit (or perhaps the burden) of guiding a "rotating team" across the three-year effort. His initial team included Hemant Elhence and Anne McPherson from McKinsey and Gina Walter from The Conference Board. His succeeding teams included Robert Proctor, Miriam Herman, Steven Kelley, Catherine Forster, Rod Bourgeois, and Jason Santamaria from McKinsey. Of course, it is not enough to simply mention Jason's role, since his Marine background was a key to our understanding the Corps. Tracy Tefertiller deserves a special thanks for integrating across multiple teams and becoming our most articulate spokesperson among her colleagues. These team members were assisted throughout by the specialized contributions of professionals like Nancy Taubenslag, Gene Zelazny, and Paul Hasse. A very special thanks goes to Debbie Shortnacy, my right arm, who received the baton from Lisa Tignor midway into the effort and managed to handle the myriad of filing, follow-up work, references, manuscript preparations, and special tasks without missing a beat.

A few of my partners, past and present, deserve special mention for their willingness to plow through my early drafts, comment on my evolving hypotheses, and introduce me to high-performing enterprises. My current partners and colleagues, Marc Feigen, Niko Canner, and Alan Culler, not only served as invaluable sounding boards, but also encouraged me to take time that might otherwise have been focused on the start-up challenges of our new firm. The Texas practice of McKinsey was particularly helpful. The leader of that practice, John Bookout, had the patience, forbearance, and willingness to provide talented associates for the research. Bruce Roberson, Warren Strickland, and Jeff Hawn were particularly helpful in securing access to intriguing companies and offering perspectives and constructive critiques on my conclusions. And last but not least, a very special thanks goes to Larry Kanarek who, as leader of McKinsey's organization practice, sponsored and funded much of the initial research.

The editors constitute a separate category that includes the Harvard Business School Press, Sagalyn Literary Agency, and my wife, Linda (easily the most dedicated and persistent of the group). Marjorie Williams deserves special thanks for giving me a second chance and for guiding me to Nicola Sabin. Nikki proved to be a gem: wise, insightful, and a pleasure to work with. Rafe Sagalyn played a very special role in this effort when rational parties threatened to reach irrational conclusions. He is indeed a master of his craft.

The final note, however, must be reserved for the participating enterprises, and particularly the individuals within those enterprises who enabled us to probe beyond the normal limits to understand their magic. Many already occupy integral parts of the book for obvious reasons, but a few stand out. First mention goes to Brigadier General Keith Holcomb and Colonel Robert E. Lee of the United States Marine Corps and Rita Bailey of Southwest Airlines. These individuals not only steered me through the warp and woof of their remarkable institutions, but eventually took a chance on the highly improbable joint workshop between leaders of the two institutions that so vividly demonstrated the validity of our original premise: "You have to really care" about each and every employee.

Several others were also instrumental in this work: Tim Lupfer and Professor "Wick" Murray, who introduced us to the reality of the Marines; Colleen Barrett, who let me under the tent at SWA; Brad Bryan, who remembered our past work together well enough to let me reopen the Marriott mysteries; and Steve Messana, who took a chance with us at The Home Depot. Special kudos to Max Watson at BMC and Ray Gumpert at Texas Instruments, who provided our pilot cases. In addition, David Novak at KFC, John Mueller at 3M, Gil Marmol at Perot Systems, Dan Barr at First USA, Carolyn Annand and Joe Douglas at Hill's Pet Nutrition—each one a busy executive—saw value in our probe and took the time to provide critical access and perspective for our work. The list goes on, and I apologize to those who deserve equal credit here and whom I may have unfairly (and unintentionally) overlooked.

It has been a challenging, stimulating, and improbable journey—and I sincerely thank all those who made it possible.

I ✦ MAINTAINING THE CRITICAL BALANCE

Figure I-1 BALANCING THE COMPONENTS OF ENTERPRISE PERFORMANCE AND INDIVIDUAL FULFILLMENT

Enterprise performance requirements

- Shareholder return
- Market share
- Customer satisfaction
- Work output and improvement
- Core capability development

Individual fulfillment needs

- Source of livelihood
- Direction, structure, and control
- Identity, purpose, and self-worth
- Belonging and social interaction
- Opportunity

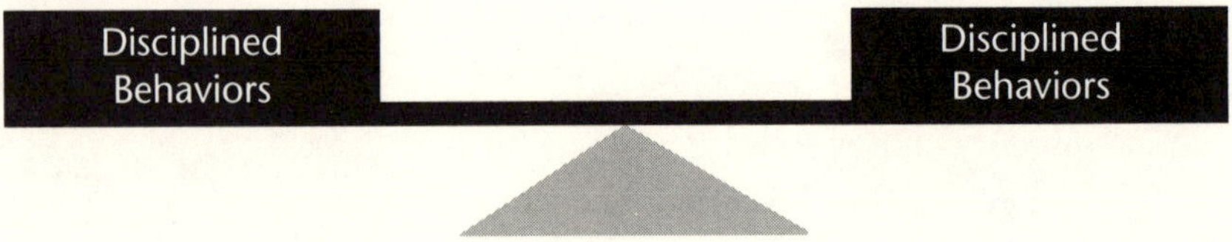

Disciplined Behaviors

Disciplined Behaviors

*N*ot *surprisingly, perhaps, the key to* the emotional commitment at the front line lies in maintaining a balance between enterprise performance and employee fulfillment. While you can certainly drive performance through intimidation, insecurity, and "good old consequence management," you cannot expect the extra energy that comes from positive emotional commitment unless employees really believe that the "gives and gets" in their work effort balance out.

The higher-performing workforces that we have explored do much more than simply pay lip service to worker fulfillment on the job. They consciously focus attention on it and are disciplined about making sure that critical segments of the workforce receive it.

The enterprises that have been successful in sustaining emotional commitment within critical segments of their workforce (usually at the front line) do not all follow the same path. There are important commonalties, of course: All believe strongly in the value of the individual worker, all strike the balance between fulfillment and performance, and all make clear choices and cultivate sets of disciplined behaviors (figure I-1). However, beyond those broad levels of abstraction, the options are many.

1 ✦ *The Power of Emotional Commitment*

In my first meeting with Steve Messana, senior vice president of Human Resources at The Home Depot, he captured the power of frontline commitment in the following simple statement:

> *We encourage all of our people to come up with their own ideas to capture the customer's attention, and to try them out—there's no need for approval here. Sure, we get some lousy ideas along the way that we would rather not have had, but that's the price we are willing to pay for the widespread individual initiative that makes this place unique.*

The Home Depot has been the leading home improvement retailer in North America for well over ten years. It continues to outpace the competition in growth, shareholder returns, and the emotional commitment of its people. Their remarkable commitment lies at the heart of the company's performance record—far more so than its strategy or unique business concept. You can talk with virtually any employee and sense his or her strong feelings about having a role in the enterprise and its success.

"JUST A MOM"

Consider Deb Burke, an associate with The Home Depot in its Woodstock store outside Atlanta, Georgia. Deb joined The Home Depot about four years ago as a "peak timer." On average, peak timers account for about one-fourth of the workforce and work less than full time, often on an unpredictable, as-needed schedule. Unlike most of The Home Depot's hires, Deb had virtually no relevant product or retail experience. Nor was she in search of extra money to help the family, since her husband runs a successful business. Deb was simply looking for interesting work outside the home. She was hired because of her positive attitude, obvious energy, and natural empathy with people, both potential customers and fellow employees.

She was assigned to Chris Fitzgerald, the assistant store manager for building products, who put her in the millwork department. Most millwork customers are construction-hardened tradesmen and carpenters—predominately macho males who think they know exactly what they want. At first Deb was terrified by the prospect of having to deal with these customers on a range of technical products with names that only a woodcutter could understand. Chris took her aside after the first day and said, "Look, the fact that you don't know anything is going to work in your favor. You can learn it right from the start. Trust me. Before long, you'll know more than anyone about millwork." He then took her through the pile of catalogs, pointing out where and how to find the answers.

For several weeks Deb found herself floundering around, doing her best to find answers for a group of customers who took great delight in confounding, if not embarrassing, her. More often than not, when under intense interrogation by a customer, Deb's last-resort response was "Look, I'm doing the best I can. *Damn it, I'm just a mom!*" That usually worked in several marvelous ways. First, since most customers had moms themselves, they went through a profound attitude change on the spot. They tried very hard to help her instead of embarrass her. Second, they were suddenly much more tolerant of her mistakes and of the time it took her to look things up. Third, they knew that although most moms don't know wood stuff, they probably know commonsense stuff. And most important, in Deb's mind at least, the customers could trust her as their very own mom surrogate. Both men and women found it hard not to trust a real-live, honest-to-goodness mom, particularly when she was so obviously trying to do her best in a difficult assignment.

By the time Deb left the department three years later (she was promoted to manager of another department), both she and Chris maintain that she probably did know more than anyone else—customer or manager—about the complicated world of millworking. Her achievement took a lot of hard work, however, under conditions of relentless pressure over many, many months. And remember, Deb didn't need or want the money. What motivated her, then, to work so hard, learn so much, and stay so long? What made her such an emotionally committed worker?

Deb's motivation stemmed from the same things that apparently motivate most of The Home Depot's associates. First, they savor the satisfaction of turning a frustrated customer into a happy one. As one associate put it, "The look on their face stays with you for days!" When asked how they would prove that they had a higher-performing workforce, Home Depot people often answer, "Look at the customer's faces when they leave here—you see lots more smiles than frowns." Second, the associates thrive on the challenge of a frantic work environment, where one never knows who, when, or what will be the source of the next challenge. They welcome the opportunity for individual achievement and personal growth. During busy periods, the place looks more like a circus than a retail warehouse store. There is never a shortage of challenges for the individual achiever. Third, the Home Depot associates become part of the honest-to-goodness in-store family of people with whom they share respect and support. Finally, they like the content of the work—hands-on problem solving that requires intricate product knowledge as well as superior customer relations capabilities. As a result, most associates can't wait to get to work, and almost hate to leave. One of Deb's colleagues said that she prefers working at the store on Saturday to working around the house at home. The place is truly fun—so much fun that Deb usually forgets to pick up her weekly paycheck until her husband, in mock desperation, blurts out, "So, did you get your check this week, or are you still working for fun?"

The Home Depot may be one of a kind in home improvement retailing, but it is not alone in depending on the emotional commitment of its front line. The performance record of KFC (Kentucky Fried Chicken), for example, is a bit more checkered than that of The Home Depot. When Colonel Harland Sanders and his wife founded Kentucky Fried Chicken in 1952, they launched a simple concept: a good family dinner that most people can afford. The idea quickly grew in the minds of thousands of franchisees, whose personal affection for the Colonel persists to this day. The early growth and performance record, however, was interrupted by a series of acquisitions by large enterprises that replaced the personal touch of the Colonel with consequence management at best—a tough management style focused primarily on financial measures and rewards.

As a result, the franchisees and frontline restaurant managers felt used and lost faith, and growth and stockholder performance suffered badly in the late 1980s. Recently, however, the company resuscitated its performance record by essentially resurrecting the Colonel into a culture that combines the personal touch of old with the consequence management principles of late. The powerful combination has clearly energized the hearts and minds of KFC's workforce and franchisees.

CONTAGIOUS EMOTIONAL ENERGY AT KFC

An Ohio River boat, the *Star of Louisville,* was the setting for my first direct encounter with the emotionally enthusiastic KFC people who represent the legacy of Colonel Sanders. Despite the size and conspicuously white facade of the boat, we had trouble finding it since it was anchored below a maze of connecting freeways and on/off ramps that converge along the emerging riverfront development of Louisville, Kentucky. As a result, we boarded just as the river cruise was getting under way. It was a beautiful evening, and both the KFC people and an unidentified wedding party that shared the boat ride were the beneficiaries of all the scenic beauty the Ohio River can offer. All evening long, the company's proceedings were punctuated with shouted slogans, Bronx cheers, inside jokes, and general hoopla. Later in the evening, a regional director of operations and recognition and the vice president of marketing made brief remarks—amid a lot of good-natured jibes from the audience. By the end of the cruise, everyone clearly had received a full measure of fun and enjoyment, as well as conspicuous recognition for his or her accomplishments. The cruise was much more than a normal sales award dinner, however. It was a floating circus—parades and all! Moreover, it was typical of many such events at KFC every month.

What explains this kind of emotional energy at KFC? Surely, the memory of a kindly Southern gentleman in a white suit is not the answer. Nor is it explained by a few simple rules and shibboleths that the Colonel promulgated—and that still characterize KFC's values. Nonetheless, KFC has recently turned itself around dramatically. Before 1994 the company had suffered five years of flat sales growth. From that point on, however, KFC enjoyed same-store sales increases of 7 to 9 percent while competitors continued to face declines.[1] At the heart of this turnaround has been KFC's blatant return to its roots to re-create what newly anointed CEO David Novak called a "restaurant-operating culture." The culture focuses on a few key measures, such as the "Colonel's Dozen," twelve rules for restaurant service. KFC leaders ensure disciplined attention to building a strong culture of recognition, celebration, frontline leadership, and semiserious internal competition. The company's current success is also firmly grounded in an integrated set of processes and metrics that not only complement the Colonel's Dozen, but also ensure both shareholder gain and marketplace performance. As Chuck Rawley, chief operating officer of KFC, puts it, "We're in the people business—we could probably sell anything—we just happen to sell chicken dinners. This is all about 'leveraging up' our forty thousand employees and the sixty thousand other people at the franchises."

The KFC approach, however, is very different from that of The Home Depot. Moreover, just as with The Home Depot, KFC's approach is not for everyone. A company has several options for obtaining an emotionally committed workforce.

IDENTIFYING HIGHER-PERFORMING WORKFORCES

The definition of higher-performing workforces—any significant group of employees whose emotional commitment enables them to make or deliver products or services that constitute a sustainable competitive advantage for their employer—implies the following criteria, which we used in selecting the organizations that we would study for this book:

+ A larger than normal proportion (i.e., more than one-third) of individual workers consistently exceed the expectations of their leaders and customers.

+ The average worker performs better than the average competitive worker—typically through a cohesive set of management systems, programs, and motivating/energizing mechanisms.

+ A strong emotional commitment to higher standards and aspirations is reflected all across the workforce and appears to create a multiplier beyond what rational systems and programs could explain.

✦ The collective performance of the entire workforce or of critical segments (typically at the front line) forms the core of the institution's competitive advantage and is extremely difficult to copy.

Unfortunately, these criteria are easier to observe and assess judgmentally than they are to measure in any quantitative or statistically provable way. Hence, we relied on a three-step approach to determine if the enterprise benefited from a peak-performance workforce. The first step was simply to track the performance of the enterprise over time, since it is difficult to meet our workforce criteria if the enterprise is not achieving superior results. The performance records of the sample are summarized in Table A-3 in the appendix. The second step was to conduct a series of in-depth interviews with executives and managers in each company to ascertain if and why they believed that the workforce was at the core of enterprise performance. The third step was to obtain as much evidence as possible (quantitative and qualitative) to confirm management's judgment. That is, we looked at whatever indicators of productivity, quality, turnover, and customer service comparisons were available. Highlights of this assessment are summarized in the appendix Table A-3. Often, we could not measure the workforce segments separately from the overall enterprise performance. Nonetheless, the research team probed until it was satisfied that the criteria for a higher-performing workforce were being met over time. In every case described in this book, our research team, as well as management at several levels, was convinced that the quantifiable aspects of enterprise performance directly resulted from a superior workforce effort grounded in the emotional commitment of individuals within critical segments of the workforce.

The peak-performance workforces that we explored are about performance from individuals themselves, rather than the process or technology with which they work. Such workforces involve both individual and collective performance and encompass much more than the efforts of "a few good men (and women)." Moreover, the most noticeable and compelling characteristics of these workers were their enthusiasm, energy, and emotional commitment to perform—which cannot be quantified. There is little doubt, however, that this extra energy at the front line explains the company's competitive advantage over time.

Although the previously listed criteria constitute a tough set of attributes to maintain, they also offer significant long-term rewards. At the highest levels of abstraction, enterprises that sustain higher-performing workforces have much in common. A company's distinctive focus and execution, however, more clearly explain its unique performance record than do its commonalties with other enterprises. In other words, examining the specific ingredients and how they are applied reveals no single "right" path for achieving and sustaining higher workforce performance. More than one way works.

Our criteria can apply to all employees or to particular segments. For example, at Southwest Airlines and The Home Depot the criteria apply to their entire workforce. In contrast, at Hambrecht & Quist the criteria apply primarily to its investment and distribution professionals—and BMC applies them to its sales account representatives and its "product authors" (software designers). In each case, however, the collective performance of these employee segments has largely determined the competitive success of the enterprise.

WHAT WE FOUND

Not surprisingly, when we looked at each institution, we found that each applies its own set of distinctive approaches, mechanisms, and tools—some entirely unique and some commonly held. The most compelling commonalities, however, were in the philosophical beliefs and practices shared by leaders at all levels, that is:

+ They believe strongly in each employee—and that the strategic value and performance potential of the workforce can determine the relative success or failure of the enterprise. This belief is focused primarily on frontline people rather than those in the managerial ranks.

+ They engage their employees emotionally as well as rationally. Enterprises that cultivate such workforces invariably go beyond rational motivation to engage and harness the emotions of employees. In fact, the employees' emotional energy is the most visible difference among the higher-performing workforces explored in this book. The energy is contagious across the enterprise and has a multiplier effect on collective performance.

✦ They pursue enterprise performance and worker fulfillment with equal rigor. They are extremely disciplined about maintaining a dynamic balance between the two over time. They insist on sets of disciplined behaviors in different places that create equal emphasis on fulfillment and performance. Moreover, the leaders maintain a balance wherein both factors are optimized—not a "zero-sum game," wherein one must be traded off against the other.

Beyond these three basic commonalties, however, many different approaches, mechanisms, events, and tools are applied to good advantage among the cases we explored. A handful of cohesive patterns or paths nevertheless consistently emerged across the cases, although some companies followed more than one path at a time. Each path was characterized by a consistently high level of workforce energy consciously channeled in ways that ensured a dynamic balance between enterprise performance and worker fulfillment.

WHY WORKFORCE BEHAVIOR MATTERS TO TOP MANAGEMENT

Unfortunately, far too few companies make any serious effort to generate emotional commitment within their workforces. Many do not believe the effort will be worthwhile, thinking instead that average workforce performance is the best one can hope for. Of those who acknowledge the potential value of using worker fulfillment to engage emotions for performance, most go about it haphazardly, usually because they do not know how. For these companies, consequence management may be the only approach that they understand.

The successful efforts at peak performance are based on a high level of commitment to fulfillment and performance. The various tools that companies use to reinforce that commitment are tightly integrated into a cohesive, synergistic approach that both generates and channels human energy.

Clearly, top management must be involved in developing an emotionally committed workforce for many reasons. First, a cohesive approach is essential, and cohesiveness demands executive leadership alignment (i.e., the actions and decisions of leaders reinforce one another's contributions to performance). Second, most of the best sources of emotional energy cannot be tapped without the efforts of executive leadership. Finally, balancing enterprise performance and worker fulfillment requires trade-offs that can only be made at executive leadership levels.

Once we realized that no single pattern for peak-performance workforces prevailed, we wondered if the explanation was always situational. The good news is that there are five patterns that work. Thus, by focusing on one or two patterns that best fit its own business, marketplace, culture, and leadership, a company can greatly improve both how top management invests its collective time and resources and the results it can expect. The bad news is that companies with only average levels of workforce performance cannot achieve higher levels without investing a great deal of time and effort—no matter what path or paths they choose to pursue.

THE CHALLENGE CAN APPEAR OVERWHELMING

Companies like Southwest Airlines (SWA) and The Home Depot energize their people in both dazzling and overwhelming ways. For example, in their highly revealing book, *Nuts!,* Kevin and Jackie Freiberg outline a seemingly unending list of what makes SWA's energizing machine work so well.[2] They include thirteen core values, eleven philosophical attitudes, and ten "values in action." Most chapters end with a "Success in a Nutshell" summary list, all of which adds up to literally hundreds of action items important to the company's success. Similarly, the U.S. Marine Corps prides itself on its abbreviated briefing pamphlets for promulgating its rules of engagement. Even the short forms, however, constitute an intimidating inventory of what the Marines consider important.

Action lists like these can be useful reminders of what it takes to achieve peak performance within large complements of people. Unfortunately, however, they are not lists that the rest of us can hope to apply—largely because we do not start from the same place. Few of us have had to fight for survival against unfriendly regulatory agencies and killer competitors as SWA had to. Nor can we resurrect the Colonel's legacy to motivate and build commitment as KFC did. And obviously, we do not face the threat of war to help us focus our hearts, minds, and souls as the Marines must. It would be folly for most institutions (whether military or business) to try to emulate SWA's hundreds of actions—or the Marines' years of tradition and valor. Instead, institutions with different cultural and business base points must decide which insights and ingredients of the winning combinations offer the best learning opportunity for themselves.

GOOD PEOPLE MANAGEMENT FALLS SHORT

Lacking such insights, most companies simply fall back on the more abstract and widely accepted principles of good people management. All good managers believe in treating people fairly, providing them with incentives to perform and opportunities to grow, and rewarding their performance with recognition as well as advancement. Good leaders also seek to recruit the best talent they can find and practice the doctrines of consequence management and individual accountability. These principles are hard to argue against, but seldom do they differentiate the higher-performing workforce from the average or normal workforce. This does not make the principles less valid, since they underlie the elements that do determine higher-performing workforces. The peak-performance quotient, however, invariably goes beyond these commonly accepted principles and engages the emotional commitment of the worker. To secure this commitment from its workers, a company must pay disciplined, consistent attention to worker fulfillment.

Moreover, the principles of good people management are so widely applied in both successful and unsuccessful workforce performance efforts that the list of good things to do has become virtually endless. Companies that try to give equal emphasis to all aspects of good people management invariably overload their system. Why, then, do the efforts of companies like SWA, KFC, and The Home Depot appear to emphasize so many elements, actions, and mechanisms? How can all these devices be integral to their success with their workers? The answer lies in the time frame.

Over time, the priorities and concentration of these companies have shifted. They have placed their primary emphasis on the few key elements that fit their circumstances during particular periods in their history. For example, SWA's legacy is much more important as a source of employee energy today than it was during the start-up period, when threats to survival dominated the scene. Sometimes this shift in company priorities occurs along a single path, and sometimes it cultivates a second, complementary path. In addition, some complementary activities just spring up in the same garden, as it were, to work in conjunction with the more formally cultivated key ingredients.

WHAT CAN BE LEARNED FROM THIS BOOK

This book is concerned with energizing people for performance and the different successful paths to that end. It describes how each path concentrates management attention on worker fulfillment to harness the emotions of many people in sustaining a higher-performing workforce. This is a different challenge than simply motivating people to meet demanding financial performance objectives. The latter is what most companies do, and it implies setting unambiguous goals, establishing clear measures, and holding people individually accountable for results (consequence management). Logical, rational motivation is certainly a good thing, but it is no match for engaged, emotional commitment. Just ask anyone who watched the New York Yankees in the 1998 playoff series games, which culminated in a World Series victory and the highest number (125) of games won in a single year by any major league team in baseball history.

Energizing people for performance elevates the game significantly, to the point that many employees go well beyond leaders' expectations, individual accountabilities, financial results, and short-term market objectives. This book describes how to unleash the full individual and collective potential of people—at the front line and across the broad middle—to achieve and sustain higher levels of performance than the workers themselves thought possible, than management or customers expected, and than competitors can realistically achieve.

Unleashing the full potential of people is undeniably a tall order; few institutions have managed to do it consistently. This book explores the approaches of those who apparently have gone far beyond any conventional notions of managing solely to meet ambitious financial objectives. It looks at how such institutions tap into worker fulfillment to develop the extra quotient of emotional commitment that deeply energizes many people to perform well beyond conventional norms.

Each successful institution we have explored pursues peak workforce performance within an integrated organization approach or path that generates widespread emotional energy and is disciplined about how that energy is channeled to yield higher performance. The energy sources and channels of alignment are supported by mechanisms that simultaneously impact performance and fulfillment.

FIVE PATHS THAT WORK

Five paths explain all the higher-performing workforce situations that we explored in depth. They are labeled "balanced paths" to reflect the critical importance of sustaining a dynamic balance between worker/enterprise performance and worker fulfillment (i.e., wherein both the company and its employees benefit by achieving distinctiveness along their chosen paths). This balance means the enterprise pursues simultaneous improvements along both dimensions; it does not trade off one against the other.

Each path constitutes a clearly different approach for energizing a workforce for higher performance. Certainly, there are overlaps and similarities among the paths, but the primary focus and value proposition of each is quite distinct:

1. Mission, Values, and Pride

2. Process and Metrics

3. Entrepreneurial Spirit

4. Individual Achievement

5. Recognition and Celebration

These labels convey the primary focus of each path as indicated by the case research. The paths were not among our initial hypotheses; nor did we select the case examples to highlight any path. Furthermore, the companies did not consciously create or decide on these paths. They emerged as dedicated leaders pursued a balanced performance/fulfillment result. We simply discovered the paths as we dissected each case to understand what was energizing the workers. As we explored further, five recurring patterns emerged in the sources of emotional energy and how that energy was channeled into peak performance. Hence, the five patterns, or balanced paths, have become the overarching concept or framework for this book.

Clearly the most noticeable difference between the higher-performing workforce and a normal workforce is in the level of energy and emotional commitment that employees exhibit. Even the casual observer can feel the difference when walking through the halls. People move faster, interact with more visible animation, communicate with more palpable emotion and excitement, listen more intently, and respond more vigorously—and really enjoy themselves in the process. They pay little attention to the clock, with most arriving early and leaving late. When they are not on the job, they are probably thinking about improving the job. Moreover, this energy seems to persist throughout the day—day after day—in various parts of the organization. Some call it fun; others describe it as challenging and stimulating. To outside observers, it can appear exhausting as well.

What generates all this energy? Obviously, it must ultimately come from within the people themselves, when something occurs that engages their emotions. A few people, of course, can turn themselves on, so to speak. But within any large group of employees, most will need some kind of outside stimulation, usually on a regular or recurring basis. It can be provided by a leader, one able to reach outside himself or herself and draw upon something other than personal charisma or influence. Emotional energy can be generated by the dynamics of a marketplace, that is, growth, customers, or competitors. It can also come from a history or legacy of remarkable accomplishments, heroes, or martyrs. Whatever the generating source of energy, the leadership system must make a consistent effort to tap into it regularly.

Not all of the more obvious sources of extra energy for an enterprise are available to every aspirant to a higher-performing workforce. To be successful, however, a company needs to use more than one source over time. The examples in part II illustrate how important it can be for a company to have more than one source and a consistent and systematic way of keeping those sources burning brightly in the employees' eyes.

Unfortunately, a surge of extra energy can be a bit like a torrential downpour that causes rivers to overflow and run amok. Unless the energy is channeled properly, it can create confusion, do a lot of damage, and divert the organization from its purpose and goals. Enterprises that would sustain a higher-performing workforce by generating extra energy cannot afford to leave the alignment of that energy to chance. By alignment, we mean individual decisions and actions that *reinforce* one another in boosting enterprise performance. Nor can they count on shibboleths like empowerment, shared values, and individual freedom to keep things on target. Instead, the companies we studied are very disciplined about maintaining certain channels of alignment supported by a wide variety of mechanisms to ensure both enterprise performance and worker fulfillment.

These mechanisms can be categorized within several alignment approaches. Moreover, it is imperative to make such a choice. In other words, an enterprise wisely picks only a few approaches, which it expects to execute with distinction. This focused distinction within a few approaches differentiates the peak-performance workforce. Different enterprises choose to emphasize different channels and sometimes vary that emphasis over time. Unfortunately, many companies today are trying to pay equal attention to far too many alignment approaches. It takes remarkable discipline—both applied by the enterprise and self-imposed by the workers—for an organization to be truly distinctive in a few approaches. Those few must also strike a dynamic balance between enterprise performance and worker fulfillment.

Certainly, engaging the emotions of employees can stimulate higher performance from them. Moreover, many factors—not all of them positive—can stir the emotions of a workforce. Nonetheless, our research indicates that three basic lines of inquiry offer richer learning opportunities for the reader:

1. What are the five patterns or cohesive paths that lead to an emotionally committed, higher-performing workforce? What do they have in common, how do they differ, and what conditions favor following one path over the others?

2. Why do the more than twenty top-performing institutions, carefully selected and studied in depth, follow different paths, and how do they generate and channel the emotional energy that their choices require?

3. How can a company use this framework to decide on the right path(s) to pursue; the sources of energy to tap; and the approaches, mechanisms, and tools to channel that energy to higher levels of performance?

Above all, we hope the reader who sees the potential in an emotionally committed workforce will become as convinced as we are about the importance of being purposeful and disciplined in selecting and following one or two of these paths.

SHAPING A BALANCED CONSTRUCT

The primary purpose of this book is to help leaders shape their own balanced configuration or path. In each enterprise that we studied, we found a few critical sources of energy and a few alignment approaches to be instrumental in creating a balanced, distinctive construct, which sometimes integrates two paths. Though each company pays some attention to most of the approaches, each also concentrates on and integrates a few defining ones.

As previously mentioned, the more surprising discovery was that five paths (or combinations of energy sources and alignment approaches) seemed to explain all the cases that we explored. These unique configurations are all characterized by disciplined and distinctive execution of a few key alignment approaches and draw on more than one unique source of energy. Whatever path they take, companies with peak-performance workforces enjoy a common feature: a dynamic balance between worker fulfillment and company performance over time.

2 ✦ Introducing the Balanced Paths

The Olympic games capture the attention of people world-wide. Athletes from almost every country in the world aspire to compete in this one-of-a-kind athletic extravaganza. The participants vary from the natural athlete to the highly specialized competitor. Some figure skaters, for example, choose to compete in the demanding short and long programs of the mandatory figures; others choose the highly specialized art forms of pair skating and ice dancing. The track and field competitors vary from long jumpers to pentathlon and decathlon specialists.

Few Olympians, however, can expect to win a gold medal in multiple events that do not share some common athletic thread. We don't see boxers competing in the pole vault, sprinters competing in the weight lifting, or even gymnasts competing in the high dive. Potential champions pick their events carefully. The events they choose must fit their intrinsic physical capabilities, their mental attitude and philosophy, and their training commitment.

Moreover, the path they must follow to win an Olympic medal varies depending on the event. Prospective medal winners work long and hard within a training regimen that fits their aspirations as well as their physical and mental condition. Of course, the basic fundamentals of physical fitness, mental concentration, and emotional conditioning are required in virtually all events. But well-conditioned, natural athletes will not win an Olympic medal unless they design and pursue a preparation path tailored to their category of events. And although every athlete will pre-pare in his or her own way, the winners tend to follow one or more of several proven preparation patterns.

So it is with creating a higher-performing workforce. Certainly, the path or paths any institution chooses must fit its business performance priorities, its marketplace circumstances, and its workforce fulfillment needs, as well as the unchangeable aspects of its culture and values. Some institutions that we have studied in depth concentrate primarily on a single path, but many appear to follow a natural combination of two paths. The combination gives them added balance and flexibility to deal with change. All these enterprises, however, are deeply committed to excel along their chosen paths.

THE BALANCED-PATH CONCEPT

The determination to strike a balance between enterprise performance and worker fulfillment is fundamental to each of the five paths. Al-though every company employs a different combination of managerial levers and approaches to sustain that balance, each combination consti-tutes a path (or culture) that leads to an emotionally engaged workforce whose members consistently deliver higher performance (i.e., value to customers and investors) than its competition does. It is hardly surpris-ing that more than one pattern works. The five have been labeled *bal-anced paths* to emphasize the underlying importance of balancing worker fulfillment with enterprise performance.

Although enterprise performance (i.e., shareholder gain and cus-tomer value) is reasonably well understood, worker fulfillment deserves some elaboration. It is based on underlying human needs, first articu-lated by Abraham Maslow.[1] The needs start with survival and proceed through belonging and self-esteem (table 2-1). The relative importance of the basic fulfillment needs will often vary by workforce segment and, in particular, by level in the organization. For example, the basic needs for a job and a reasonable amount of structure and control are usually more important at the lower or entry levels (or within segments of unskilled workers). Conversely, the needs for personal growth and opportunity become more important at higher levels. Although each company develops its own approach, every enterprise with a higher-performing workforce applies some fairly obvious fundamentals.

Table 2-1   GENERIC FULFILLMENT NEEDS

Basic Subsistence (a job)	Structure and Control	Identity and Purpose	Belonging	Opportunity
Work for a paycheck	Control your own destiny	Stand out from a talented crowd	Be part of a respected group	Learn and grow as a person
Work in a safe environment	Know what is expected	See value in your work	Feel a part of something special	Be challenged
Feel secure in your job	Know *why* things happen	Take pride in your skills and abilities	Feel like an owner	Try something new and different
	Know what may change and what will hold constant	Do good for others	Enjoy the camaraderie of co-workers	See personal progress
	Feel competent to do what is expected	Receive the respect of others	Feel like you fit	Know that opportunities are waiting
		Receive fair recognition	Trust those you work with	Have a positive self-image
	Control your immediate work environment	Receive fair reward (pay and other)		

Shading denotes needs that are notable in higher performing workforces.

What is most important, each of these enterprises has a straightforward workforce value proposition that makes clear what "gives and gets" employees can expect. Although the value proposition is unique for each company, those following a particular path reflect a similar value proposition that goes well beyond monetary awards and sometimes varies with particular segments of the employee population. In each successful case, individual workers have little doubt about what is expected of them, as well as what they can expect in return, and they ultimately find that the trade-offs are worthwhile. The execution of this value proposition results in feelings of worker fulfillment that significantly enhance worker performance. The credibility of this value proposition in the workers' minds is what sustains their long-term emotional commitment.

Beyond their determination to sustain this balance, however, the companies in our research diverge markedly from one another in the balanced paths they followed. Each path can lead top management to a focused, integrated set of values and actions that generate emotional commitment within critical segments of the workforce—provided, of course, that the leaders at several levels believe such commitment to be a core element of the company's competitive advantage. The balanced-path concept can help top management think about its options. Following a balanced path, management can choose where the enterprise should concentrate to become truly distinctive in the worker's eyes, aligning the hearts and minds of employees to produce a peak-performance workforce over time.

As we explained in chapter 1, we did not start out with this five-path concept in mind. In the beginning, we were searching for the common threads that would lead to a single pervasive pattern or to a common set of best practices that could be tailored to fit specific conditions. Although we could have described such an overarching pattern, we found it too abstract to be of much value in understanding key institutional differences and how to deal with them.

LIMITATIONS OF THE CONCEPT

Despite the usefulness of the balanced-path concept, its application has some obvious limitations. As mentioned earlier, many companies that have achieved a truly higher-performing workforce appear to be pursuing more than one path at a time. One path tends to be the "dominant eye" that focuses their efforts at any given point. But several enterprises pursue a second path that they master as well—and that complements their dominant path. Southwest Airlines, to cite the extreme example, which had its roots in entrepreneurial survival, now pursues three other paths with exceptional proficiency (i.e., Mission, Values, and Pride; Individual Achievement; and Recognition and Celebration). Nonetheless, a single path pursued with rigor and discipline can deliver emotional commitment and peak performance in the workforce. We will illustrate this point in part II with case descriptions of BMC Software, Inc.; Hambrecht & Quist; and the U.S. Marine Corps.

Although each path is distinctive in its own right, the five are neither mutually independent nor comprehensively inclusive. The concept of five paths is a useful framework, but not a perfect one. Because of unavoidable overlaps and duplications among the primary paths, the framework is not free of ambiguity. Moreover, companies following the same paths may generate the emotional energy from somewhat different sources and employ different approaches for channeling that energy to achieve a dynamic balance between worker fulfillment and enterprise performance.

Each of the five paths presents difficult balance challenges over time. They all demand unusual clarity of focus and concentrated effort by leaders at all levels. Otherwise, the critical balance between enterprise performance and worker fulfillment cannot be achieved or maintained. When imbalance occurs, the consequences can be disturbing; those who stray from their chosen path often have trouble finding their way back. The critical factor in sustaining the emotional commitment of the workforce, of course, is not the path(s) you follow, but the balancing of enterprise performance with worker fulfillment—whatever that takes. Table 2-2 presents a composite summary of the paths, comparing them in four dimensions: conditions that favor each path, likely sources of energy, alignment approaches frequently applied, and notable examples.

This chapter will provide an overview of the five paths, which will be illustrated with case studies in more detail in part II of the book. The following sections describe each path in four parts: (1) the basic beliefs or workforce value propositions that guide how top management will

Table 2-2 COMPOSITE SUMMARY OF THE FIVE PATHS

Balanced Path	Conditions That Favor a Particular Path	Most Likely Sources of Energy
Mission, Values, and Pride	• Rich history employees are proud of • Noble purpose in the eyes of employees • Value-driven leadership • Ample team opportunities	• Magnetic leaders • Compelling legacy • Impossible dreams
Process and Metrics	• High value in behavioral consistency • Clear measures for business priorities • Maturing marketplace conditions • Priority on continuous improvement • Accessible and credible database	• Unrelenting customers • Dynamic marketplace
Entrepreneurial Spirit	• Plentiful high-risk, high-reward opportunities • Significant employee "ownership" potential • Rapidly growing, dynamic marketplace • High value in individual initiative and risk taking • Hands-off leadership philosophy	• Magnetic leaders • Impossible dreams • Dynamic marketplace
Individual Achievement	• Highly ambitious individuals predominating in the workforce • Individual growth and achievement of prime importance to enterprise performance • Attractive earnings potential without significant personal risk • Highly competitive and mobile marketplace for members of the workforce	• Dynamic marketplace • Unrelenting customers
Recognition and Celebration	• Performance of "average" workers is critical • Work is not intrinsically stimulating • Monetary rewards are constrained • Marketplace for people is very competitive • Labor pool is largely unskilled	• Magnetic leaders • Dynamic marketplace • Compelling legacy

Most Frequently Applied Alignment Approaches	Notable Examples
• Creating broader pictures • Articulating what matters most • Making purposeful selection • Showing people their true value	• U.S. Marine Corps • Marriott International • 3M
• Providing performance transparency • Distributing leadership broadly • Enhancing the work itself	• Avon Manufacturing • Hill's Pet Nutrition • Johnson Controls
• Creating widespread opportunity • Distributing leadership broadly • Making purposeful selection • Providing meaningful recognition and rewards	• Hambrecht & Quist • BMC • Vail Ski School
• Articulating what matters most • Providing performance transparency • Making purposeful selection • Creating widespread opportunity	• The Home Depot • McKinsey & Company • First USA
• Showing people their true value • Generating collective energy • Providing meaningful recognition and rewards	• KFC • Marriott International • Southwest Airlines

generate and channel emotional energy, (2) the characteristics that distinguish the path from other paths, (3) an illustrative example, and (4) imbalances that can occur.

THE MISSION, VALUES, AND PRIDE PATH

It is hard to find any established company that does not have a "vision and values" statement of some kind. Most of these statements are posted on walls, printed on wallet cards, and distributed in glossy promotion pamphlets to all employees. The executives who promulgate them do so with pride and a bit of bravado, most of which is pretty much lost on the broad base of employees. If nothing else, frontline workers are realists; it is extremely difficult to fool them with lofty rhetoric that denies marketplace reality. Nonetheless, the leaders of all too many companies proudly point to well-crafted aspirational statements that have little to do with what goes on in the marketplace. Not surprisingly, very few of them can claim peak-performance workforces.

The situation is very different within an enterprise that excels along the Mission, Values, and Pride (MVP) path. Members of the workforce take great pride in the aspirations, accomplishments, and reputation of the enterprise. They also take pride in the achievements of their immediate work groups and in the specific contribution they make to those groups. Often, the history and legacy of the company have become powerful sources of pride and emotional energy. The MVP path invariably spawns an abundance of team opportunity and distributed leadership roles throughout the organization, including the front line. It all starts with the leadership philosophy or basic beliefs at the top of the enterprise.

Leadership Philosophy

The top management leadership philosophy of the MVP path is based on the following underlying workforce value proposition:

Employees will feel truly proud of what this enterprise stands for, what their specific work group can accomplish, and what they can contribute, both collectively and individually; their pride will be continually reinforced with external and internal recognition.

Leaders of institutions that follow the MVP path are sometimes characterized as dreamers. In one important sense they are. They envision a noble purpose for their enterprise that transcends any short-term profit or financial gain. As businesspeople, of course, they recognize that the piper must be paid, that is, shareholders must benefit. But responsibility to shareholders is seen as almost a necessary evil offering little motivational or energizing value to them or their workforce. Philosophically, the business leaders dream of product and service offerings that will literally "delight the customer," as well as make all employees deeply proud of what they make and how they make it. Creating a legacy is often more important to such leaders than creating wealth. Not surprisingly, "hard-nosed" executives from other companies sometimes call them dreamers behind their back.

Company values are deeply ingrained throughout the enterprise, and people who cannot embrace these values invariably leave. To outsiders, these values typically sound like the meaningless platitudes that everyone mouths. To insiders, however, such values take on powerful meanings that determine organizational behavior at all levels. The leaders believe that the company's core values are inviolate guidelines of action and behavior that determine the quality of product, the way customers are treated, and the behaviors that employees adhere to. Values are not simply nice words to mouth; they are mandatory guidelines reflected in disciplined sets of behaviors.

Distinguishing Characteristics

What differentiates the Mission, Values, and Pride path is not found in the formal statements, claims, and pride of top management; rather, it is in a current and recurring set of accomplishments that constitute a rich legacy that frontline employees can take pride in. A long heritage of marketplace accomplishments engages the emotions of numerous people throughout the organization; it is replicated in current achievements. A widespread sense of pride in collective accomplishment also ensures an environment where people enjoy working together. Consequently, team opportunity and real team performance abound.

Such a heritage, however, takes years to develop, even when the organization is launched to meet an exciting national priority like putting a man on the moon, the challenge assigned to the National Aeronautics and Space Administration (NASA). In the eyes of the employees, the history evolves seamlessly into a "noble purpose" that reflects and is consistent with the legacy. In fact, leaders at all levels make a point of drawing on the legacy to reinforce the company's basic values. Consequently, the leadership is widely distributed and value driven.

Attitude is another characteristic of the MVP path that distinguishes it from other paths. People have a lofty view of what they are about and often disdain the efforts of competitors to approach their levels. Although this sometimes breeds denial, more often it creates an attitude of positive aspiration that lends credibility to even the most menial tasks. An attitude of selflessness prevails that often causes employees to subordinate their personal interests for the good of the enterprise and in the consistent support of their co-workers. Though never completely eliminated, of course, self-interest has far less influence in a true MVP environment than in most other commercial situations. This is virtually the opposite of what occurs along the Individual Achievement path and the Entrepreneurial Spirit path.

An Illustrative Example

On July 4, 1997, millions cheered the televised pictures of the *Pathfinder* and *Sojourner* rover adventures on Mars. To many, it was reminiscent of Neil Armstrong's walk on the moon—only this time without human life at stake. As one observer noted with a straight face, however, "This is the first time anyone has driven a car on Mars!"

Many people witnessed and vicariously experienced what *Time* magazine cleverly labeled "J.P.L.-ation," after the Jet Propulsion Laboratory technology that enabled the *Sojourner*'s Mars excursion, in widely distributed pictures (video and magazine). Some may recall the image of Chief Engineer Robert Manning leading a highly energized group of his Jet Propulsion Laboratory cohorts in various cheers, physical demonstrations, and other emotional displays. It was a celebration dance more typical of high school students whose team had just won a state basketball championship. We were witnessing a bunch of emotionally committed and higher-performing workers in action.

Obviously, average workers performing at average energy levels do not create, launch, or drive remote-controlled vehicles in outer space, regardless of the size of the funding. The *Pathfinder/Sojourner* act was a truly remarkable proposition to begin with, especially considering the huge budget reductions and funding constraints imposed on this program. *Pathfinder's* predecessor "probers" (*Vikings 1* and *2*), for example, had the benefit of $3 billion that funded two launches, two orbits, and two landings. *Pathfinder's* solo launch and landing action was achieved at less than one-tenth of the cost. No wonder the "extraordinary, ordinary folks" working at the space center were energized by the sheer magnitude of their mission and the deep-seated pride in what they were accomplishing. And no wonder this compelling event generated every bit as much employee energy as did the early NASA programs of putting men on the moon. Such events, though rare, can produce contagious energy, focus, and alignment within the actions and decisions of large numbers of people.

Consequently, both programs benefited from a critical mass of peak-performance workers at several levels. Though hardly surprising news, these higher levels of performance over extended periods were probably not the result of simply executing some series of good people management practices. In fact, NASA leaders didn't worry about whether they would get a higher level of performance from these groups of people; that was simply assumed. Instead, the NASA group was completely focused on achieving their truly remarkable space exploration proposition—landing and operating a scientific recording vehicle on Mars. They did not need a lot of special motivation, beyond the clear and compelling mission, the ingrained values of quality and teamwork, and the pride of accomplishment. The rest of us can only marvel at the boldness of the original proposition, not to mention the ultimate accomplishment of the JPL team.

Even this brief vignette of the Mars space probe captures the essence of why a compelling MVP approach can energize people for performance. Chapter 4 explores two more detailed examples of how the Mission, Values, and Pride path actually produces peak-performance workforces under less dramatic circumstances.

Mission, Values, and Pride Imbalances

Straying from the MVP path is a common problem for companies that let pride in past accomplishments blind them to gradual erosions in their competitive effectiveness. Many well-known names, including

KFC and the Marines, have fallen into this trap. At KFC, the loss of the Colonel's persistent emphasis on customer service produced variations in delivery that lost both customers and franchisees. This erosion of customer-service emphasis was masked by strong feelings of pride in the past. Unfortunately, the new owners' initial attempts to regain lost market position were largely numbers-driven—in pursuit of a Process and Metrics path—which only caused the company to stray further from the MVP path. By the time David Novak appeared on the scene, the old MVP path was virtually invisible, and the emotional commitment of both franchisees and restaurant general managers was rapidly disappearing. It took three years to right the ship and effectively integrate the two paths that now sustain the critical balance.

The U.S. Marines suffered a similar fate during and after the Vietnam debacle. Forced to take in far too many marginal recruits and thus overwhelmed by the growing numbers of nonbelievers, the emotional commitment of their front line eroded badly. Alfred Gray's unlikely appointment as commandant in the 1980s was indeed fortuitous. He snatched back the warrior spirit legacy and returned the ship to an even-keel balancing of performance and fulfillment as only the Marines can do.

Imbalance on the MVP path is typically caused either by a complacency that grows out of failure to consciously fuel the legacy, or by an overconfidence that causes people to ignore significant marketplace changes. In the first case, the legacy is lost on the newcomers, who have no direct connection to it; in the second case, people simply overlook the need to adapt behaviors within their historic framework of core beliefs. They assume that change is unnecessary.

THE PROCESS AND METRICS PATH

At the other end of the forest is the Process and Metrics (P&M) path. This path works too. On the surface, however, it looks a lot like the well-trodden, consequence management approach of most well-managed enterprises, which seldom generates emotional commitment and energy at the front line. We all recognize this approach. It is based on the sound principle of individual accountability and thrives on a set of well-defined measures that translate corporate objectives into individual goals at all levels. With consequence management, everyone knows the few metrics that matter in their jobs, as well as how those metrics add up to deliver shareholder and customer value. In addition, well-defined management processes ensure that individual behaviors produce the most efficient work and materials flows from suppliers to customers. Workers who follow their process guidelines and score well on their metrics are systematically advanced. Those who deviate and fall short are relocated, and those who waffle in the middle are expected to shape up or move out in due time. It is a demanding, efficient environment that keeps people's noses to the grindstone. They may not particularly like it, but at least they know what to expect.

This is not, however, the same as the Process and Metrics path, which leads to an emotionally engaged, peak-performance workforce. Here, the enterprise also has a clearly defined set of performance measures that translate readily into individual goals. These goals emphasize specific outcomes rather than activities that may or may not lead to outcomes. Well-defined processes guide the efforts of people at all levels, but these processes provide for worker fulfillment as well as performance effectiveness. Moreover, the workers themselves invariably play a key role in the selection and design of the processes and metrics that affect them. Such processes enable initiative and innovation as well as ensure compliance and cooperation. The walls of various company facilities are adorned with charts and reports of achievements against metrics that are meaningful to individual workers and to the enterprise overall. People are highly energized by clear evidence of the company's achievements that reflect their own contributions. They are rewarded (and penalized) in direct relation to the measures of their own performance, and they constantly strive to achieve new levels of their individual best. Although this path often characterizes manufacturing operations, it is by no means confined to such situations. For example, both Marriott and KFC are nonmanufacturing illustrations of mastering a P&M path that yields strong emotional commitment within critical segments of their workforces.

Leadership Philosophy

The top management leadership philosophy is based on the following underlying workforce value proposition:

Employees who consistently meet and exceed their metrics and adhere to the critical process requirements will be recognized and respected by their peers and conspicuously recognized and rewarded by management.

Leaders of institutions that follow the balanced Process and Metrics path believe in going well beyond any simple notion of consequence management. Philosophically, however, they remain dedicated to the principle of "a few closely watched numbers." They go to great lengths to ensure that overall corporate objectives are both measurable and translatable into key measures for individuals at all levels of the organization. They hold people accountable for meeting their numbers, and they develop numbers that will create both customer and shareholder value that exceeds what competitive institutions can achieve. Most importantly, the numbers they emphasize are credible to the workers who must meet them; people understand the *why* of the critical measures.

These goals are accompanied by meaningful rewards, which are often nonmonetary. Leaders believe that recognition must come from fact-based evaluations, multiple managerial judgments, and customer-validated quality. As a result, the workers become energized by meeting and exceeding their metrics even though the metrics are continually being extended and stretched. Workers often see metrics as challenges that bring out their individual best, and they are energized by that challenge. When they can see productivity rates climb, yields increase, quality improve, and worker skills enhanced, they are energized to do more.

Leaders who rely on the P&M path for fulfillment as well as performance are careful not to create a fear of failure among the employees who occasionally miss their numbers. They go to great lengths to ensure that people are encouraged to try for demanding metrics even if they must fall short—as long as the effort is genuine and the improvements over time stand up against the marketplace. What is most important, employees believe that the metrics and process "constraints" within which they work not only are necessary and fair, but will also enable them to excel in personally meaningful ways.

Distinguishing Characteristics

Few consequence management efforts ever result in a truly energized workforce; in fact, most proponents of this management style do not worry about emotional commitment at the front line. The difference lies in the focus and balance of how the Process and Metrics path is pursued—and in the leaders' determination to engage the positive emotions and rational compliance of the workers. Companies that have energized and elevated their workforce performance through process and metrics do not simply track financial numbers and enforce only what is quantifiable. They pursue and track simultaneous improvements in worker fulfillment and customer reactions, which is in stark contrast to the financially driven efforts of most other companies. Moreover, the achievement of the increasingly challenging goals and metrics (particularly those that go beyond financial numbers) stimulates constructive competition and extra effort, even among average employees.

The conditions that favor the P&M path tend to be found in large, mature organizations that highly value behavioral consistency in the design, production, and marketing of the products and services. Clear measures for assessing progress toward the key business priorities typically already exist in the company or can be readily developed. The company also shows a capability of developing integrated measures across the many parts of a complex operating environment. The marketplace tends to be a maturing one with well-known, established competitors.

Perhaps the most critical difference between the normal approach to top-down consequence management and the Process and Metrics path is the "bottom-up" design and monitoring of the P&M path. All kinds of things get measured, posted on walls, and calibrated against standards—but most of them are influenced heavily, if not determined, by the workers themselves. A Richmond, Indiana, manufacturing plant of the Hill's Pet Nutrition Company, the leading manufacturer of prescription pet foods sold primarily through veterinarians and veterinary hospitals, is a good illustration.[2] The plant described below is a clear leader in quality and productivity within the industry as well as the company.

An Illustrative Example

The Hill's Pet Nutrition operation in Richmond is one of the better, but less well known, examples of how a Process and Metrics path was both created and pursued successfully over time. To begin with, the company maintains a philosophy of open-book management, wherein every employee can obtain information on any subject relevant to his or her role. Joe Douglas, who runs the Richmond plant, brings all plant employees together once a year to spend a day understanding the competitive environment.

When you enter the plant, you are met with a flood of operating information and activity announcements posted on every wall:

✦ Weekly packaging efficiency rates, targets, and trends by production line

✦ Special process control charts for moisture and density for each of several extruding machines

✦ Training classes calendar

✦ Sign-up sheets for multiple sessions of "Biz Wiz" training

✦ Meeting notice for "communities of practice," including packaging, batching, and processing

✦ Invitations for joining the packaging "community of practice"

✦ Quarterly plant profit-and-loss statements (with explanations) blown up to poster size and hanging in the main hallway

These kinds of wall postings at first appear randomly placed and a bit excessive. As you walk through the plant, however, and ask various workers about them, three things become clear and compelling. First, each worker knows exactly what the various charts represent and what the numbers and graphs on them mean with respect to his or her particular job. Second, the workers have had a strong hand in how the information will be displayed and what will be done with it. Last, they are visibly excited about meeting their daily and weekly targets. This process and metrics approach reflects every bit as much input and influence from the bottom up as it does from the top down. As a result, the workers are more than interested in the displays; they are emotionally challenged to impact the results—not unlike teenagers constantly trying to master higher levels of achievement in their favorite video game.

Process and Metrics Imbalances

Straying from the P&M path is a common problem for companies that overemphasize financial numbers and short-term performance results. In fact, most companies suffer from such an imbalance along this path for very understandable reasons. The constant emphasis in the business press and the financial community about quarterly earnings growth and head-count reductions makes it difficult to define consequence management in any other terms. Unfortunately, these terms are seldom fulfilling to members of the frontline workforce.

Dozens of stories of this kind of imbalance appear in the business press every year. For example, consider Apple's well-publicized pursuit of streamlined operations to compensate for the marketplace impact of lack of product uniqueness, or the many megamergers whose proponents cite cost reductions and financial legerdemain as the key benefits. Again, such metrics fall on deaf ears within the ranks of large workforce contingents—and sooner or later many of these agglomerations pay the price of disgruntled workers and excessive turnover in critical areas.

Most often, imbalances along the Process and Metrics path are caused by an overemphasis on short-term financial numbers or on a failure to balance those metrics with another set of metrics that gives equal attention to accomplishments that are meaningful to employees. It is also possible, although less common, for companies to under-emphasize short-term financial numbers and explain away serious performance shortfalls as unimportant in the long-term scheme. Such companies often fail to make it to the long term. The difficulties of sustaining a balance within the P&M path alone are one reason that most of the P&M cases we explored were striving to integrate a second path.

THE ENTREPRENEURIAL SPIRIT PATH

"We need more entrepreneurs in this company" is an all too common cry from top executives frustrated by the lack of individual initiative, risk taking, and new product introductions in their companies. The fundamental problem, of course, is that the true entrepreneur simply would not last long in most large enterprises. Nevertheless, many large corporations persist in believing that some kind of corporate entrepreneurial spirit could really energize their people. The truth is, it could.

Creating an Entrepreneurial Spirit (ES) path in an established corporation, however, is a significant challenge. First, the members of the workforce must perceive a high individual earnings opportunity based on building something of unique value. The path is characterized by high-risk, high-reward situations—plus the opportunity to share significantly in the ownership of whatever the enterprise is becoming. People on the ES path are typically energized by a dynamic, growing marketplace, a high individual earnings potential, and a unique opportunity to "build something of my own." They enjoy a great deal of independence in how they do their job, as long as the results are compatible with broad enterprise aspirations.

Unfortunately, this approach takes root much more readily in new ventures than it does within large established corporations. The few established companies that pursue the ES path invariably stumbled across it very early in their journey and somehow managed to retain important vestiges of it as they grew larger and became much more complex enterprises. Examples include BMC, Hambrecht & Quist, Southwest Airlines, and The Home Depot. For all these companies, the Entrepreneurial Spirit path was well established during their very early years. Moreover, most of those well-known entrepreneurial start-ups have chosen not to rely only on the ES path as they have grown. Thus, the basic leadership philosophy and differentiating characteristics are probably much more likely to come from small beginnings.

Leadership Philosophy

The top management leadership philosophy is based on the following underlying workforce value proposition:

> *Employees will be rewarded directly in proportion to what they create and the personal risk they incur; those rewards have virtually unlimited upside financial and ownership potential.*

Entrepreneurs are a fascinating combination of market seers, risk takers, fortune hunters, and institution builders. To know one is to marvel at his or her emotional energy, insatiable optimism, relentless determination, and outright luck. This is not a game for the faint of heart or the weak of stomach.

Although a corporation probably cannot expect to develop true entrepreneurs deliberately, it can certainly create an environment that energizes its employees through the conscious generation of an entrepreneurial spirit. The basic leadership philosophy that characterizes such environments starts with a strong belief in letting talented people have their head in the pursuit of new marketplace challenges. The company may pay little attention to how the challenge may be pursued, or even what the specifics of the challenge might require. Its only interest is in enabling independent initiative, creativity, market responsiveness—and results reasonably consistent with the enterprise's aspirations. Moreover, the opportunity to own an important piece of what you create is very real. Sounds easy enough, but it implies a much higher degree of confidence in people to simply follow their nose to find the gold. Not many corporate leaders can hold to this philosophical bent when pressed by their shareholders for gains in quarterly earnings.

Differentiating Characteristics

In situations that favor the Entrepreneurial Spirit path, high-risk, high-reward opportunities abound. Invariably, the ES approach flourishes in a high-growth environment, with a great deal of marketplace dynamism and uncertainty, which adds to both the excitement and the anxiety of working there. People at all levels pursue some kind of ownership opportunity that offers both earnings and institution-building benefits. The enterprise highly values individual initiative, idea generation, and eagerness to take risks to exploit new ideas.

Time is a scarce commodity in entrepreneurial situations, for many obvious reasons. The marketplace is exploding with competitors and product offerings; a few weeks' delay in a new product can result in disaster. With tight funding for the enterprise, the results must be produced before the money runs out. People are impatient for their ideas to be recognized and acted upon, and will bolt to other places if they believe they can get faster action.

A coherent strategy is hard to find in such situations and is seldom considered necessary. At Southwest Airlines, the CEO openly disdains the term *strategic planning,* which he views as completely counter to the kind of on-line thinking, frontline initiative, and market responsiveness that have built SWA into a clear industry leader on several dimensions.

An Illustrative Example

BMC Software is a unique software company founded in 1979 as a pure start-up by Scott Boulett, John Moores, and Dan Cloer (whose last initials gave the company its name). It has grown dramatically in both sales and shareholder returns to reach a market capitalization per employee that rivals that of Microsoft. BMC's initial offerings turned out to be *killer apps,* that is, breakthrough products that enabled IBM customers to squeeze more performance out of IBM's database products and mainframe computers. This strong value proposition, targeted to a relatively narrow customer base (that requires little hand-holding), allows BMC to rely on a telesales model. It also enables the company to literally hard-wire individual incentives to specific product results for both sales representatives and software designers.

BMC thus constitutes a simple entrepreneurial model that does not depend on the existence of an overall goal or mission to focus the workforce. Nor does it depend on an inspiring leader to energize people. The model also clearly segments the workforce and focuses BMC's energizing efforts primarily on two critical groups: the product authors (or software designers) and the experienced telesales professionals. Top performers in both groups can and often do make more cash compensation than the CEO does, in any given year.

BMC clearly gets higher performance from these segments of its workforce. In fact, the company has one of the highest productivity records in the entire software industry. These results, along with the energy sources and alignment approaches that comprise BMC's Entrepreneurial Spirit path, are described in detail in chapter 5.

Entrepreneurial Imbalances

Straying from the ES path is a common problem for companies that found the path a natural one during their start-up days, but rapidly outgrew it and stifled it with excessive process and bureaucratic controls. It is difficult for large companies to provide the high-risk, high-reward opportunity to create "your own thing" that the true entrepreneurial situation represents. Many large companies pay lip service to entrepreneurialism, but are a far cry from providing it.

As mentioned previously, many start-ups provided great entrepreneurial opportunities until size and scale took over. IBM, Microsoft, and even Hewlett-Packard typify this phenomenon. Amazon.com, America Online, and Starbucks will probably encounter a similar fate unless they disaggregate aggressively. Southwest Airlines is an excellent example of a company that got its start within the ES path, but quickly developed, mastered, and shifted to other paths to sustain the emotional commitment of its people. Today, Southwest is one of the few companies that integrates and excels along three paths (Mission, Values, and Pride; Individual Achievement; and Recognition and Celebration)—but one of them is *not* the ES path.

A few entrepreneurial ventures have sustained the emotional commitment of key segments of the workforce even as size and scale became important. Most companies, however, find that an ES path works best in the early stages of their development. As a result, the path is often combined with another path that is more sustainable over the long term.

THE INDIVIDUAL ACHIEVEMENT PATH

Members of the workforce along the Individual Achievement (IA) path perceive great opportunity to excel and develop as individuals. Personal growth is as important to their fulfillment as is the personal recognition and reward they receive for their performance. People on this path are energized by the abundance of personal growth opportunities they perceive around them, as well as by their own individual achievements. The primary focus of the enterprise is that of tracking and rewarding individual performance and ensuring that high achievers have ample advancement or job enhancement opportunities.

The IA path bears some similarity to the Entrepreneurial Spirit path just described. However, it is clearly distinguished from the ES path by a lower-risk profile, more limited ownership and earning opportunity, and a sharper focus on individual achievement and personal growth opportunity. Nonetheless, the IA path creates a different sense of ownership that comes from taking personal responsibility for one's own development and for making an individual impact on enterprise success. This is not, however, the same financial ownership that entrepreneurs get when their name is on the door, their individual fortune can be made, and their personal net worth is at stake. For example, except at relatively senior levels in most individual achievement situations, it is unlikely that more than 30 percent of an employee's compensation would be "at risk."

Performance-based terminations are also less common along the IA path, because people tend to depart from a company more of their own volition. For example, at The Home Depot, one of the better examples of a well-executed IA path, there are only three "deadly sins": using drugs, abusing people, and dishonesty. If an employee has not committed one of them, the organization will bend over backward to work with him or her. Even at McKinsey & Company, another well-known enterprise that pursues the IA path, few would describe employment there as a high-risk proposition, given the multitude of other opportunities that a stint at McKinsey opens up. Nonetheless, both The Home Depot and McKinsey offer relatively attractive financial rewards to those who stay the course—but they are by no means get-rich-quick situations.

Leadership Philosophy

The top management leadership philosophy of the Individual Achievement path is based on the following underlying workforce value proposition:

Employees will be recognized and rewarded directly in proportion to their personal accomplishments. They will be well paid and advanced based on those contributions, and they will work alongside talented individuals in the field.

IA path leaders believe that the key to enterprise success is attracting the best possible people—"world class talent"—to fill every important position in the company, and then energizing them to achieve their individual best in that position. An important corollary element of this philosophy is providing such individuals with enough latitude and "solution space" to make whatever they wish out of their jobs through personal growth, individual initiative, and creative outreach. Based on their accomplishments and potential, the better people are promoted frequently in such environments. They are, however, also encouraged to make the most of their situations without waiting for job changes or advancements. Individuals often have considerable influence on the shaping of the content and conditions of their own jobs.

Moreover, the leaders of IA organizations are emotionally committed to giving their people every opportunity to achieve and grow as individuals. They devote significant time to helping people develop themselves to the fullest extent possible. Individual roles are broadly defined, and extensive efforts are made to equip each individual with the knowledge and skills required to fill these roles—and to move beyond them. These investments in people often carry over from the professional domain to the personal domain. It is not unusual, therefore, to see an IA organization going to extraordinary lengths to help an employee confronting a family emergency.

Distinguishing Characteristics

The attributes and conditions that differentiate the Individual Achievement path come from people's inherent need to stand out as individuals, to influence their own destiny, to be associated with other top individual achievers, and to advance and grow personally. In the IA path, these fundamental human needs receive a much higher priority than do other fulfillment needs, such as being part of a group or sharing in collective or joint accomplishments. The path offers abundant opportunities for personal growth and individual advancement. A worker, for example, has opportunities to fill a variety of roles, learn different skills, work on a range of issues, and significantly impact both customers and the enterprise. Consequently, the IA workforce tends to include very ambitious individuals.

Individuals in an IA workforce are also likely to be talented and in short supply. Moreover, the criteria for judging the talent pool can include a wide range of characteristics not necessarily determined by academic credentials or test scores. Both Southwest Airlines and The Home Depot have thousands of people applying to join their workforces, and both of them pay much more attention to attitude, personality, work ethic, and other nonacademic characteristics than to intellectual credentials. However the talent pool is defined, these organizations are clearly relentless in their pursuit of the very best.

So why doesn't every peak-performance worker want to be on an IA path? The simple answer is that it requires a lot of hard work and unpredictable hours. Individual performance shortfalls are jarringly obvious (if not painful), personal anxieties run high, and the peer pressures on under-performers can be very intense. Although the financial earnings opportunities may be attractive, situations that are more entrepreneurial offer better earnings and ownership opportunities. Individuals are expected to understand the aspirations and intent of the leadership of the enterprise, although most consider these as guidelines rather than constraints.

The IA path provides individuals with an unusually broad and varied "solution space" plus a freedom to act that is accompanied by a clear sense of individual accountability for results. Leadership is not a matter of formal responsibility, because it is expected of people at all levels, regardless of their job title. Virtually all employees clearly understand the overall enterprise mission and values and how these affect their individual roles. In an IA situation, individual growth and achievement prove to be a key determinant of enterprise performance over time.

An Illustrative Example

The Home Depot prides itself on the so-called customer obsession of its employees. As a result, it is not surprising to hear a Home Depot associate claim he or she will do whatever it takes to delight the customers, and individuals at all levels constantly generate new ideas to that end. During our visit to The Home Depot near Atlanta, Jim Wargo, the store manager, and his associates were hard at work, generating new ways to attract and keep their customers. For example, Chris Fitzgerald, assistant manager for building products, was quite taken with his deep-fried turkey idea. Deep-fried turkey is exactly what it sounds like. A whole turkey (plucked and cleaned, of course) is dipped into a deep-fat fryer of substantial proportions and cooked to succulent perfection. "What it does," he explained, "is coat the outside so there's no moisture coming out." Not only is it delicious beyond description (according to Chris), but it creates a seductive aroma that lasts for hours. Chris planned to launch the turkey fry in the middle of The Home Depot parking lot on the next busy Saturday, so that the tempting scent will waft its way into nearby parking lots of competitive stores, luring any wayward customers back to The Home Depot. As Chris noted, since The Home Depot already sells the fryers, it was just a question of getting the turkeys. Nonetheless, in Chris's mind, it was his idea and his opportunity and will be part of his individual contribution to building the institution—and he was clearly energized by it!

Individual Achievement Imbalances

Straying from the IA path is a common problem for companies that either over- or underemphasize the compensation and advancement aspects on which this path is based. Moreover, these mistakes in emphasis are all too easy to make because the right level of compensation and "fast-track" advancement varies by industry, company, and workforce segment within each company. When compensation and position become overly dominant, greed and power will overpower the more constructive motivations of individual achievement and growth. Many investment banks and high-growth situations like Microsoft provide examples of this problem.

Conversely, when there are serious constraints on compensation and advancement opportunity, an enterprise must look for complementary ways to satisfy worker fulfillment needs. Government agencies such as the State Department and the Federal Bureau of Investigation (FBI) that are unable to offer high pay have to draw instead upon pride in their mission and the role they play in society. NASA is a good example of integrating Individual Achievement with the MVP path to counterbalance the economic constraints the institution faces.

Imbalances along the IA path usually occur because of an overemphasis on individual compensation and an unhealthy competition between talented workers to "out-achieve" colleagues with whom they need to collaborate and support. As a result, this path often works best when it can be integrated with another complementary path.

THE RECOGNITION AND CELEBRATION PATH

The Recognition and Celebration (R&C) path is described last for two reasons: First, although enterprises often dabble at recognition and celebration, only a few really achieve a level of distinction along this path. Second, the R&C path invariably works best in combination with another path. At one point during the evolution of our study, we thought of recognition and celebration more as a channel or mechanism to support another path, rather than a cohesive path itself. However, as we explored how much integrated attention, discipline, and thought R&C requires in companies that excel at it, we concluded that it deserves separate consideration as a path in its own right.

Members of an R&C path workforce are constantly being recognized for all their achievements in meaningful and conspicuous ways. Both individual and group accomplishments are celebrated and rewarded regularly. These events are part of the management processes and are integral to the informal construct of the enterprise. Moreover, the non-monetary aspects of this effort are much more important than the formal compensation program. The overall atmosphere created is one of friendliness, enthusiasm, and fun—all within the context of achieving peak performance standards. Magnetic leaders often provide a key source of energy. As we mentioned earlier, however, in our case studies, the R&C path was always combined with one or two other paths. It was never the primary path.

At the heart of a R&C path is a unique leadership philosophy at the very top of the organization, without which the celebrations, frivolity, and merriment become more diversionary than purposeful and effective. These efforts must be relentlessly pursued over time rather than simply practiced as convenient. The celebrations must become an integral part of the management process, not a handful of random events arbitrarily skewed to the whims of a few merrymakers and back-slappers. When the recognition is done right, of course, it is particularly meaningful to the best performers, even though it cascades across most people in the organization. The activities are inclusive across several levels and clearly show a lot of forethought.

Surprisingly, perhaps, the celebrations are not particularly costly. At SWA, for example, employees often sponsor a fund-raiser to support their Halloween spectacular (which you have to see to believe!). Despite all the frivolity and fun, companies that integrate such celebrations into their path make sure that there is a persistent focus on what really matters most to both employees and the company. They reinforce both performance and fulfillment priorities.

Leadership Philosophy

The top management leadership philosophy is based on the following underlying workforce value proposition:

Employees will be recognized, rewarded, and celebrated in dozens of ways—by supervisors and colleagues as well as top management—for their collective and individual contributions. As a result, they will work in an environment alive with enthusiasm, excitement, and fun and wherein formal compensation is of secondary importance.

The underlying philosophy of the leadership in these companies is not unlike the carrot-and-the-stick or banana-and-the-whip fables of old, except that money is never the carrot or banana. These old bromides would have us believe that you can get much more work out of a donkey or a monkey if you reward them positively and frequently. So it is with the leaders of the R&C path. People respond more positively to heartfelt, credible, nonmonetary recognition than they do to financial rewards. However, the leadership of these companies ensures that the efforts are thoughtful, purposeful, and constantly improving, rather than something that becomes viewed as trivial, repetitive, or "off the shelf."

They also believe that it is important, perhaps essential, for workers to enjoy themselves during work—even to the point of having fun. Moreover, these efforts are initiated and supported by line management rather than by staff assistants with nothing better to do. The line managers at all levels are convinced that a happy workforce will be a more productive one, and they make every effort to make sure that it happens.

Distinguishing Characteristics

Companies that rely on this path invariably face the challenge of motivating large numbers of frontline employees who bring only a modest capability and work ethic to their jobs. Monetary rewards and incentives are constrained by the economics of the business, and the work itself is seldom intrinsically stimulating. Job requirements do not demand high levels of education or special skills. Nonetheless, the marketplace for people can often be very competitive.

Much attention must be paid to nonmonetary recognition and reward for both individual and group accomplishment. This recognition goes well beyond leaving it to chance or relying solely on the instincts of a few individual managers; it is an integral part of the overall leadership process. Special events provide primary platforms for visible recognition and celebration. They also act as forcing devices that ensure consistency over time. Although the special events may have common formats, their approach and content are notably innovative and emotionally engaging. As one leadership trainer at Southwest Airlines remarked, "It really feels like I'm still experiencing the best parts of being in high school."

Throughout the critical segments of the R&C workforce, energy levels are visibly higher than normal, sustained by consistent encouragement from peers and formal and informal leaders. A celebration may look like impromptu fun, but it is the result of purposeful hard work at several levels. Much of the work is done off-line and on people's own time—just because they like doing it! Virtually every manager pays special attention to the accomplishments of his or her people. This kind of recognition and celebration becomes so contagious that colleagues and peers pay as much attention to the accomplishments of people as do the supervisors and managers. Everybody gets caught up in celebrating everybody else's contributions, both big and little.

An Illustrative Example

A visit to a facility (not airports) of Southwest Airlines is strangely reminiscent of a visit to an elementary school art fair. In both cases the walls and hallways of otherwise simply designed buildings are adorned with pictures, posters, placards, and mementos of all shapes and sizes. Everything imaginable is displayed if it somehow illustrates some special moment of accomplishment or celebration.

The SWA headquarters building at Love Field in Dallas has literally thousands of events framed on the walls or mounted on the desks and coffee tables. It also has many fun mementos, such as the white wooden statue of Abraham Lincoln that appeared in a TV commercial with CEO Herb Kelleher. It doesn't really stand for anything, but it brings many smiles to the faces of visitors and associates alike.

In addition, it is hard to miss the recorded pictorials of countless celebrations that permeate SWA's culture. The airline will celebrate anything of meaning for its people. Such enterprises truly care about their people and make sure that all their people know how much they care. You cannot put a dollar figure on either the costs or the benefits of such efforts—but you would have a hard time convincing this enterprise that these efforts are not absolutely essential to its ability to achieve and sustain higher performance among its frontline people.

Reward and Celebration Imbalances

The R&C path invariably is used in combination with one of the other paths—primarily because it is difficult to achieve the appropriate performance balance. KFC combines R&C with the P&M path, Marriott combines it with the MVP path, and Southwest Airlines combines it with the IA path.

Companies that have strayed from this path include many who simply "overload the system" in an attempt to carry out every good people management practice imaginable. The celebrations in such companies are invariably forced, and employees find ways to avoid them. The recognition tends to be tenure-based and does not differentiate on the basis of critical elements of performance. Worst of all, the effort has a randomness that provides little cumulative impact on the performance of either the workforce or the enterprise. It becomes much ado about nothing.

Unfortunately, companies can easily become overly enamored with the R&C path and lose sight of their performance end game. It is also easy to pursue the path randomly if not superficially. In both cases, this is caused by a lack of the disciplined behaviors required to make the recognition and celebrations truly meaningful to employees and truly complementary to enterprise performance.

WHERE THESE FIVE PATHS LEAD

This chapter gives a brief, integrated overview of the five paths that characterize all the cases we have explored in depth. The five paths constitute a composite framework of options that allows top management to make several important choices, namely, where and how to generate emotional energy and what approaches to use in channeling that energy to achieve higher performance. The number of choices these paths represent, however, can be confusing, if not overwhelming. Hence, leaders must be both selective and disciplined in developing a coherent path for generating and channeling emotional energy.

The peak-performance workforces invariably draw on energy sources like past heroes or fierce competitors that already exist rather than attempting to create new energy sources from scratch. Nonetheless, the sources that they draw upon are unique to their situation and point in time—rather than being any prerequisite of the path or paths they follow. In other words, each primary source of energy can be found in several different case examples, regardless of their particular path emphasis. Most companies have at least one of these sources of energy, but are simply not disciplined about identifying them or tapping into them effectively.

Channeling the emotional energy generated for performance can be an equally challenging problem. The case studies uncovered several approaches for channeling emotional energy, any of which can be used to help stimulate complementary improvements in worker performance and worker fulfillment. Again, the multiplicity of choices here places a real premium on obtaining disciplined sets of behaviors in a few places. In that context, the enterprises we studied had been purposefully selective to execute distinctively within a few alignment approaches.

In order to make those choices wisely, however, an enterprise must understand the role of disciplined behaviors that we found to be critical along each of the five paths. Without the discipline to be selective and focused, an enterprise cannot follow a coherent, balanced path successfully. All the higher-performing workforce situations we explored exhibited very disciplined behaviors in their efforts to accomplish the following:

✦ Build top management commitment to a value proposition that balances enterprise performance with worker fulfillment.

✦ Generate emotional commitment within critical segments of the workforce by systematically tapping more than one energy source.

✦ Channel the extra emotional energy by being selective and focused enough to excel in a few alignment approaches.

Part II explores several case examples in some depth to illustrate how different enterprises accomplish these three fundamentals within their chosen paths. The value of any path lies in how it enables top management to selectively focus the emotional commitment and energy of critical segments of its workforce.

II ✦ EXPLORING THE FIVE BALANCED PATHS

Figure II-1   CHARACTERISTICS OF THE FIVE BALANCED PATHS

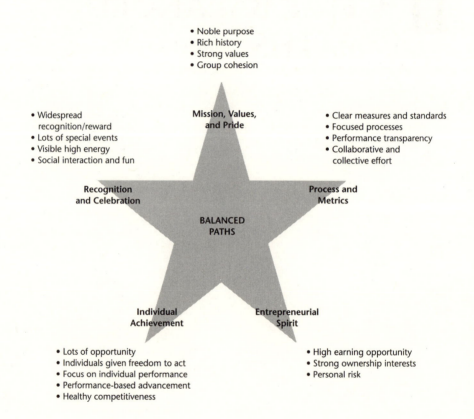

- Noble purpose
- Rich history
- Strong values
- Group cohesion

- Widespread
  recognition/reward
- Lots of special events
- Visible high energy
- Social interaction and fun

**Mission, Values,
and Pride**

- Clear measures and standards
- Focused processes
- Performance transparency
- Collaborative and
  collective effort

**Recognition
and Celebration**

**Process and
Metrics**

**BALANCED
PATHS**

**Individual
Achievement**

**Entrepreneurial
Spirit**

- Lots of opportunity
- Individuals given freedom to act
- Focus on individual performance
- Performance-based advancement
- Healthy competitiveness

- High earning opportunity
- Strong ownership interests
- Personal risk

The five paths that lead to an emotionally committed, higher-performing workforce have the underlying similarities described in part I. That is, each applies sets of disciplined behaviors to ensure a dynamic balance between enterprise performance and worker fulfillment. How that balance is achieved, however, differs to some degree in every case, as one would expect.

Fortunately, five patterns can help explain each case and are helpful in considering what combination of approaches and mechanisms makes the most sense for any particular situation (figure II-1). Several companies follow more than one path, although each path will lead to a higher-performing workforce. The advantage of having multiple paths to choose from is that, if well integrated, they reinforce and strengthen one another in ensuring balance over time. The disadvantage is that integrating across more than one path complicates the task. The importance of choosing, however, cannot be overemphasized; trying to excel at all five paths precludes distinctiveness along any one path. The choice is what allows the leaders of an enterprise to concentrate its efforts and resources in ways that lead to distinctiveness in the eyes of the employee.

3 ✦ The Mission, Values, and Pride Path

Those who succeed in energizing workers along a Mission, Values, and Pride (MVP) path invariably benefit from an existing legacy. It is very difficult to sustain frontline enthusiasm for high aspirations without a credible history consistent with those aspirations. Nonetheless, the path has wide appeal with many pretenders to the throne, but only a select few see real results. Often, the MVP path has been pursued in conjunction with a second or supportive path that helped provide the extra energy and alignment required until a reasonable legacy could emerge. The Home Depot, Southwest Airlines, and Marriott International are all good examples of this integrated, dual-path approach. The best example of a pure MVP path, however, is the U.S. Marine Corps—with over two hundred years of successfully "defending our country's honor" to draw upon. Our work also suggests that much of what the Marines do to fuel their front line warrants consideration by members of the corporate world.

THE MARINES: OVERCOMING THE INSURMOUNTABLE

The U.S. Marine Corps (USMC) has certainly earned a place in any serious discussion of the MVP path. No other organization—military or civilian—demonstrates the power of a noble purpose and core values as well. My father was a Marine during World War I and, like all Marines, proud of it. He kept his dress uniform pressed and ready to go until he died, even though he had not been on active duty for over fifty years.

Although he told me stories about his time in the Marines, I never fully appreciated their remarkable history and legacy until writing this book.

Historical Perspective: An Incomparable Heritage

The Marine's MVP path is like most great journeys—simple to describe and begin, but extremely challenging to complete. Their dual mission highlights this challenge: "We win battles. . . . We make Marines." The Corps is a premier crisis response force that must be in a constant state of readiness, "24 hours per day, 7 days per week, 365 days per year." Marines must be well prepared to handle a variety of missions on short notice, under any circumstances, with a global reach—and to win decisively. The rich history of the Corps speaks for itself (table 3-1 shows a few highlights). It continues to provide a powerful source of energy that its leaders tap into consistently and purposefully. They align that energy through the disciplined execution of a few basic approaches: distributing leadership broadly, clearly articulating what matters most, and sharing collective energy at all levels. It is a simple formula that yields a very powerful balance between personal fulfillment for individual Marines and consistently superior performance for the Corps.

Why the MVP Path Makes Sense

Perhaps the primary rationale behind the MVP path for the Marines was and is survival—as a military institution. As the leaders are quick to remind you, the USMC is the only "unnecessary" branch of the armed forces; hence, it must earn as well as demonstrate its right to exist in every congressional budget review. Within this unique military survival context, however, is the same set of factors that explain why a particular path makes sense for a commercial enterprise, that is, performance priorities, marketplace realities, workforce fulfillment needs, and other cultural factors.

Performance Priorities. The performance priorities of the USMC include more than winning battles in wartime, when individuals must respond under fire and deal with unexpected chaos and life-threatening situations. The Corps must also maintain a very high state of readiness and proficiency in peacetime—and demonstrate their value to a Congress whose priorities vacillate between leading the free world and concentrating on domestic issues. To achieve such divergent goals, the Marines must stay at the forefront in understanding political and social conditions, weapons technology, and military strategy and tactics, as well as changes in human resource characteristics. Their strategy is to be "the most ready at the least cost."

Table 3-1   U.S. MARINE CORPS CHRONOLOGY

Date	Significance
1775	The U.S. Marine Corps is born in the Tun Tavern in Philadelphia "over a few beers"
1820–1859	Commandant Archibald Henderson demonstrates to Congress his unyielding commitment to cost discipline by repeatedly *returning* funding allocated to the Marine Corps
1820–1866	Three attempts in Congress to disband the Corps
1918	World War I: Marines are such fierce fighters at the Battle of Belleau Woods that the Germans began referring to them as *teufelhunde,* "devil dogs"
1941–1945	World War II: At the Battle of Iwo Jima, Marines raise the flag atop Mount Suribachi. Admiral Chester Nimitz describes the thirty-six days of fierce fighting: "Uncommon valor was a common virtue"
1950–1953	Korean War: The First Marine Division defends against eight Chinese army divisions in minus-twenty-degree temperatures in the Battle of the "Frozen" Chosin Reservoir
1989	Commandant Al Gray serves combat rations at an official dinner, shocking attendees who include members of the Joint Chiefs of Staff and high-ranking Department of Defense officials
1991	Bangladeshi flood victims refer to the Marines who provide them with disaster relief as *faresta,* "sea angels"
1995	Marines rescue U.S. Air Force pilot Scott O'Grady after he is shot down in Bosnia

This strategy leads to important performance priorities for the Marine Corps in two areas: superior leadership and tactical innovation. An unsurpassed commitment to developing superior leaders is a primary determinant of the Marines' success to date. It is based on selecting high-caliber individuals with solid leadership potential, instilling them with the basic values of Marine Corps philosophy, and developing each individual's leadership style through practical experience and coaching/mentoring.

Tactical innovation—fighting smarter—enables the Corps to realize its strategic objectives despite its scarce resources. Marines match an enemy's superior size and strength with speed, agility, and ruthless opportunism. They exploit his critical vulnerabilities with a carefully crafted plan that maximizes firepower and brings a custom-tailored fighting force to the battle. Over the years, the Marines have been consistent innovators in maneuver warfare ("hit as quick as you can and as hard as you can"), operational pace or tempo ("so rapid the enemy cannot react"), and combined arms and task organization ("put the enemy in the horns of a dilemma").

Marketplace Dynamics and Realities. The "marketplace" of the USMC is the global geopolitical environment, with all its unpredictable elements of tension, intrigue, instability, and change. Marine leaders tailor the composition of operational forces to meet the challenges of the assigned mission. For example, if a Marine commander were facing a mechanized threat in the desert, he would bring tanks, artillery, and attack helicopters to the fight. If he were to defend an embassy in a heavily wooded area, he would deploy foot soldiers, military police, and transport helicopters. To use business terminology, Marines serve each market with a highly tailored approach.

Workforce Fulfillment Needs. The Marine "workforce" includes a disproportionate number of people from dysfunctional circumstances that result in significant gaps in basic human development. In other words, many individuals enlisting in the Marines lack a positive self-image, self-discipline, and other basic attributes, as well as a sense of belonging and a desire for opportunity. Turnover is a major problem, especially given the tremendous investment the Corps makes in its Marines. Achieving a balance between institutional performance and workforce fulfillment is a constant, unrelenting challenge for the Corps. The challenge is exacerbated by a dwindling national defense budget, which affords scarce funding for recruiting, training, and replacement of outdated equipment.

Cultural Factors. The USMC culture is based on much more than military discipline. It is a culture of change, innovation, and continuous improvement as well. At the same time, it is a not a growth culture—in fact, the Marines have managed to create remarkable emotional energy and commitment even during extended periods of budget cutbacks and declines in size. The culture reflects the Marines' strong beliefs in the importance of their mission to be prepared to defend their country's interests in any kind of battle or defense scenario. It also reflects a compelling need for real team performance to exploit multiple leader options and ensure collective support and flexibility in battle. As a result, the Marines are constantly modifying the scenarios they expect to encounter and seeking new ways to deploy and mobilize their forces. They have cultivated a sense of openness within the organization that actually encourages constructive self-criticism (as any issue of the *Marine Corps Gazette* will attest) and leads to continual improvement, innovation, and change. I was surprised to find that many of the Marines' frontline leaders met the criteria for real change leaders better than did most commercial enterprises I have studied.[1]

The best way to illustrate how the USMC uses the MVP path to achieve this balance between institutional performance and workforce fulfillment is within the context of our visits to Parris Island, South Carolina; Quantico, Virginia; and Camp LeJeune, North Carolina. Each visit provided useful examples of how the balance is achieved.

Parris Island: Establishing Core Values

We started our tour of the Parris Island training facility in the so-called yellow footprints, the spot where all new recruits must stand when they step off the bus at the processing center for their first encounter with a drill instructor (DI). The yellow footprints are where the discipline begins, as a DI shouts out initial instructions. It was also the beginning of our exposure to the relentless, repeated inculcation of the Marine Corps "core values." All Marines carry a small card that reminds them of what matters most in the Corps—"Honor, Courage, and Commitment"—and the clear, powerful meanings those simple words convey to the Marines. There is little question that the Marines epitomize the Mission, Values, and Pride path. Their mission is to defend their country against any kind of external or internal threat; their values are to do it the right way—with honor and caring for one another. They take great pride in their mission and values, and that pride constitutes the primary source of energy for their "workforce." At Parris Island, the direct purveyors of that energy source are the DIs, who personify the core values in appearance, word, and deed. These values are also what characterizes the personal change that takes place in most recruits who make it through the Parris Island ordeal (officially known as the Marine Corps Recruit Depot—MCRD).

The stated mission of MCRD (and its companion group, the Eastern Recruiting Region) is to "recruit young Americans and make them Marines." Unlike most other military services, the Marines put the bulk of their initial efforts into value shaping, not skill building. The vast majority of recruits enter without a clearly defined set of personal values. And some who enter are on the verge of adhering to an unhealthy set of values for themselves as well as for society. Changing these personal values is what the Parris Island experience is all about. Those who cannot adapt their personal values to fit the Marines' core values will not make it. The Corps cannot maintain its superior performance in the defense of this country unless the personal behaviors of Marines at all levels reflect these values. The history and legacy of the Corps provide ample evidence of this. Correspondingly, an individual Marine cannot find fulfillment in the Corps without embracing these values. In the course of embracing them, most recruits also find new self-confidence and respect for themselves. They accomplish more—as individuals and in teams—than they ever thought possible; they attempt physical and mental feats they did not believe they could do; they develop skills they never imagined they would master. As one DI observed, "Every recruit benefits when he pushes himself beyond his former limits. . . . We give them higher standards and greater confidence in themselves along with higher values."

So why don't other educational institutions have a similar effect on their "recruits"? Clearly some do, but their task is much more difficult because they do not have the advantage of the closed system that Parris Island provides. Brigadier General Keith Holcomb is the first to admit that he would be hard pressed to accomplish the transformation (or perhaps more accurately, the conversion) that takes place in Marine recruits without the benefit of a closed system. From the yellow footprints to the graduation ceremony twelve weeks later, the recruit is constantly in the system and within the personal purview of the drill instructors.

The Pickup: Unforgettable Role Models

After a day or two of scrambling for gear, bunks, and other essentials, it's time for the *pickup,* the time when the recruits are turned over to the specific DIs who will shepherd them through the next three months. It is a memorable event that begins the process of clearly articulating what matters.

We were introduced to Captain Fennell and his officer and NCO assistants before the pickup, and then slipped in the back door of the barracks to observe the event. Along each side of the room were the bunks of the recruits with their gear properly stowed. The recruits themselves—about thirty-eight of them—were seated cross-legged in the middle of the floor with their backs to us. Since their heads had just been cleanly shaven and they were grouped in no particular height order, I had the impression of bobbing water-polo balls of many colors. Racial diversity is not an issue at Parris Island—although racism is an ever-present threat that must be moderated constantly, if not eliminated entirely.

Captain Fennell addressed the platoon with all of the sharp articulation and clear delivery of a practiced speaker—only a bit louder and faster. With rapid-fire precision, he focused his lecture on heart and core values to the rapt attention but obvious bewilderment of the bobbing, occasionally nodding, heads. Fennell stopped in midsentence to sharply upbraid a recruit for apparently nodding off. Of course, there were far too many things for the recruits to remember, much less contemplate doing in real life. Nonetheless, Captain Fennell made his central point that this place is mostly about values. He also made it painfully clear that they were recruits, not Marines, and that to become a Marine would require an incredible amount of effort on their part. Each would have to earn the right to wear the emblem and share the legacy. At the same time, he worked hard at making each of them believe they could do it: "When you complete this course—and you *can* complete it—you will become my brother. . . . You may give up on yourself more than once during the next eleven weeks, but we will never give up on you!" And he means it.

Throughout the lecture, he made pointed use of key words in the new language that the recruits would have to master. Henceforth, they would always refer to themselves in the third person; walls would become bulkheads; floors would be decks; and windows and doors, portholes and hatches. They would also have to master an endless list of acronyms that make for efficient communication among experienced Marines. It is the beginning of a common language that permeates and characterizes the culture. More importantly, the specialized language helps bond Marines and reinforces their commitment to the core values. The lecture ended with a pointed summary of the Uniform Code of Military Justice (UCMJ) and how it differs from the civilian legal system the recruits were used to. Any act of disobedience, disrespect, and dishonesty, for example, is a violation of the code. Or as the captain put it even more succinctly, "Anything that disrupts the good order and discipline of the Corps is punishable under the UCMJ."

The captain then introduced his assistants, who each marched in quick cadence to the center of the room, executed a flawless salute, faced the recruits as he was introduced, made a sharp right or left face, and marched off to one side of the barracks. Attired in flawlessly pressed uniforms and executing their moves with snap and precision, they presented a memorable role model image that the recruits would not easily forget. Many that we talked with afterward made the unsolicited comment, "When I first saw those DIs at the pickup, man, I knew that I wanted to be like them!" So begins the recruit's personal commitment to become a Marine, based on a clear visual image of what that means. It is also the beginning of the remarkable bonding that develops between recruits and DIs.

That bonding may be the most important element in the Parris Island formula. Certainly, the DIs are impressive role models for how a Marine should look, think, and behave. Only the top 25 percent of the Corps is even considered for DI assignment. The Marines want only their best to be responsible for training new recruits in basic values. The DIs are personally interacting with every recruit under their command every day. DIs are there when the recruits tumble out of their bunks each morning, and the DIs' lights can be seen burning long after lights-out in the recruit barracks. What sometimes starts as recruit hatred for the early intimidation, personal embarrassment, and intensity of the schedule that the DI personifies ends up invariably as respect that transcends the DI's Parris Island role. Few Marines of any age do not cherish fond memories of their DI or credit the DI for some of the truly defining moments in their life.

The DI Team: Feeding off One Another

"We use every tool we can," said Sergeant Sheffield in response to my question about motivating the recruits. Every recruit poses a different motivational puzzle, and it is the DI's job to solve that puzzle. The best DIs know when and how to shift from intimidation to encouragement, or from interrogation to fear. "Whatever works" could well be the DI motto. They become masters at engaging the emotions of recruits.

As we probed in our later discussion with a group of five DIs, we were impressed with their insight as well as their frankness, as shown in their own words:

They all need someone who can see through their weaknesses to their strengths.

We have to take away their "me-ism." . . . The power of a common goal makes them work together. . . . There is no I in T-E-A-M.

Shared hardship is what brings Marines together as powerful teams in the fleet. . . . That's why we want recruits to experience so much shared hardship here.

As DIs, we have to work as a team (even though our platoons compete). . . . We "feed off each other" for motivation.

The recruits will see through you if you are wrongly motivated for yourself.

In the final analysis, the DIs are motivated by the noblest of purposes: to make each recruit a self-sufficient person, resourceful enough to survive in any situation, and dedicated to making sure that his or her buddies survive. Wick Murray, a military historian now working for the Smithsonian Institution, recalls the Chosin evacuation story from the Korean War. Apparently, U.S. Army and Marine units of similar complements were cut off behind enemy lines under virtually identical circumstances. Many Army units essentially fell apart and suffered heavy casualties before getting back to friendly forces. In marked contrast, the Marines held together and even brought out their dead. Marines simply cannot imagine leaving wounded comrades behind. This ingrained value of "never let your buddies down" is implanted and takes deep root at Parris Island.

Several DIs told us that a powerful source of energy in real battle conditions is fear. When that kind of fear runs rampant, however, it can also be paralyzing. Not surprisingly, this paralysis by fear is what the DIs want most to prevent. They were not referring to a physical fear of death or personal injury, however. They were speaking of the more powerful emotional fear of letting your buddies down when they really need you. This is one of the more powerful values (within the overall category of courage) that the Parris Island formula inculcates into every graduating recruit. It also helps create a team culture within a rigorous chain-of-command structure that has few equals in the corporate world.

My colleague Brad Berkson correctly observes that the Parris Island formula requires almost no outside source of energy, because the recruits are energized primarily by their role model DIs, who are energized primarily by their recruits' transformation and fulfillment. The skeptic might argue that *transformation* is too strong a word for such a relatively short program, but there is little question that most, if not all, recruits undergo a sea change in their beliefs about themselves and the world and in how they behave. Perhaps the change is more like a religious conversion than a physiological transformation, but whatever the label, most recruits that become Marines will never be the same again. The well-known Marine expression "Once a Marine, always a Marine" is far more than just a slogan; former Marines savor the memories for most of their lives. Ask the close friends and family of any Marine—and watch the feelings of pride well up in their eyes and faces.

Shared Hardship in the Crucible

The "Crucible" constitutes the ultimate challenge as well as the ultimate team event in the Marine's basic training program. It was added only recently when the commandant of the Marine Corps asked General Holcomb and a group of other officers to design an event that would become the emotional culmination of the training for the recruits. To that end, the officers changed the next-to-last week of the program to create a mentally and emotionally demanding set of challenges, with minimal sleep and maximum "teaming." Brigadier General James Battaglini, who is in charge of Parris Island, describes it as "a team event based on shared hardship." Holcomb says the commandant wanted it to be the defining moment in the entire program—"a core values practical application challenge."

The Crucible is all of the above in fifty-four hours of continuous evaluation and testing. It is designed around a series of sixteen "warrior stations," each named after real heroes (Medal of Honor winners) whose acts of heroism are described at the station on plaques and by DIs before the event. Each portion of the Crucible requires the recruits to work as a team—each with a different recruit serving as the leader. Not only do the DIs go through the muck and mire with their recruits, but they make sure that the recruits continue to learn from their mistakes as they go.

The final event of the Crucible is a grueling nine-mile "hump" (run) with full packs and weapons after the recruits have gone without sleep or rest for more than two days. It ends symbolically at the Iwo Jima Monument at the entrance to Parris Island, where each recruit receives the Marine Corps official emblem, pinned on by his or her DI. Few manage this award without tears—including several DIs.

Even in retrospect, the recruits describe it with obvious emotion as "molding, mentoring, and motivating at its best," and "the hardest part is staying motivated all the time. . . . We could never do it without the first eleven weeks of preparation." Clearly, the commandant got his defining moment as the program culminates in a classic engagement of the emotions of recruits and DIs alike. It stays with them throughout their career, if not their lifetime.

The New Cohesion Teams

"Every Marine, a rifleman" is a slogan that reflects another time-honored practice within the Corps. No recruit gets through Parris Island without mastering the rifle, and no Marine goes through skills training at Camp LeJeune without going through live-ammunition infantry drills. The infantry Marines are organized into *cohesion teams* that will stay together for their entire four-year enlistment. Each cohesion team consists of twelve people, although the Corps is experimenting with smaller units to make it more practical to keep the units together over the four-year period.

These units are impressively disciplined like real teams, in that all members are expected to lead and function and work alongside one another like members of a team. During the drills and exercises, the leadership shifts within the group—both formally and opportunistically as situations develop. The members learn when and how to follow the leader, to lead themselves, and to shift from one mode to another. There is continual mixing and matching with respect to roles and skills. It is a real team capability in short supply in the corporate world, and it feeds off of the collective pride at the heart of the Marines' balanced path.

The cohesion teams also provide a formal structure within which Marines can easily talk with one another about problems, pressures, and things they need to learn. The real team's natural learning attributes are particularly valuable during this period of the Marine's development.

Many Marines we talked with believe that the combat skill training is actually more difficult than the Parris Island values and discipline training. "Boot camp is actually more of a mental game than this combat training. . . . This is a day and night effort over much more extended periods."

A significant part of the difference between boot camp and combat training stems from the focus on simulating actual operating conditions in the fleet. Moving from accelerated training to actual fleet operations is bound to produce a different atmosphere, time frame, and mode of behavior. The routine is different, the players are different, and the adjustment is difficult. The cohesion units are expected to help a great deal, simply because the return to the fleet will be with a team that has learned to solve problems together. It is the beginning of the collective energy they must learn to generate and regenerate themselves under the difficult if not life-threatening conditions of battle.

Obviously, the Marines are not a natural peak-performance workforce model for the corporate world. To begin with, the Corps is not a business and does not require commercial skills; its performance does not have a profit motive. Members of the "workforce" make mistakes all the time. For example, low-flying Marine pilots cause civilian deaths; individual Marines break both military and civilian laws; the Corps loses some of its best talent to better jobs on the outside. Moreover, one would hardly call most of the work that the Marines do "fun." Nor is their organizational and leadership system some kind of exciting new paradigm of empowerment that we should all be trying to emulate. Marine values are not for everyone.

Nevertheless, after studying the USMC relative to other peak-performance workforce situations, I believe that all the aforementioned differences between the Marine Corps and the business world matter not a bit. The Marines know how to engage the positive emotions and modulate the negative ones. They demonstrate a unique capability to balance enterprise performance and workforce fulfillment that most business organizations would do well to understand and learn from. Much of what they do is readily transferable, even though it is part of a uniquely integrated and fairly closed system.

Energy Sources and Alignment Approaches

As illustrated earlier, the Marines' primary source of energy is their rich legacy and history, literally unmatched by any other enterprise that we have studied. Moreover, they are diligent and purposeful about tapping into that source, and hence they derive more frontline energy from their history than almost any other institution, civilian or military.

Interestingly, however, their legacy has not been their only source of extra energy. During the late 1980s, a badly needed and powerful supplemental source of energy emerged in the form of Commandant Al Gray. In the aftermath of Vietnam, the discipline, values, and commitment of many Marines were showing serious signs of deterioration. It was not the Corps of old. Moreover, the Marines might not have survived that critical period in their history without Al Gray's determination to rekindle the warrior spirit throughout the Corps. Even though he formally retired as commandant in 1991, his magnetic image remains fresh in the minds of Marines at all levels. Clearly, he has provided the Corps with a powerful source of energy that recharged their collective pride when they needed it the most. The Marines are truly distinctive in aligning this energy with three complementary approaches or tools:

Distributing Leadership Broadly. Contrary to the conventional image of a hierarchical, command-and-control organization, the Marines succeed in distributing leadership very broadly. Drill instructors, infantry fire team leaders, and staff sergeants alike are expected to "know the intentions of leaders two levels above them" and take actions and initiatives consistent with those intentions, no matter what the formal commands may have been. Even the lance corporal in the streets of Haiti facing angry civilian mobs has to be a leader in knowing if, when, and how to use his weapons and authority—consistent with the intentions of his leaders.

In this context, it is significant that the focus of the Marine Officer Candidate School in Quantico, Virginia, is as much to evaluate leadership potential as it is to train new officers. To that end, the school applies a template that differentiates several types of leadership potential (e.g., being assertive, collaborative, insightful, and supportive); most corporations are content with only one. The Marines intend to get all the leadership possible at each level and position in the institution. They develop different combinations of leaders who "will ensure mission accomplishment and place the welfare of their Marines before their own." Such leaders constitute incomparable role models for their troops.

Articulating What Matters Most.   The first things every recruit must learn are the precise meanings intended by the Marines' values of honor ("integrity, responsibility, accountability"), courage ("do the right thing in the right way for the right reason"), and commitment ("devotion to the Corps and to fellow Marines"). Marines are legendary in their determination to never leave a wounded buddy behind.

These values take on an obvious criticality during battle, but as mentioned previously, since the Marines are usually not involved in battle, the values must be meaningful in peacetime as well. To that end, not only are their preparations continuous, but they also invoke remarkable realism. The anxiety and fear that recruits feel throughout their training is very real. So is the pride they feel in each accomplishment. Marines constantly "practice" engaging the constructive emotions in peacetime to evoke the same feelings of anxiety, fear, and pride that will occur in wartime.

In return for their devotion to these values, the individual Marine has always been regarded and treated as the most precious asset of the Corps: "Our ability to win our nation's battles rests, as it always has, on the individual Marine. Regardless of the relentless pace of technology, people, not machines, decide the course of the battle."[2]

Spreading (and Regenerating) Collective Energy. Marines feed on one another to sustain their energy and commitment during the long periods of peacetime preparation. For example, the recruits are energized by the role-model behaviors of their drill instructors, who in turn are energized by the positive changes in the self-image and pride of the recruits. Newly commissioned officers are most anxious about the reactions of the "troops" they will soon command, who in return will be motivated by the actions of the new leaders.

In addition, the Corps makes the most out of all achievements, advancements, and accomplishments of its people, both as individuals and in teams. The Marines are among the best practitioners of real team discipline that I have ever observed. No accomplishment goes unnoticed, and no individual or team achievement goes without meaningful recognition and positive attention. For an institution that has not been growing for over ten years now, it creates a remarkable number of opportunities for learning, skill development, and personal growth.

It is an elegantly simple recipe that for over two hundred years has enabled the Marines to make the most of what they have had to work with. Nor should one overlook the importance of how well they use discipline and good order to build self-image and confidence as well as ensure performance in battle. The amount of genuine caring for one another in peacetime as well as during war is unusual for a military organization. Many regard their fellow Marines as family.

3M: THE PERPETUAL INNOVATORS

The Mission, Values, and Pride path serves a few other institutions almost as well as it does the Marines—although none can point to such an impressive performance record over time. Many companies, of course, would profess to be on this path, but only a few successfully use it as the foundation for a peak-performance workforce. Among those that have succeeded is 3M, the $15 billion producer of everything from consumer office supplies to medical devices and cleaning products. Although 3M does not rely as heavily on this path as does the USMC, the company's distinctive application of its MVP path is worth understanding. There are some interesting parallels between these two institutions—but there are some even more interesting differences.

In 1953, a 3M laboratory assistant was working on the development of a liquid coolant. She spilled on her shoes a few drops of the coolant, which proved virtually impossible to clean off despite her scrubbing efforts with soap, alcohol, and various other solvents. In a flash of insight that 3M employees have become famous for, she wondered if the coolant's water-resistant properties would make it a good rain repellent. Might its imperviousness to solvents somehow be used to protect fabrics from stains? Thus was born the entire family of Scotchgard protectors used today on clothing, carpets, furniture, wood, and leather. As 3M is quick to point out in its Web site on "Who We Are," "Not all of our new products come about through lucky accidents. We take innovation seriously. . . . To really understand 3M, you have to know our imaginative people, working together to find practical ways to make life better."

Post-it Notes are one of 3M's more remarkable products that make my own family's life at lot easier. I suspect we are not alone, since the product is one of the five top-selling office products in the United States (as well as a best-seller worldwide). At home, we use it for everything from reminders on the refrigerator door to page markers for books, reports, and the like. For those few lost souls not yet familiar with the product, it is note paper that comes in various sizes and colors that has a self-sticking (repositionable) strip enabling the user to apply and detach it several times without a trace. How versatile can you get?

First introduced on the U.S. West Coast in 1980, Post-it Notes were "invented" by 3M researcher Art Fry, who became irritated that scraps of paper often failed as bookmarks for his choir hymnal—apparently, they wouldn't stay in place between choir practices. Recalling that another 3M scientist had invented an adhesive that had been rejected because of its impermanence, Fry deduced with clairvoyance that a "temporarily permanent" bookmark would be an ideal use for the glue.

Fry is a typical hero in the world of 3M innovators (which, like the Marines, includes many innovators as well as heroes—even if you restrict your criteria to the breakthrough products like Post-it Notes). He grew up in a small Iowa town and attended school in a one-room schoolhouse. Showing a very early inventiveness, he dreamed of becoming a chemical engineer like his father. He started working at 3M while still a student over thirty-five years ago and has remained there ever since. He remarks with some pride that he needed at least as much ingenuity to sell the idea as he did to create Post-it Notes in the first place: "It was hard to sell the concept that people needed a note pad that would sell for a premium price compared to ordinary scratch paper."

One year after their introduction in 1980, Post-it Notes were named 3M's Outstanding New Product. Fry was promoted to division scientist in 1984 and then to corporate scientist—the highest level on the technical side of the company—in 1986. One cannot help but wonder how many other large corporations would have even listened to Art Fry's foolish dream.

Historical Highlights

Founded in 1902 to make grinding-wheel abrasives, 3M has evolved into one of the world's most admired companies, selling more than fifty thousand products in over two hundred countries. The business picture for the company is a complex mosaic filled with dozens of different markets, channels, brands, distributors, competitors, and customers. 3M's Web site and internal literature are filled with examples and facts like the following one that illustrates the emergence of the kind of product innovation that permeates the company's history:

✦ The company first was able to pay a dividend in 1916, after completing a turnaround that had been a struggle since 1902. 3M has paid quarterly cash dividends on common stock without interruption ever since. The credit for the turnaround was due in large part to a product that was an extension of the company's original interests in abrasives—soon to translate into staggering quantities of sandpaper used in World War I.

✦ Opportunity knocked when, in 1920, vice-president William L. McKnight received a curious letter from a printing ink manufacturer, to wit: "Please send samples of every mineral grit size you use in manufacturing sandpaper." . . . [T]he writer, Francis G. Okie, had invented a new sandpaper that was waterproof! [It] gave the company an industry "first" and repositioned 3M as the industry leader with its product Wetordry . . . which continues to offer important solutions to 3M industrial customers worldwide.[3]

William L. McKnight joined the company in 1907 as an assistant bookkeeper and became its president in 1929 and chairman of the board in 1949. Many believe his greatest contribution was as a business philosopher, since he created a corporate culture that encourages employee initiative and innovation and provides secure employment. His basic rule of management was laid out in 1948:

> *As our business grows, it becomes increasingly necessary to delegate responsibility and to encourage men and women to exercise their initiative. This requires considerable tolerance. Those men and women to whom we delegate authority and responsibility, if they are good people, are going to want to do their jobs in their own way.[4]*

This philosophy is behind 3M's myriad accomplishments, honors, and formal recognition for both accidental and "on-purpose" innovations. In 1995 3M was awarded the National Medal of Technology for "nine decades of innovation."

Why the MVP Path Makes Sense for 3M

The company's continued emphasis on the MVP path has been a conscious and natural choice. Several factors unique to its situation in the following four areas have contributed to that choice: business performance priorities, marketplace dynamics, workforce fulfillment needs, and other cultural factors.

Performance Priorities.   3M's performance requires product innovation and customer service initiatives from everyone: "Innovation is more than products; . . . it's the way 3Mers do business."[5] Profiled as one of the truly visionary companies in *Built to Last,* the company holds to an informal rule that 30 percent of all sales should come from products developed in the last four years.[6] As stated in its Web site, "At 3M, we pride ourselves in forming innovative relationships within our organization, with suppliers and customers, between domestic and international business units."[7]

A few examples of 3M's more recent successful innovations illustrate the point. A new single-use clinical thermometer introduced in mid-1997 significantly reduces the risk of infection. Personal electronics and dashboard displays now shine more brightly with Durel Corporation (a 3M customer) EL lighting systems, thanks to products made possible by innovative technology from 3M. A new 3M Privacy Film allows window manufacturers and their customers in the construction industry to install frosted windows that become clear with the flip of a switch.

Marketplace Dynamics and Realities.   3M's marketplace is filled with fierce competitors and demanding customers: "3M serves an extraordinarily diverse group of markets. . . . We are able to do this because we think of markets as customers to be listened to."[8] This diversity creates a constant development and spin-off of innovative ideas, processes, and products. As a result, 3M has to perform in a very versatile manner to meet its customer needs. In fact, 3M people are masters at applying a great many technologies to develop products that often anticipate unrecognized customer needs, as well as satisfy current demands.

Innovation at 3M starts with the customer. Its customer-focused training process is labeled ACT, an acronym for the three steps in that process: assessment and analysis, curriculum content, and training transfer. Getting customers into the ACT is a constant and changing challenge, as Jack Tencza, director of training for 3M, points out:

> *The number one issue is that we need to find better ways to serve the customer, in particular, finding other ways the customer can use our products—and that translates into doing a better job of knowing the customer's customer.*
>
> *[A second issue] is the hassle factor. . . . We're a big company, and many customers would rather talk to fewer people to simplify the process. . . . A third issue is keeping promises.*[9]

The realities of 3M's marketplace are in a constant state of flux, not only because of the diversity of customers, but also because of the increasingly large and aggressive competitors it must deal with. With almost no end to the competitive onslaught facing people throughout the workforce, it is critical that the more than fifty thousand employees of 3M respond quickly, consistently, and innovatively. It is a tall order that 3M does not underestimate.

Workforce Fulfillment Needs. The company wants the spirit of innovation surging throughout every department, operating business, and geographic location across the globe. That means that individuals throughout the workforce need to believe they can be innovative. They also want the encouragement to be creative, to share knowledge freely and openly, and to act on their own initiative. Certainly, they need to be recognized for those efforts, but they also need to be unafraid of making mistakes for the right reasons.

The workforce at 3M consists of people who thrive on collective accomplishments; hence, teams are a vital part of its work environment. One team leader with whom we spoke at 3M captured the importance of team performance, as well as the fulfillment needs that team leaders must address if team performance is to thrive. Tom Herzberg is a team leader in the Specialty Chemicals Division at 3M. He joined 3M in 1982, first during his undergraduate chemical engineering program at the University of Iowa. When he graduated in 1985, he came to 3M full-time and has worked as a team member or team leader in the same area, Specialty Chemicals, since he joined the company.

Tom plays several roles in his job today. As a team leader, he works on *process development support,* taking new products from the laboratory stage to full production. Tom is a technical team leader in this area and focuses on the technical and manufacturing aspects of new product development. He describes his role on the team as that of a player-coach who does both a significant share of the real work himself (e.g., analyzing data, performing lab tests) as well as managing and motivating the work of other members of his team.

As a team member, Tom represents the technical functions on larger new-product-introduction teams that include sales, marketing, manufacturing, and so forth. He splits his time between these two roles on an as-needed basis, as he says, "fighting fires" wherever they occur. For example, he recently finished working on the hydrofluoroether product introduction, a chemical designed to replace chlorinated fluorocarbons (CFCs) as they are phased out because of environmental concerns. Tom acted as both a team leader on the technical side and a member of the multifunction team responsible for the total introduction process.

As a team leader, Tom believes it is critical to communicate frequently to build relationships among the team members. Placing great importance on building relationships through informal conversations, he "makes the rounds" of the people on his team and "just talks about whatever they want," whether it is business (e.g., how the team is progressing) or personal. He believes it is important to spend time "translating. . . . You need to get inside their heads and see what they're thinking."

Cultural Factors.   Almost from the beginning, 3M's leadership philosophy has been based on delegation and initiative. As early as 1948, William McKnight explained that 3M was determined "to delegate responsibility and to encourage men and women to exercise their initiative." The company promotes an atmosphere of continuous learning and growth. The employees know they have the freedom to take risks. In technical areas, for example, most employees are encouraged to devote a certain amount of their time to trying out their own fledgling ideas. Many of these dreams have turned into successful products, sometimes even breakthroughs.

Many employees have a long record of service. There is considerable potential for both upward and lateral mobility within and among the many business units of the company. As a result of this promote-from-within culture, higher-level positions are invariably filled from the existing experienced pools of talent within the company.

Company literature for new employees says that the number one expectation for new hires is their desire to make a difference. Whatever the individual's functional role, his or her job is to find new and better ways of contributing to 3M's success: "Creative thinker, problem-solver, challenge seeker—you're expected to be all three . . . [and] avail yourself of the many opportunities for fulfillment as a member of the 3M team."

Energy Sources and Alignment Approaches

Behind its remarkable legacy, which is a primary source of workforce energy, is a clear mission and set of values that help align people's actions and decisions, as well as build upon the legacy. The corporate vision and mission is to be the most innovative enterprise and the preferred supplier to its customers. It is not the content or appropriateness of 3M's mission and values that makes the company so effective in its pursuit of the MVP path, however. It is a relentless consistency in keeping the 3M legacy alive and in consciously drawing upon it to energize and align workforce initiatives through collective pride.

3M's most important second source of energy is its dynamic marketplace settings. Because of its devotion to innovation of all kinds, the company finds itself in dozens, if not hundreds, of constantly changing markets. The customers and competitors in these markets are uppermost in the minds of employees, who take great pride in satisfying, if not delighting, the customer with new product and relationship ideas. Many of their ideas come from the customers themselves, and virtually all of 3M's successful innovations have roots in the priority attention that employees give to anticipating customer needs. To channel the energy that it derives from its legacy and market situations, 3M remains truly distinctive in its execution of four complementary alignment approaches.

Distributing Leadership Broadly.   Although 3M is certainly decentralized, its broad distribution of leadership is not limited to structural roles. Through the widespread use of teams, its emphasis on new ideas and innovations at all levels, and the basic philosophy of its early leaders, the company encourages and obtains leadership contributions from hundreds, perhaps thousands, of employees. As James Collins and Jerry Porras detail in *Built to Last,* 3M's broad-based leadership system, not an elite few at the top, explains this company's relentless marketplace success: "The beauty of the 3M story is that . . . they created a company—a mutation machine—that would continue to evolve independent of whoever happened to be chief executive."[10]

Showing People Their True Value.   The leaders at 3M truly believe in the value and potential contribution of people at all levels. Again, this is a core belief with deep roots. William McKnight made this clear as early as 1948: "Mistakes will be made. But if a person is essentially right, the mistakes he or she makes are not as serious in the long run as the mistakes management will make if it undertakes to tell those [people] exactly how they must do their jobs."[11]

This philosophy still prevails. Employees throughout the company continue to believe that they are highly valued for their ideas as well as their work efforts, and that they can take appropriate initiatives to improve things without fear of reprisals if the result does not always parallel the intent.

Creating Bigger Pictures.   The company goes to great lengths to make sure that all its people understand what their part of the business is about: economics, customers, competitors, and performance gaps. But it also goes to great lengths to explain the meanings behind the business specifics—at both the overall mission and values level and the more pragmatic marketplace-dynamics level. Mike Hornelty, a frontline team leader in the Chemicals Group, illustrated this for us by providing what he called

> the salesman's view of this thing. This is [about] communicating with cus-
> tomers and competitors. These are our people, they want to know what's go-
> ing on, and they want the truth. They're not powerless, they want to win
> just as much as I do, even if it's just the clerk in charge of the widget wash-
> ing. If you just tell him what's going on, and where you want to go, he'll
> help you get there, he'll help you win.

Articulating What Matters Most.   Like the Marines, 3M captures what matters most in its simple set of values: First, satisfy customers with superior quality, value, and service. Second, provide investors an attractive return through sustained, quality growth. Third, respect the social and physical environment. Perhaps the most important value is the last: "to be a company employees are proud to be a part of."[12] Not only are these values known to all workers, but they are personalized by how each person applies the value in his or her specific part of the business.

Some financial analysts might question 3M's financial performance from time to time, but few would question its remarkable ability to obtain innovative performance from its workforce. At the heart of this performance is its balanced pursuit of the Mission, Values, and Pride path.

A DEMANDING PATH

3M is a far different institution from the USMC; the parallels, however, are worth noting. Both care deeply about their people, eulogize down-the-line heroes, believe in their mission and core values, and actively cultivate team efforts throughout their organizations. Moreover, both have experienced extremely difficult times in pursuit of their noble aspirations: The Marines were deeply scarred by the Vietnam War, and 3M recently encountered one of its most difficult performance challenges, as highlighted in a 1999 *Business Week* article:

Analysts and investors are angry that management has missed annual earnings projections for two years running. Sales, at $15 billion, are essentially flat, and net income dropped 44.6% in 1998 to $1.2 billion. The stock has lost a third of its value since 1997. . . . It's a bruising fall from grace for 3M.[13]

In such cases, the emotional commitment of the frontline people gets severely tested. The Marines recaptured it through the remarkable efforts of General Al Gray to relentlessly return to the basics of disciplined behaviors and the warrior spirit. The Marines held closely to the MVP path.

It is too soon to know how well 3M will weather its performance shortfalls. Perhaps it too, like the USMC, should simply rededicate itself to its basic mission and core values. If so, it behooves the company to be as diligent as the Marines were after Vietnam in refocusing attention on disciplined sets of behaviors that reinforce their core values along a performance dimension. For example, though team performance is important to both institutions, the Marines are much more disciplined about getting real teams where they matter most. As a result, there are few "compromise units" in the Corps. In contrast, because team performance at 3M is left largely to the instincts of good managers, they achieve it somewhat randomly and are more often victimized by compromise units. The difference lies in how the two organizations enforce the critical elements of team discipline.

Sindy Burke at Southwest Airlines broke down the meaning of the word *discipline* to help us understand why it is so important to companies seeking to energize their people through pride in their mission and values: "Discipline comes from the word disciple, which means to lead, to guide, to follow. That basically sums up what we look for in all of our people, and what we all strive to do." Without this kind of discipline, you cannot stay on the MVP path for long.

A final factor regarding 3M's current performance challenge is its principal reliance on the MVP path. In our research, only the USMC, NASA, and 3M relied primarily on the MVP approach. All other commercial enterprises that excel on the MVP path—namely, Marriott, The Home Depot, SWA, and Avon—have chosen to excel along another path as well. Perhaps it is time for 3M to consider that option.

4 ✦ The Process and Metrics Path

Every good company pursues a process and metrics approach to some degree. It is based on sound principles of accountability and consequence management. The primary attributes include clear measures and standards for performance, a set of coordinated and integrated processes for delivering value to customers, and performance transparency (people know and can see how they and others are performing). Performance goals are set, and revenue, cost, and profitability measures are established, tracked, and compared. Competitive position and market share are reported frequently. Often, a management-by-objective process attempts to measure and monitor important nonquantitative elements of performance. Sound familiar? It should, since most of us work in a world of multiple metrics.

It is significant, however, that the higher-performing enterprises that emphasize a Process and Metrics (P&M) path invariably pursue one or more other paths to complement and help balance that effort. Johnson Controls Automotive Systems Group and KFC, for example, complement their Process and Metrics with widespread Recognition and Celebration paths. Marriott and Avon integrate their P&M path with a Mission, Values, and Pride approach. In this chapter, we will explore how Avon and Hill's Pet Nutrition follow a P&M path in sustaining their peak-performance workforces. Neither company is in very exciting businesses per se—and their manufacturing operations (where we decided to focus our attention) are anything but naturally appealing high-tech systems. Even the locations of their plants are uninspiring, if not hazardous. Nevertheless, both companies have still managed to generate the kind of emotional energy that characterizes the peak-performance workforce.

AVON: A GLOBAL HOUSEHOLD NAME

Much better known for its 2.6 million "Avon calling" direct sales representatives than for its higher-performing manufacturing operations, Avon is a worldwide brand of incomparable recognition and value in nearly one hundred countries. The company has annual sales of over $4 billion across a range of products that includes cosmetics, perfume, and costume jewelry. And although the efforts of both manufacturing and sales are complementary parts of the Avon aspiration to be the world's leading beauty products company, the U.S. manufacturing mission is clearly aimed at a more explicit target. This target lends itself to well-integrated processes and compelling metrics, namely, "to deliver quality products and services, defect free, on time every time, and at the lowest total delivered cost to our sales representatives and customers."

Historical Perspective: A Story of Struggle and Success

I was fortunate to be working with Avon when James Preston and Robert Pratt launched an effort to reshape the Avon vision in 1989. They and their executive colleagues labored for several months developing the ideas and crafting the words of a new vision that would recapture the feelings, energies, and imaginations of their people. Those were difficult days for the company, whose early history had been truly unique in the corporate world. Avon had wandered a bit from the powerful roots cultivated by David W. Mitchell, who had led the company in the creation of one of the most pervasive direct sales operations in the world.

Hicks Waldron and Jack Chamberlin, who succeeded Mitchell, had become enamored with diversifying into a strange array of health-care equipment and products, fragrances, and financial services businesses. The diversity and the diversion of resources and the confusing set of priorities that accompanied it nearly undid the company during the early and mid-1980s. Fortunately, when Jim Preston became CEO, he engineered a return to Avon's roots and refocused the company's aspirations and strategies on its traditional beauty products global market. Today's manufacturing effort reflects that focus.

Preston played a unique leadership role in the eighties. During and after his cosmetic and beauty products apprenticeship, he cultivated widespread respect and admiration among the Avon reps—historically the core of Avon's distinctiveness. He not only engaged people's emotions and excitement about returning to their basic vision, but also launched changes in distribution channels and product emphasis that were embraced by the global sales force. This new energy and hope spread across the world of diverse sales representatives and customers, and it now permeates the manufacturing as well as sales and marketing employees.

Why the P&M Path Makes Sense

We explored the Process and Metrics path that Avon follows in three very different plant situations: one in Morton Grove (near Chicago), where cosmetic products are made; and two in Puerto Rico, where costume jewelry is manufactured. Despite the different product lines and plant situations, we found the P&M path key to the higher performance of the workforces in each. The crux of the matter, of course, is engaging the emotional as well as the rational commitment of the associates.

We will use the Morton Grove plant to illustrate how this path works within Avon's manufacturing operations, and why it makes sense. The conditions that favored a process and metrics approach at Morton Grove are summarized in the following four sections.

Performance Priorities. The broad-market cosmetics business demands close attention to quality as well as cost. Quality gaffes can cause health hazards and are therefore subject to close scrutiny internally and externally. Any defects not only hurt current sales, but also erode future customer confidence. To compete effectively in this business, a manufacturer must set quality standards carefully to reflect the price competitiveness of the market—and it must adhere to these standards. Any defect can significantly affect the customer's reaction to buy again and can sometimes pose serious health risks. These priorities cannot be met unless the individual workers are positively engaged and willing to be measured and evaluated against precise standards.

Marketplace Dynamics and Realities. The market for the outputs is intensely competitive on a global scale. The cosmetics business constantly pursues new product ideas and attributes; it is a constantly changing style game that demands quick response from manufacturing sources. Styles and customer preferences can change overnight, and the ability to respond to those changes is essential to maintaining a leadership position in the marketplace. The determination of market preference is a constant challenge that depends on astute market segmentation, research, and style sensitivity. The manufacturing operation must be capable of meeting those demands against stringent time constraints and product specifications. Well-designed process and metrics approaches are absolute necessities in this kind of environment.

Worker Fulfillment Needs. The individual fulfillment needs of the Morton Grove workers had a lot to do with job security and group support, as illustrated by the following comment from an associate in one of our group discussions: "Most of us want to retire from Avon, so we need to be sure this plant stays on top of the pile. Our goal is for everyone to be a top performer."

Other issues at play in worker fulfillment are worker involvement and expression, the strong need for group approval and acceptance, and the desire to influence one's own destiny.

Cultural Factors.   The family culture of Avon prevails throughout the company, along with Avon's long legacy of caring for its employees. The company's global reputation in the marketplace is a source of pride in manufacturing operations as well as marketing. People believe that the company's reputation is second to none, and they are proud of being a part of that kind of enterprise. Many employees can trace their family roots to relatives who have worked as sales representatives or within earlier plant situations. A real feeling of "family" among the workers is evident within the plant, and that encourages people to report their accomplishments and progress to one another in visible ways. As a result, they feel more comfortable expressing both pride and disappointments to one another than one might otherwise expect.

Convincing Performance at Morton Grove

Avon's manufacturing history in Illinois dates back to 1946, when warehousing and shipping operations began at Chicago's North Pier terminal.

The branch operations were moved to Morton Grove ten years later, when manufacturing was added to a facility that now also houses sales, finance, and customer service for the Avon North Region. Morton Grove is the largest of Avon's three manufacturing facilities in the United States, with a diverse employee complement of roughly five hundred and an average seniority of fifteen years. The workers who make it through the first-year probationary period typically stick around, since it is now regarded as one of the best places to work on Chicago's north side. Not only are the work environment and the pay considered attractive, but Avon has a well-deserved reputation for caring about its workforce.

The walls of Morton Grove are adorned with dozens of displays that attest to the facility's workforce performance, including both formal award plaques and weekly posted performance metrics placards. The awards include internal and external recognition for the workforce's achievements in productivity, quality, and customer service. As a result, Morton Grove is also Avon's leading facility on new technology products and serves as a primary training center for managers from the company's international operations (in over forty countries). It received the 1995-1997 Global Micro Merit for achievement of zero microbiological rejects (i.e., its products were basically germ-free) on world-leading production rate of 15,000 annual day lots. This resulted in an unprecedented 50,000 germ-free day lots, equivalent to 800 million units of production. Simply put, the plant had a three-and-one-half-year run without a single microbiological reject in a complicated process that literally *invites* such microbes! At the same time, the plant has reduced its Occupational Safety and Health Administration (OSHA) recordable incident rate 59 percent over the past four years and its lost-workday cases by 56 percent.

The performance metrics displays in the Morton Grove facility may not be as colorful or obvious as the formal plaques, but they take up a lot more wall space. Every processing station, assembly line, and packaging operation has huge placards that display the relevant metrics on daily and weekly production, quality, and safety activities. Most machines also display the daily volumes, run rates, and downtimes on electronic screens as they occur. If something matters to product quality, productivity, or customer service, there is a metric display for all to see and track against. Moreover, the workers take great personal and collective pride in keeping these metrics on a positive slope.

Credit the Associates

William A. Baronti has been the general manager at Morton Grove for the last five years, but he credits the associates (Avon's term for its employees) with most of the accomplishments. They are the lifeblood of the business, in his view, and he spends a lot of time encouraging and listening to them. "If I really need to know what's going on in a problem area, I go first to the [frontline] associates working the territory," he says. He admits that he has to be sure that he doesn't inadvertently intrude on a supervisor's territory, but he wants to hear the story straight from the horse's mouth whenever possible. What is most important, he has established an environment where people feel free to raise problems, describe frustrations, and advocate change.

In addition to the informal interactions, there are formal discussions and processes that keep him close to the action—*touching the associates* is his term for it. Every Thursday a series of mini-meetings are conducted in a very open atmosphere. All associates are encouraged to voice concerns and put forth ideas for improving any process in the plant, be it formal or informal. Baronti tours the plant monthly to formally "grade" the housekeeping efforts of all sections. Somewhat reminiscent of a military white-glove inspection by commanding officers in its attention to detail, it is done with an attitude of constructive improvement that most associates respect. In fact, he makes the inspection personally because the associates and their leaders prefer it that way. "No one else can be as unbiased as Bill," we were told. And, of course, Baronti's monthly housekeeping ratings are posted and tracked right along with the other metrics of performance.

Baronti is a tall, handsome father of five whose graying hair, pleasant demeanor, and ready smile belie his relentless attention to detail and discipline. The specifics of the plant's performance results tumble off his tongue in surprising detail and accuracy; he knows what's going on in every corner of his "land-locked" facility. Bounded on two sides by freeways, and another by a railroad, there's little room left to expand. Hence, productivity improvements are even more mandatory for the workers who want to keep earning the right to a big share of Avon's U.S. cosmetic production within their facility. Baronti walks the plant floors with a spring in his step that tells even the casual observer that he really enjoys the job. He likes these people—all of them—a lot. He also knows and speaks to most of the five hundred "permanents" by their first name, as well as several agency (temporary) workers, who are seldom around for more than a few months at a time.

Baronti staffs Morton Grove to meet a base level of expected volume and uses agency or contract employees for surges. At present, nearly 35 percent of the workforce is made up of these contract workers, but he is aggressively trying to drop that percentage closer to 20. Both he, his advisors (the official term for supervisors at the plant), and most experienced associates believe strongly that the advantages of agency workers (i.e., variable direct cost and no benefit cost) do not offset their typically lower levels of commitment, work ethic, and value variation. Contract workers are a cost-effective, but not necessarily a performance-optimizing alternative over the long haul.

A Rich Legacy Less Recognized by New Hires

Avon's unique history and incomparable brand image are clearly important to management, although the legacy seems less apparent to several newer associates. The workforce is somewhat bimodal in this respect. Experienced associates are more articulate about the company's history, and a few still remember the rough seas the company went through in the 1980s, when diversification, diversionary programs, and reengineering layoffs dominated the scene. Some still soberly recall how close the plant was to being shut down.

As Baronti tells it, "Morton Grove was on the bubble" when he took charge in November 1993. He had to make several immediate changes to make sure that they didn't slide off the bubble on the wrong side. The toughest change was adding the third shift, which most associates and advisors dislike. Baronti would still like to find a way to drop back to two shifts, but maintaining a positive performance slope makes that impossible to do for now. He believes that the workforce understands this. In our interviews and group discussions, we encountered few complaints about it. In fact, most employees recognize that it is essential to maintaining their leading position within the Avon manufacturing system.

Overall, most employees—even the newer ones—take pride in the company history and particularly its survival of the early 1980s. Clearly, the vast majority of associates, new and old alike, are proud of Avon's unique global reputation for quality, stability, and caring about its people. Its early history may not be the source of energy it once was, but it remains an important reason that people feel good about working at Morton Grove. For this and other reasons described, the voluntary turnover rates are very low.

Managing the Tensions

Certainly, Morton Grove is not without its workforce tensions. Over half of the workforce has fifteen or more years of tenure with Avon. What is important to the new hire may not be as important to the more tenured worker. A natural tension also exists between the desire for open communication and interaction and the need to get the job done as efficiently as possible. Strong supervisory actions can sometimes get in the way of more interactive team disciplines, and self-directed work teams are not always the best way to handle unexpected problems with tight time frames. Rewarding people for individual efforts can sometimes directly conflict with team norms. It is also hard to draw meaningful financial distinctions between top performing teams (or individuals) and the average performers.

The performance review process has changed quite a bit since Baronti took over. These changes have sounded a wake-up call for some of the more comfortable, experienced people. Nonetheless, it has not been easy to get rid of the perpetual foot-draggers, particularly if they have long tenure on their side. The workers are well paid relative to other jobs in the area, but the compensation is not the primary source of motivation for most of the people with whom we spoke.

They are more influenced by the open environment that Baronti maintains. Workers are all encouraged to speak out, take initiatives, and offer new ideas for improving both productivity and the working environment. Not all workers, however, step up to these kinds of informal leadership roles; some are content, and actually prefer, to let others take the lead. For example, some processing operations delegate a "safety-spoke" role that is typically rotated among the shift team. Many people do not like that role, because of the extra work and potential pressure that it creates. The same can be said for the fire-marshal and spill-response roles.

For the most part, however, the better workers not only accept these difficult, sometimes unpleasant, assignments, but regard them as ways to make their jobs more challenging and stimulating. They might grumble a bit about not getting paid enough for all they do, but most would rather have the variety and the opportunity than not. Many processes and metrics are designed to promote that kind of variety along with the productivity discipline that prevails.

The Advisor Role

The approximately forty-five supervisors at Morton Grove are now officially called professional advisors. Although the title may have changed more than the role, the position has some important differences in attitude and expected behavior. The intent was to shift supervisors into a coach and team leader mode, and thereby eliminate unnecessary hierarchical tiers in the organization. To understand this shift, we talked with Laurie and Mike, both of whom are in the advisor role now.

Laurie is part of the Avon family in more ways than one. Her mom was an Avon representative for twenty-seven years, and Laurie has been with the company for over twelve. Mike reached his fifth anniversary in May and actually started his career working for Laurie. Both have held various positions, from warehousing supervisor and packaging manager to process redesign leader. There is an obvious amount of mutual respect between the two, now peers within the Morton Grove organization system. The system consists of only three layers: leaders, advisors, and associates.

Mike emphasized that many of the more tenured supervisors could not make the shift in attitude and behavior intended by the advisor role. Ingrained mind-sets and habits are hard to break. Laurie speculated that as many as two-thirds of the former supervisors have trouble mastering the new advisor role, and some will undoubtedly fail. A supervisor who knows how things should be done, and has a well-established pattern for getting it done, is not easily converted to the notion of letting the less-experienced people work it out together. Moreover, the team approach clearly works best in the smaller units; larger units need more structure and direction.

Both Mike and Laurie agreed that while compensation might be an important factor in attracting and keeping the better worker, it is not the primary motivator. Some people, of course, are largely self-motivated. Most, however, respond to the pride of accomplishment and the Avon image and legacy of quality and brand recognition. Laurie explains:

"You'd be amazed at what people around here (even the newer ones) know about Mitchell and the early days. A lot of hourly associates apparently are also sales reps for Avon or have reps in their families."

The company also has open forums and presentations on the mission and values. As one associate put it, "they are discussed to death." This openness is a legacy of James Preston, one of the more inspirational leaders in the eyes of the Avon workforce and representatives.

Positive team motivations, however, are a much more pervasive factor. Self-directed work teams exist in most of the plant's operations, and many of them—particularly the small ones—do function as real teams. Mike and Laurie told us of the "cream team" that was set up this year to provide a single-line focus. This assembly team performed outstandingly in making line improvements to achieve both productivity and ergonomic benefits.

Avon's processes and metrics are designed to capitalize on the desire of individuals and teams to understand their goals, measure their progress, and know how they stand relative to others. The internal competition, mostly constructive and positive, is an important element of the P&M path at Avon. The company measures the productivity and quality results of departments, process lines, and teams. The metrics are on display for all to see.

Associates Speak Out

Not surprisingly, the associates have a somewhat different perspective on the process and metrics emphasis at Morton Grove. In our discussion sessions with them—both individual and group discussions—we were impressed with their openness and insight.

Our first small group session with associates was reflective of that openness and insight and typical of what we heard from others. It was a diverse group in age, experience, tenure, and ethnic backgrounds. Carol Noser has been with Avon for twelve years and works in the testing department. Gail Tanner was one of the long-tenured participants in this group, having joined the company in October 1981. She likes the benefits, sees the job as "pretty stable," and likes the opportunity she has been given to learn different skills. But her eyes light up when she refers to her current group situation: "Tubers is my team!!" (Tubers refers to a production group that works with cosmetics in tubes.) Ulysses Fernandez has been with the company only since April 1993, but he likes how easy it is to relate to people there. Tom Sullivan has been in Morton Grove for about six years and is a maintenance technician. Sullivan came in from the agency force of temporaries. Joe Lynch and Tom Duncan both have over twenty years with the company, and Tom's mom worked at Avon before he did.

It was a congenial, open, and articulate group. They identified a number of motivational factors:

Now I believe management [Baronti and his leadership team] really cares about us. . . . Before, you were just a number who was never listened to. We are lot more involved now.

I like the opportunity you have here to learn a lot more—and I like knowing where I stand. . . . All I have to do is look at the charts on the walls.

They are teaching me how to present my ideas and conclusions more clearly, so management can learn as well. . . . Managers come and go, so the associates have to help the new ones learn their jobs.

I take a lot of personal pride in the quality of our products . . . particularly the products that I work on.

The group was equally frank about what is not working so well at Morton Grove. Nor were they particularly inhibited about describing some of the negatives that troubled them. It was obvious that Baronti's work environment expects and encourages them to speak out about things that aren't what they could be—as long as the discussion is constructive. Some of the group's criticisms follow:

I really don't understand the "college requirement" for advancement. I'd like to see them promote more up from the ranks. . . . I know they try it once in a while, but they give up too soon.

It's good that they push responsibility down to our level, but sometimes it's too much. . . . We have to concentrate more, and have less time to socialize.

If [people are] not pulling their weight, then ask them to leave. . . . A bad apple drags the whole barrel down.

They need to differentiate more, based on the results we track. . . . Why not pay the people and teams who do the best job a lot more?

. . . doesn't have to be money. . . . The recognition around here is not nearly enough. . . . Putting numbers on walls is not good enough for top performers.

Touring the Facility

No visit to Morton Grove is complete without the plant tour, and we were fortunate to have Baronti himself as our guide. He takes great pride in how the plant seems to literally sparkle despite its age. His associates and advisors are constantly finding ways to improve the productivity, quality, ergonomics, and cleanliness (all of which are measured with metrics displayed on the walls). Easily the most memorable parts of that tour were the dozens of small improvements that the associates had visibly and simply made on the production line. The activity of one machine shop at the back of the first floor, for example, mostly centers on jury-rig fabrications for the ideas and experiments that workers are constantly coming up with.

Whatever the idea, however, Baronti insists that it be pilot tested before being applied. "You'd be surprised what you learn that you'd never have thought of without a disciplined piloting process." The testing is just one more formal process that ensures the optimal performance gain from any prospective change—and also avoids careless and costly mistakes or miscalculations. A good example was in the palletizing warehouse, where Baronti had recently installed an impressive automated racking system. "It really didn't cost all that much [about $200,000], and it more than pays for itself in a year." The racking system saves space and manpower; it also reduces lost or damaged products. Even though the system was a no-brainer, based on the statistics provided by the maker, Baronti still insisted on the pilot process. As a result, the facility changed several of the system's dimensions, as well as the areas in which the system would be used.

There are three basic levels or floors devoted to manufacturing and storage. The top floor contains large mixing vats where the compounding takes place. The finished compounds are then transferred to the second floor, where they remain in large storage tanks until packaged on the first floor. It is a simple operation, but the tremendous variability in products makes it a huge technical-process challenge. Although Baronti takes great pride in how well this process challenge is being met, he recognizes that his Process and Metrics path requires constant attention and discipline.

Energy Sources and Alignment Approaches

Two sources of extra energy were important in Avon's manufacturing operations. Obviously, a helpful source of energy has been the company's rich history and legacy of accomplishment and caring about its people. In addition, the workers are not far removed from another powerful energy source: the dynamic global marketplace for beauty products. They take collective pride in their ability to beat the competition on quality and cost. They also take pride in elevating their relative position within the Avon manufacturing complex. Baronti is a master at both building and capitalizing on that pride through participation, recognition, and hands-on interaction.

In addition, Avon has had the benefit of two magnetic top leaders along that way, both of whom have been powerful sources of emotional energy and commitment throughout the organization—and particularly among frontline workers. The impact of both men has been most noticeable among the millions of "Avon calling" reps around the world; however, that energy has been an equally powerful source of emotional energy within the manufacturing operations. David Mitchell remains an icon in the minds of many old-timers in the company, but James Preston has assumed an equally charismatic role in recent years. It will be interesting to see how the company adjusts to Preston's recent retirement. Certainly, the emotional commitment he has generated will need to be sustained, either by another source or perhaps by creating another icon of history.

The energy that these sources generate is aligned by three complementary approaches, at which the Morton Grove employees believe the company excels. These approaches are detailed in the following sections.

Distributing Leadership Broadly. The effort to distribute the company's leadership starts with the simple notion of changing the names of *workers* to *associates*, and *supervisors* to *advisors*. It continues with the strong commitment to have only three levels in the plant (leaders, advisors, and associates), and to encourage all three to lead in the introduction of new ideas for improvement and initiatives for change. It extends and expands the leadership capacity through the disciplined use of teams, which enable more than one member to lead. The teams also provide a strong sense of worker fulfillment in member support and collective achievement.

Baronti and his leadership group believe strongly that they must obtain initiative and new ideas from their workers, even within the essential structure of their strong P&M path. Without such inputs from many workers, the leaders could not continue their quest for both perfect quality and process improvement. As a result, Baronti and the other leaders encourage suggestions and innovations from individuals and groups, virtually on a daily basis. The previously mentioned machine shop, dedicated primarily to testing the workers' ideas, shows the importance that Baronti gives his associates' initiative. What's more, many of these innovations have become improvements conspicuous on every line.

Articulating What Matters Most.   The measures and metrics throughout the plant are carefully thought out and clearly articulated for employees at all levels. Workers are very clear on what is expected and how they are to deliver on the job against clear points of performance focus. People share a common understanding of "how we do things around here," a message constantly reinforced by multiple sources, namely, plant leaders and advisors.

The workers themselves play an important role in determining how things should be measured and reported and, sometimes, what the most important measures should be. Above all, however, the standards for cost and quality are truly essential to the success of the plant operations—and hence to the security of the worker's job. No one wants his or her plant, or line for that matter, to be the one not meeting the targets that set the pace for plant performance. The workforce is justifiably proud of how well their plant performs compared with overall Avon performance and outside competitor performance.

Providing Performance Transparency.   The walls at Morton Grove are covered with performance results that correspond to the primary points of performance focus. This open display of performance information provides clear, quick, and direct feedback—both positive and negative. The feedback is based on a heavy dose of facts, but intangibles also come into play; it is much more than a numbers game. The feedback builds collective pride and gives the workers a clear sense of accomplishment and fulfillment.

Last, but not least, these sources of energy and the key alignment approaches are carefully integrated into a construct that reinforces both performance gains and worker fulfillment needs with equal vigor. Management works hard to recognize and reward achievement. Leaders and advisors alike constantly nourish Avon's legacy of caring about its people. It is a discipline enforced by strong feelings of peer pressure and self-compliance to achieve the targets and measures that matter.

HILL'S PET NUTRITION

Hill's Pet Nutrition, Inc., is the world's leading supplier of premium pet food sold primarily through veterinarians and pet stores. The company manufactures over fifty different formulas and applies strict standards for quality and cleanliness. We explored workforce performance at its plant in Richmond, Indiana, which has 260 employees and competes for workers with numerous other manufacturers in the local market. The Richmond facility produces dry pet food and maintains a three-shift operation. It serves as the prototype for developing a *high-commitment work system* being adopted by other plants in the United States. Like the Avon manufacturing plants, Hill's pursues a Process and Metrics path to sustain a peak-performance workforce. Both insiders and outsiders agree that Hill's workforce meets that challenge well.

The company has been widely recognized for its accomplishments by businesspeople, politicians (it received a special productivity award by the U.S. Senate in 1993), and others.[1] Despite a doubling in the number of products, and a 70 percent increase in volume between 1992 and 1996, the Richmond plant has achieved $28 million in cost savings, a 52 percent increase in manufacturing productivity, a 32 percent increase in throughput, a 20 percent reduction in downtime, and a 72 percent reduction in overtime. In addition, the plant has had a 65 percent drop in OSHA-recordable safety rates.

The Richmond "prototype" plant is also distinguished for its greater production flexibility. It runs more formulas than does any other plant and is used for swing production when other plants are at capacity. The plant enjoys very low turnover, for example, just 5 percent per year for technicians compared to other area manufacturers, whose turnover rates run as high as 17 percent per *month*.

Richmond Plant History

Marc Swartz can talk for hours about Hill's Richmond manufacturing facility. Richmond's first plant manager, Marc told us the story behind the conception and design of the plant.

Not surprisingly, Swartz takes great personal pride in what the Richmond effort has become. In spite of his natural modesty, he exudes pride in his own role in the creation of the facility. A graduate of the University of Missouri in 1970, he then worked for Procter & Gamble for ten years. He believes that this experience gave him a great foundation for "building a different kind of place at Richmond . . . [in terms of] spirit, feelings, and approach toward people." In 1980, Swartz started his own construction company, which he ran until 1989, when he joined Hill's as the project manager for the Richmond plant. He says that running his own business taught him how to rely on people. Joe Douglas (vice president of operations, and sponsor for the new business venture) appointed Swartz as the facility director in May 1990. Joe gave him "a short charter and blank sheet of paper." The charter was this: "You will have a team-based plant with technicians that are self empowered." Swartz's reaction was, "Okay, good plan. Now what the hell do we do?"

In early 1990, Joe, Marc, and Jerry Krueger (director of human resource development) began to develop a vision, mission, and strategy for the Richmond plant and all of Hill's manufacturing. Krueger also found a consultant named Paul Gustavson, who introduced Hill's to a socio-technical system–based organization planning and design (OPD) process that the plant adopted. Marc described several plant design choices directly resulting from their OPD principles. For example, Hill's has created a "vision wall," on which every employee writes a page on how he or she feels a part of the aspirations, principles, and values of the plant.

The company goes to considerable lengths to eliminate hierarchical symbols or barriers. For example, the facility has only one entrance. Everyone dresses the same; there is no employee of the month and no plant manager parking. "If you want a good spot, get there first."

Moreover, many opportunities are provided for people to interact and network with one another. The facility contains extrawide corridors so that people can walk shoulder to shoulder instead of one behind the other. Marc believes that some of the greatest ideas come out of the informal networking afforded by such an open atmosphere. Open or glassed-in offices (if they are closed to reduce noise) help everyone see where everyone else is. Since keeping the plant running is the number one priority, easy access to everyone in the plant is important. Swartz explains the idea behind the open-office system: "If you need me, come in and get me, even if I'm in a meeting. How many times do you go up to a door, it's closed, and you don't feel like interrupting, so you go away?"

Most important, Hill's is extremely disciplined, purposeful, and selective in its hiring. Marc sees it as largely a "self-selection process." The end of the hiring process is a session focused on the issue of fit: "Do you share these beliefs? Because we will expect you to behave according to these beliefs."

A Perspective from the Middle

Debbie Carter is a typical middle manager at the Hill's Richmond plant. She is a graduate of Purdue University, with a degree in Food Science and Technology. Her first professional work was a one-year stint as a quality management trainee at Carnation Pet Foods. From there she spent ten years at Purina in quality management and manufacturing services. She liked it well enough but saw little room for personal growth. In early 1990, she received a call from a headhunter about Hill's Richmond plant. As soon as she began interviewing, Debbie knew that the workplace would be different—it was exciting; people talked about "what we stand for"; there was a vision. The emotion in Debbie's eyes and voice as she describes the contrast was convincing, to say the least.

Debbie's first job at Hill's was as a quality team leader. Initially she was involved primarily with hiring and training the new hires. She conducted business, technical, and social training. She also did more technical work like developing the line's sanitation and quality program. At the same time, she was learning for herself about the self-directed work team approach on which the Hill's Richmond plant relies so heavily.

After a year and a half, Debbie moved to an operations team leader role, a direct team leadership position rather than her earlier support role. In this new role, she worked with her team on its self-management (e.g., developing its schedule and working approach), performance evaluation process, and setting of its own "curbs." She explained that in this position, she did a lot of managing and leading on the fly: "I learned more in that job than in my previous eleven years of work experience."

Debbie's current position covers plantwide quality and lab operations. Every operations team already has a member who handles quality management. Debbie and her group provide assistance, services (e.g., lab tests), and training in statistical process control techniques to these individuals. Like most people in the Richmond facility, Debbie has worked in a variety of positions and roles and feels a strong commitment to the team process that pulls it all together.

Debbie points to several reasons why the plant's high-commitment work system design results in more productivity. To begin with, there is less formal management, a higher ratio of technicians to managers, and a clear process for team interaction and assessment. The process also provides for more uptime on the production line because the process enables technicians (Hill's term for its plant employees) to do their own preventive maintenance and repairs (rather than waiting for a maintenance person to arrive). Basically, the technicians have more control over their own destiny.

The technicians develop a broad base of knowledge and an ability to use advanced statistical process control (SPC) techniques, which results in less waste, better product consistency, and less production line downtime. There are clear indications of better day-to-day decision making, largely because decisions are made by cross-functional groups or teams rather than any single person. As a result, people have a real sense of belonging to, and acceptance within, a group that they can respect and trust.

Most important, perhaps, everyone works at a skill and responsibility level one or two positions higher than his or her formal position. Debbie believes she is at what would be a plant manager level at most workplaces. She also believes that many technicians would qualify as supervisors elsewhere. Consequently, people develop a stronger self-image as well as pride in what they can do. In making these observations, Debbie draws on her ten years at Purina as a point of reference. She finds the management approach at Hill's much more trust based, wherein one's own team sets production targets and holds themselves mutually accountable for meeting them. People know all the goals and performance levels: output, costs, yield, efficiency, and so on. Moreover, they know them for the other Hill's plants as well as for Richmond.

Why the P&M Path Makes Sense

The basic conditions that led Hill's to pursue its P&M path are reflected in its business performance priorities, marketplace dynamics, workforce fulfillment needs, and other cultural factors at the Richmond plant. These are summarized and illustrated in the sections that follow.

Performance Priorities. As the number one supplier of specialty pet food not sold in grocery stores, Hill's places an extremely high premium on quality for all its products. The company considers it critical to monitor product quality as well as production efficiency.

According to Marc Swartz, the basic premise of the plant production model is that "you're only there as a plant because people external to the plant want you to be there." As a result, the process consists of four steps, all driven by clear business priorities:

+ Define externally driven objectives. These include business, community, and customer service objectives. The challenge lies in balancing and prioritizing among objectives and constituencies.

+ Derive the behaviors that can fulfill those objectives. In other words, everyone would work together toward common goals. Although Marc would call this a team, he is really thinking of a much larger, but equally cohesive group that includes the entire plant—a broader notion than that of a focused real team.

+ Set principles that would lead to desired behaviors. Everyone must see himself or herself as part of the same cohesive group effort and believe in a set of principles that all can support and follow.

+ Make design choices that are consistent with principles. As Marc bluntly contends, "Never violate a guiding principle." Otherwise, consistency suffers, trust is eroded, and the entire system is threatened.

Marketplace Dynamics and Realities. Hill's strategy of selling through pet stores and veterinarians means that the company must satisfy unusually demanding customers, namely, professional veterinarians.

Specialty pet foods are a growing market, and other competitors are becoming more of a threat. Hence, Hill's must stay on top of its market and its value delivery proposition for its target customers.

Workforce Fulfillment Needs.   The individual fulfillment of the needs of its "new workforce" favors team and group approval; it is equally important, however, to provide individual growth and development opportunity. From the point of view of the employees, Debbie Carter believes that the Richmond team-based process works because of three simple things: trust, a well-functioning team, and "getting out of the lab."

Trust is what underpins the whole work environment. People have to trust the team processes as well as each person in the team. Maintaining that trust is the biggest challenge of operating the plant.

An equally important element, however, is a well-functioning team. When a team is functioning well, it means less pressure and greater freedom. Members are less tied up with routine problems and have more time to do "strategic stuff." A critical part of this process is having teams that address their own performance issues. Carter maintains that issues are dealt with more effectively and performance improves faster when problems are addressed peer-to-peer. The plant's *social module* provides workers the tools they need for such direct dealings. The social module is a multistep process for addressing interpersonal issues and individual performance problems and is designed to provide direct, specific, and nonpunishing feedback and intervention. However, the intervention is neither easy nor comfortable for most individuals to do initially, and some teams are simply not sufficiently developed to deal with such peer-to-peer intervention.

Carter's final point, "getting out of the lab," is not a trivial point. As with any support function, the people in a quality and lab group should not be confined to their workstations and simply toss their results and analysis "over the wall" in the hope that someone will pick up and use them. Debbie makes sure her people are out working with operations teams and with the quality management people on those teams. Debbie herself walks through the entire plant twice a day, which gives her daily at least two hours of direct observation and interaction.

Cultural Factors.   The current leadership philosophy emphasizes continuous improvement and disciplined adherence to the principles of the system. The workforce also has a strong sense of pride in the unique reputation of the company and the quality of its products. It is important to have measures and processes that will continue to support that leadership philosophy and ensure the continued strong reputation of the company and its products.

As enthusiastic as Debbie is about the P&M path at Richmond, however, she recognizes that it is far from perfect—and that things can easily go awry in the newly evolving Richmond plant culture. For example, it was probably a mistake in the beginning for management to give too much latitude to teams before they were ready. Management did not fully understand the various stages of team development, the basics of team discipline, or the need for leaders to take a more active role at the start.

Debbie is also concerned about the lack of good followers. The selection and assessment process is excellent ("the best I've seen"), but it places so much emphasis on leadership that it attracts too many would-be leaders and not enough willing followers. In fact, the person who worked quietly, effectively, and steadily as a good follower ends up getting "dinged" by the system. The current assessment process has been modified based on the understanding of the need for willing followers as well as leaders.

Energy Sources and Alignment Approaches

Obviously, the P&M path at Hill's creates a dynamic balance between worker fulfillment and enterprise performance. This path is closely integrated with a Mission, Values, and Pride path, and the combination serves the company well. Their pursuit of the high-commitment work system results in an environment that expects more of, and gives more to, its workers. People are governed by guiding principles based heavily on trust and respect. The earlier descriptions by Marc Swartz and Debbie Carter tend to highlight the technicians' point of view, but there is ample evidence of performance discipline that favors shareholders and customers as well. For one thing, everyone talks of doing what is right for the business; clear dedication to the business comes first. For another, the critical business performance metrics are both visibly displayed and well known to all.

The primary sources of the extra energy in the Richmond plant are twofold: its demanding customer base (professional veterinarians and retail pet stores) and a collective pride in the mission, values, and aspiration of creating the ultimate *learning organization,* that is, a manufacturing system that would be a model of quality and learning. The company also can draw upon its rich legacy of being the very best in its field.

The Richmond technicians see themselves as members of a flagship plant within the company and a key source of management and leadership talent for both Hill's and the parent company (Colgate-Palmolive). Team members are proud of the quality that Hill's stands for in both its products and its people, as well as what they themselves contribute to that quality. The Richmond effort at Hill's achieves an ongoing balance between performance and fulfillment, as well as integrated support of their two balanced paths by being clearly distinctive in its execution of the five basic alignment approaches discussed below.

Showing People Their True Value.   All team members at Hill's must always show respect for all individuals. This is at the heart of the trust that Debbie emphasizes in describing what works. In addition, the leaders at all levels attempt to place importance on every job. The work environment is based on mutual trust and respect. For example, there is no clock punching, and putting in your eight hours of "contribution" is viewed as a personal commitment (like the honor system at leading universities). All technicians are trusted with all operating information, and admitting mistakes is viewed as the right thing to do.

Management is committed to open communications, widespread involvement, fact-based decisions, and paying attention to people. The team-based work structure fosters openness, involvement, and real empowerment. The plant manager spends 70 percent of his or time just dealing with people; the manager often sits in on meetings primarily to show that he or she cares about the issue at hand. All managers pride themselves on always being open and available to employees and are willing to change decisions when given the supporting facts.

Distributing Leadership Broadly.   Like Avon's hierarchy, Hill's hierarchy has only three formal levels: strategic team, coordinating team, and operating teams. The entire operation is organized around both task teams and cross-functional, problem-solving teams. Five clearly delineated stages of team development warrant the empowerment of these teams. Each stage has clearly defined team leader roles and decision-making processes.

Moreover, like the associates at Avon, all frontline workers have a single title and position: technician. In fact, many technicians act more like supervisors or managers. "We work at a level above our [formal] position," explains Carter. Technicians handle day-to-day supervisory tasks and production problems. People self-police individual behavior issues using structured processes like the social module for the direct feedback described earlier.

During our frontline focus group, four technicians responded to two-way radio calls or had to step out of the interview to deal with issues on the plant floor. They also seemed to have a bit more preoccupation with thinking ahead and anticipating problems. This preoccupation characterizes the best middle managers and change leaders.

Enhancing the Work Itself.   Much attention is paid to ensuring that the work activities themselves are enjoyable, meaningful, and satisfying. Multiple roles are common among the technicians. For instance, a maintenance person can also occasionally act as "budget owner," inventory keeper, "diet owner," or "tour guide." The employees have many opportunities to switch jobs, work on special projects, and participate in communities of practice. As one technician said, "There is always something different to do and something new to learn."

Additional training is available each time an employee is given a new role or position. The balanced personal development of technical, business, and social skills of team members is encouraged, supported, and evaluated. People are also afforded reasonable time flexibility for working on special projects or taking care of personal problems. In addition, the space, facilities, and tools to support team needs are readily available. For example, a two-story, glass-walled "team center" in the center of the plant provides ready access to meeting rooms, white boards, and personal computers. There is even a PC-based asset model that anyone can access to run "what-if" scenarios for production planning.

Making Purposeful Selection.   Determining who becomes part of the Hill's organization is a critical decision. Determining where they work within the organization over time is equally important. There is unusual clarity on the prime qualities required of job candidates.

The start-up hiring process for the Richmond plant was both disciplined and purposeful. There were two overriding selection criteria: the ability to learn and the ability to work in a self-directed, team-based environment. The company actually screened nearly ten thousand applicants to fill two hundred positions! This took six months to complete. In a classic bit of understatement, one candidate said, "Patience was an important part of the process." Hill's is equally purposeful about its ongoing hiring and screens close to one hundred applicants for every position. The company's selection criteria now include problem solving, teamwork, judgment, motivation, integrity, planning and organizing skills, and overall fit with the job and workplace. Most of these are intrinsic characteristics that Hill's believes cannot be taught or trained; they must be evident upon hiring.

Emphasis throughout the hiring process is on "self-selection and mutual selection . . . You can tell from the hiring process that this is a different place and a different kind of job." Moreover, the recruiting and evaluation continue even when the plant is not in a hiring mode. The plant's reputation attracts a wider pool of better candidates (e.g., teachers, former military), and eighty to one hundred candidates apply for every open position.

Providing Performance Transparency.   All employees have a keen understanding of how performance is measured and what current performance is expected of them, their work unit, and their part of the company's business. There is information everywhere—"We are addicted to information." For example, a poster-sized plant profit-and-loss statement hangs in the main hallway. Weekly production results along with targets and trends are displayed on team room bulletin boards. Statistical process control (SPC) charts are posted for all processes and machines.

The awareness of goals and performance levels is complete and widespread. Teams are responsible for breaking high-level goals into production plans and day-to-day performance targets. Everyone is expected to know targets and performance on all aspects of production, such as costs, yield, quality, efficiency, and overruns. This awareness even extends to the objectives of the operations in other plants.

Each technician at the plant has an individual performance agreement that is used as the basis of his or her performance evaluation. Within the performance agreement, several types of objectives are included:

+ high-level production targets for the side of the operation where the individual is working (e.g., 17 million pounds, 92 percent yield, 77.5 percent efficiency for packaging lines)

+ specifics related to other, nonproduction roles that the individual also fills (e.g., budget owner for lubricants, diet owner of one product)

+ training and certification objectives (e.g., forklift maintenance, cardiopulmonary resuscitation)

+ personal skills training (e.g., use of Microsoft Word and Excel)

+ special projects and completion dates

Performance against these objectives does determine bonuses. A 6 percent bonus is awarded every three months if overall plant targets are achieved. Every six months, each person is reviewed and evaluated by a group consisting of three peers and the individual's team leader. In addition to reviewing the specifics of the individual's performance agreement, the group also makes an assessment based on set criteria, including troubleshooting, problem solving, safety, motivation, and the employee's role in and contribution to the team. A rating of 1 to 5 is given on each of these criteria, and written notes are made of the individual's assessment.

The people at Hill's had to pass a tough screen to get there in the first place—and they have to work hard to stay there. They take pride in their accomplishments, which are measured and displayed prominently for all to see. They have high aspirations as individuals and as part of a carefully selected workforce. As a result, they are more critical of themselves and their system's shortfalls than outsiders—and they are constantly energized to improve and make their workplace even better than it is. The simple, integrated construct achieves a powerful balance between plant performance and worker fulfillment over time. This actually summarizes Hill's employee value proposition which is, of course, similar to the generic value proposition for the P&M path from chapter 2, namely, *employees who consistently meet and exceed their metrics, and who adhere to the critical process requirements, will be recognized and respected by their peers, and conspicuously rewarded by management.*

A DOUBLE-EDGED SWORD

Most well-managed companies have some form of a process and metrics system and strive to enforce time-honored principles of consequence management. The essential difference between these companies and

those like Hill's and Avon lies in the attention given to the worker fulfillment aspects of process and metrics. That difference results in the emotional commitment that leads to a higher-performing workforce.

The clear measures and standards, focused processes, and performance transparency that characterize consequence management systems provide a logical rationale for peak performance. These mechanisms seldom, however, engage the emotions of the workers unless
something more is done. That is why we often find the P&M path used
in conjunction with either the Recognition and Celebration path (as is
the case at Marriott and KFC, discussed in chapter 7) or with the Mission, Values, and Pride path that we saw at Hill's and Avon.

Part of the challenge in using a P&M path to engage the hearts and
minds of workers stems from the historical association of process and
metrics with top-down control philosophies. As long as that mind-set
prevails, it is very difficult to obtain the extra, positive emotional energy
that a peak-performance workforce requires.

5 ✦ The Entrepreneurial Spirit Path

Entrepreneurs are a special breed. Few of us have the determination, courage, or creative attributes required both to envision a unique business opportunity and to incur the personal and financial risks required to bring it to fruition. It is truly a high-stakes game in which the pressure never subsides. As Cristina Morgan, senior managing director of Hambrecht & Quist (perhaps the leading generator of new equity financing and underwriting for Silicon Valley), puts it, "I know I couldn't do it—could *you?*"

People who pursue this path do so not only for the obvious wealth creation potential, but also because they want to "create their own thing." If successful, they achieve a level of independence that can seldom be attained in other ways. It can be an appealing dream, to say the least—and it is at the heart of the *new economy,* a term that has recently emerged to characterize high-growth industries.

Entrepreneurial work is intrinsically attractive to many people who believe they should be free to do whatever they like as long as their efforts produce the appropriate marketplace reaction, that is, to wow the customer and devastate the competition. Their attitude is "Nobody tells me what to do or how to do it as long as I get results." Obviously, the true entrepreneur is found mostly in start-up situations, rather than established enterprises. Nonetheless, executives in large companies frequently talk about how they need to inculcate more of an entrepreneurial spirit among their people. Few succeed in doing so, however, and even fewer can retain that spirit over time, as the natural growth in bureaucratic controls—much like ivy—snuffs it out.

Danny Rimer is a typical example of the entrepreneurial spirit at Hambrecht & Quist. A graduate of Harvard University, he and some of his fellow students began their own business while they were still in school. They wanted to "leverage the Internet," which was just emerging onto the scene, and decided to develop a product and service offering that would appeal to cultural segments of the economy (e.g., museums and art galleries). Like most early ventures, this one failed. But as with most entrepreneurs, one failure did not dissuade Rimer from continuing his quest to build his own Internet business. Four years later, after a couple of other abortive attempts, he now is on track to creating a $100 million fund for getting Internet services into uniquely attractive market segments. The surprising part of the story, however, is that he is doing this entirely within the corporate structure of a unique investment banking firm.

This chapter looks at Hambrecht & Quist (H&Q) and BMC, two very different companies that have managed to both cultivate and sustain a higher-performing workforce based primarily on creating high-risk/high-reward environments well beyond the start-up stages of the typical venture-capital play. As a result, they obtain a higher-performing workforce by following the Entrepreneurial Spirit path.

H&Q: THE "I-BANK FOR ENTREPRENEURS"

Founded in 1968 by George Quist (now deceased) and William Hambrecht, H&Q has grown with Silicon Valley in interesting and unexpected ways to become a significant leader in financing rapidly growing entrepreneurial companies, as well as a technology specialist. Originally targeted as a high-technology venture-capital firm, it now focuses on growth companies in four sectors: high technology, health care, branded consumer, and professional services. The company offers a full line of investment banking services.

Hambrecht & Quist aims to serve growth companies by mirroring how they operate: being entrepreneurial in their approach to business, taking greater risks, and operating with fewer resources than do more established competitors. It builds its business by finding high-growth-potential companies at an early stage and offering them financial services throughout their growth cycle—from private placements to merger and acquisition and corporate finance services. Its more well-known IPOs (initial public offerings) have included both Apple and

Genentech in the 1980s, as well as more recent high-profile companies like Amazon.com, Rambus, Starbucks, Siebel Systems, and Netscape. A listing of H&Q's clients closely resembles a Who's Who of Silicon Valley's hot prospects.

The firm's business performance results speak for themselves in several areas:

+ Ranked first in number of technology IPOs from 1995 to 1997

+ Ranked first in aftermarket IPO performance in 1996; second in 1997

+ Professional staff productivity typically twice that of big investment banks (half the staff to do the same-sized deal)

+ Professional staff turnover of 12 percent in 1996 and 15 percent in 1997, compared with Wall Street benchmarks of nearly 20 percent

+ Tripled revenue and doubled employees between 1993 and 1998; revenues in 1998 were $373 million

These kinds of results, plus the intrinsic attractiveness of the firm's entrepreneurial portfolio, have made recruiting at all levels relatively easy; top talent seeks the company out. In fact, the firm had no priority-focused recruiting effort at major business schools until recently. In addition, since the leaders of the firm prefer to recruit very bright people with relevant industry business experience, rather than professionally trained investment bankers, the business schools have not been prominent in their recruiting strategy. As one managing director explained during one of our group sessions at H&Q:

You have to be able to relate to entrepreneurs at a personal as well as business level to succeed here. As a result, most of our people—certainly all of the best ones—literally have a passion for working in the entrepreneurial segment. That's what makes it fun for them in such an otherwise volatile and high-pressure situation.

Historical Perspective: Born of Silicon Valley

To some extent, H&Q stumbled onto the ES path out of necessity as well as a natural legacy from its founders, George Quist and William Hambrecht, who first met in the mid-1960s. Quist had been something of an entrepreneur as president of Mandrel Industries, a precision-instrument manufacturer that grew from $600,000 to $20 million before it was sold to Ampex. For a while after the sale, Quist was president of the venture-capital division at Bank of America.

Hambrecht found the lure of high technology through his work with Security Associates, a Florida investment bank. When the bank was acquired in 1965 by Francis I. Du Pont & Company, Hambrecht was asked to open its corporate finance office in San Francisco. The two founders collaborated on several venture-capital deals before deciding to form their own investment bank. Because of their location and their previous work with new technology ventures, it was natural for them to continue that focus. To cover their operating costs, however, they also underwrote equity offerings for companies that larger investment banks found too small or risky, or both. The equity market downturn in 1974 brought them close to disbanding and caused them to liquidate much of their venture-capital portfolio. According to *Fortune*, Quist commented in 1981: "In 1974 we used to sleep every other night."[1]

They survived that period by taking the same kinds of steps that entrepreneurs take during difficult periods. They cut overhead to the bone, worked out of sparse office space, and required their sales people to pay for half of their expenses, including assistant's salaries, phone bills, and travel. The firm grew rapidly during the late 1970s and early 1980s, but it was seriously threatened again when the technology market went sour in 1984. As the firm's business declined, it experienced significant turnovers of people. CEO Dan Case remembers this period:

> *It was a very difficult time for H&Q. Basically, the firm divided into two groups—one group consisted of people who were new or less committed to H&Q who quickly washed out. The other group consisted of loyalists to H&Q and Bill Hambrecht. . . . At the age of thirty, I was put in charge of investment banking. . . . [As] the seventh head of Corporate Finance in seven years, I had twenty-one people reporting to me, and turnover was running at about 40 percent. It sounds pretty bad, but in many ways it was still fun. I like new things and fixing things that are broken, and we had plenty of both.*

Naturally, H&Q has thrived in the 1990s, with the bull market and overall rise of the new economy. (H&Q defines *new economy* as businesses with growth rates, fueled by creative ideas and innovations, that far outpace the traditional economy.) In addition, the firm made a very smooth leadership transition from the founders to a new CEO, Dan Case. The firm went public in 1996 to provide additional capital for growth and to provide liquidity for the founders and other owners. As of 1998, H&Q remains fiercely independent despite an acquisition wave by commercial and larger investment banks that has snapped up all of H&Q's peers (namely, Robertson Stephens & Company by BankAmerica Corporation, and then BankBoston; Alex Brown & Sons by Bankers Trust; and Montgomery Securities by NationsBank). Though H&Q continues to prosper, a 1998 Harvard Business School case raises concerns about how long H&Q can continue to thrive at its size and yet maintain its entrepreneurial, family-feel culture.[2]

A fundamental reason for the firm's increasing growth and success lies clearly in the caliber and energy of its people—at all levels. Management has remained sharply focused on hiring people who will complement and reinforce its distinctive culture, which a few partners described as an entrepreneurial and collegial place, where politics and bureaucracy are truly minimized. Specifically, they claim that the firm is

a closer-knit, more cohesive place to work than other investment banks. There is a real effort by most of us to carry out Case and Hambrecht's philosophy that our people be able to balance the tension between internal pride and external arrogance by working together in a collegial way.

Cristina Morgan argues convincingly that the H&Q culture presents a mirror image of the clients they serve. Certainly there are differences, but the similarities are at least as compelling. The culture starts with a nonhierarchical, open-door atmosphere where even the most junior employees are not reluctant to walk into any managing director's office to discuss both professional and personal issues. We also learned that a few people with less than one year's tenure have been assigned to work directly with Morgan and Case, not to mention other managing directors of significance.

When asked what was most energizing about working at H&Q, a three-year professional named Sanu Desai made a powerful point about the level of impact he believes that he and others can have very early in their careers:

We work on rapidly growing companies that have the potential to significantly impact the economy on a global scale. More importantly, we work with them at the early stages of their development where our impact is really critical. As a younger person, I have the personal opportunity to influence and help young executives in these organizations directly. That's a lot of impact for someone my age at this early stage of my career.

Intensity and Clarity of Focus

We started our interview probes into the H&Q culture in a newly acquired twelfth-floor conference room, which the previous tenant had endowed with the dubious design feature of full-length glass corner walls and glass doors separated by mahogany paneled walls. In a fairly dramatic but unexpected way, this design configuration symbolized the people's focus and concentration at H&Q. Five of the first eight people whom we interviewed were so focused on their work that they ran smack into one of the plate glass corner walls on their way into our interview area. Luckily, no one was seriously injured, although a few head bruises were sustained. Several people told us that this new conference room (modest by most corporate standards) was a bit fancy for H&Q, whose facilities are supposed to be more in keeping with the plain pipe-rack approach of the frugal entrepreneurs the firm serves.

What characterizes the firm more than anything else is its passion and clarity about enabling entrepreneurs—both externally and internally. Cristina Morgan and David Golden (codirectors of investment banking) say they pointedly discuss this characteristic in their interviews with prospective candidates. To every candidate, they convey this message: "Don't come here unless another one of your dreams is to run your own business—we will expect you to act as if you own H&Q, and the values and reward systems here are structured just like those places!"

As Morgan's earlier quote suggests, however, the environment is not nearly as harsh or unforgiving as the aforementioned quote might have you believe—nor are the personal risks as high. Nonetheless, the motivations are very similar, namely, participating in the creation of something new and exciting. In addition to regular compensation, the firm provides ample opportunity not only for stock ownership in H&Q, but also for individual investment in the specific ventures that become clients of the firm. Not all of the younger professionals with whom we spoke were completely comfortable with this three-piece source of earnings opportunity, two of which are more than modestly speculative. This discomfort was particularly true for those who still saw themselves in an interim position with the firm and who therefore place a higher value on annual cash compensation or "W-2 earnings opportunity." Nonetheless, the firm's managing directors have stuck to their formula, and it seems to be working. H&Q boasts the lowest turnover of any of their competitors—as well as one of the best talent pools.

This focus on entrepreneurial market segments provides a closed loop of energy not unlike the one we found in the Marines. (Marine recruits are energized by the values and behaviors of their drill instructors, who in turn are energized by the value transformations that take place in their recruits.) At H&Q, employees are energized by the entrepreneurial aura of the firm's client portfolio, as well as the direct client interactions that the portfolio provides, and the clients are attracted, if not energized, by the unique passion of H&Q's people for serving them. Undoubtedly, the firm has created a culture that energizes its people by applying the attributes of the ES balanced path. These include a high but uncertain financial earning opportunity, the chance to build and own something unique and valuable, and the freedom to do it in whatever way will produce attractive returns.

Why the ES Path Makes Sense

Again, we see the entrepreneurial pattern so evident in the firm's evolution. H&Q's basic strategy is based on a set of core values and beliefs captured in the following quotes from several partners:

> *Reveal to the market the true economic value of the emerging businesses of the new economy.*

> *Help entrepreneurs and [their] investors take advantage of the opportunities presented by the new economy.*

> *The new economy is entrepreneurial—so are we.*

> *We are not your usual investment bank or financial advisor.*

> *We are interested in more than the deal.*

Obviously, the Entrepreneurial Spirit path best fits the investment-banker segment of H&Q's workforce. It is the same pattern of determined, courageous survival that continues to shape so many of H&Q's target clients. Not surprisingly, then, H&Q people believe it is no accident that they understand that market better than most. Their dedication to the ES path, however, is a function of the firm's business performance priorities, its marketplace dynamics, the fulfillment needs of its employees, and other cultural factors summarized in the following sections.

Business Performance Priorities.   The firm's strategy and core beliefs determine its business priorities. The first priority is to encourage insight into the implications of new technologies. How H&Q encouraged Dan Rimer's Internet efforts is a good example of this priority. The firm also puts high priority on the rethinking of evolving industries, such as the semiconductor industry. The firm is committed to research that results in a deep understanding of its target clients; it goes well beyond standard financial analysis. H&Q strives to assess risk at an earlier stage of industry and company development—sooner and better than more traditional advisors do. It is also committed to finding creative approaches for funding high-growth businesses. H&Q goes to great lengths to position the firm as an entrepreneurial company focused on investment banking rather than an investment bank looking for entrepreneurial business. In this respect, the company takes coleader positions on deals when that best serves the clients, and it continually emphasizes its commitment to the development of the new economy, not just earning fees anywhere lucrative deals are found.

Since the new economy is at the core of its aspirations, H&Q constantly scans the market to spot the "next great little company." Building relationships early, H&Q grows with the winners by helping them through the financial cycle that includes venture funding, IPO financing, follow-on public offerings, and the like. The partners also can take personal stakes in companies in which they really believe, and they staff assignments with people who identify with entrepreneurial CEOs and owners. They sometimes characterize themselves as "high-IQ wing nuts" with diverse backgrounds and deep passions for the businesses they work on. The firm draws on thirty years of relationships that go back to the early days of the Silicon Valley gold rush.

These business priorities have three basic implications for their workforce performance requirements:

✦ Performance is defined by more than deals done and fees earned—something of longer-term value must be created in the process.

✦ The usual investment-bank pedigree is not necessary or sufficient—a special sort of attitude, insight, and zeal is needed.

✦ An entrepreneurial approach is required for serving entrepreneurs.

Marketplace Dynamics and Realities. Although H&Q is now the only remaining independent high-technology investment bank, that arena is no longer the sole province of small-niche players. As a result, competition for deals is becoming fierce and includes the major investment banks of Wall Street. Initial public offerings, in which H&Q does well, carry smaller margins than do second-round offerings, in which H&Q often loses clients to the bigger, full-service players. In addition, the economics of coleader arrangements (H&Q's common position on deals) are dramatically deteriorating. The coleader share of fees has dropped from 50 percent to 25 percent or less. Thus, many observers remain unclear about the viability of H&Q's current size and independence. Some wonder if the firm is too small to be big and too big to be small.

To address these challenges of market size and competition, H&Q has responded in various ways.

✦ Maintaining H&Q margins requires deeper, longer client relationships, which means a workforce dedicated to more than mere transactions and short-term personal gain.

✦ Growing H&Q places a premium on finding the next generation of winning companies, which implies finding and energizing new individuals with new insights to cover new sectors.

✦ Opportunity exists to distinguish H&Q in the talent market, provided the firm continues to sustain an enjoyable and fun culture, to look beyond the usual pedigree, to screen for those with longer-term interests—and to remain independent.

Workforce Fulfillment Needs. The labor market is equally challenging for the firm. With talent at a premium, even smarter, sharper, and more highly energized people are needed to retain the firm's distinctiveness. At the same time, the financial boom of the 1990s has increased the number of bidders for such talent. Industry recruiting focuses on a set pedigree (top schools, financial work experience, plus an MBA). Turnover rates averaging in the midteens require a constant inflow of new, experience-ready talent pursued by attractive employers that include high-growth companies as well as consultants and bankers of all kinds.

Investment banking is infamous for its brutal culture, commonly characterized as aggressive, self-serving, arrogant, and macho—an image that clearly drives some talent away. Moreover, *free agency* is typical among mid-tenured professionals and often leads to an individual's moving from firm to firm, looking for the highest W-2 income. Firms willingly play against each other in the bidding wars for experienced talent. Clearly, H&Q sets some demanding performance standards for its workforce. As a result, it requires sharp, experienced talent who will take the long view, pursue value rather than transactions, and work to broaden and deepen their capabilities. This implies people who take responsibility, who deliver better work with fewer resources, and who work collegially across different areas. They also must not waste energy on politics, turf, and hierarchy. It's a culture in which everyone has to do real work, both individually and collectively.

The fulfillment needs vary by position and role in the enterprise, with frontline associates seeking responsibility, exposure to entrepreneurs, and experience, whereas partners and managing directors seek independence,, flexibility, and freedom from unnecessary structure or process. At all levels, employees seem to benefit from the family feel and collegiality of the firm, which is truly unusual in this industry. And, of course, everyone thrives on the abundance of opportunities that the new economy presents.

Cultural Factors.   H&Q's culture is clearly unique in many ways, some of which have already been illustrated. The deeply ingrained entrepreneurial approach grows out of the firm's history of weathering multiple downturns and crises, working around the edges of conventional strategy, staying flexible, and focusing on growth. While clearly ready and willing to accept change, H&Q retains a strong, healthy wariness of the constraints of additional structure and formal process. This hesitancy to add needed processes can sometimes frustrate people when routine things take longer to get done.

A leadership bias for taking the long view with respect to both clients and financial rewards usually works in H&Q's favor. This bias was forged out of the adversity of the 1987 market crash and the MiniScribe crises (an H&Q-backed disk-drive company convicted of fraud) in the early

1990s. As a result, the managing directors have a proven loyalty to the firm and to each other. By sticking that crisis out together, they developed deep mutual trust and goodwill reflected in their willingness to defer compensation to build the firm and save for the next rainy day.

Dan Case's leadership has effectively superseded that of the founders, while preserving a strong sense that the legacy is still alive and opportunities still abound. People are zealous about finding and serving the next great company, about preserving a collegial and informal environment, and about giving early responsibility and opportunity to people at all levels. Obviously, the culture thrives on the belief that the firm will never run out of "great, little companies" to be financed and cultivated.

Not surprisingly, all of this has led H&Q to focus its workforce performance efforts on the Entrepreneurial Spirit path. Other paths get little serious consideration. The good news is that the firm has mastered this path and derives substantial workforce energy and performance therefrom. The bad news is that changing circumstances (size, competition, acquisition threats, and resource constraints) may soon make it necessary to look to other paths for support as well.

A Richness of Choices

Within their Entrepreneurial Spirit path, H&Q creates a richness of choices for its people. As a result of this variety, other paths have been less needed. Virtually all career options, however, are focused on what H&Q calls "taking the low-beta and rich-reward route to being an entrepreneur." By that it means using the H&Q platform to create a rich portfolio of opportunities that offer high earnings potential without excessive personal risk. H&Q's people can participate in private syndication opportunities that come their way, as well as enjoy the stimulation that comes from working in several companies annually rather than only one. In addition, they work in an environment populated by smart, interesting, and exceedingly diverse people. Within that overall context, the following are examples of choices available to most professionals at H&Q:

- ✦ Prepare to play your own game one day by learning from your clients and by picking up ideas and lessons from your colleagues.

✦ Build a business within H&Q, and help build a great firm by participating directly in creating new groups and businesses.

✦ Work directly with real entrepreneurs and share in their challenges
and successes.

✦ Innovate in your field and reshape the industry's playing fields by
being a thought leader who influences key sectors of the economy.

Energy Sources and Alignment Approaches

The primary source of extra energy for H&Q's balanced path is, of
course, its relentless customers, the entrepreneurs of Silicon Valley and
beyond—"cool companies" about which H&Q's workforce can feel passionate because they are at the cutting edge of the new economy. The
products and services of these enterprises are in emerging, exciting areas. Because these companies are relatively small, they are still in the
formative stages and are ready for change. As a result, H&Q can greatly
influence the ultimate success of these companies, many of which are
becoming significant, if not great, in their field. New hires can clearly
envision having a personal role in the public launch of the next head-
line-grabbing act! Few can resist it.

Moreover, the kinds of people within such companies are hard to
find elsewhere. They are real entrepreneurs—deeply committed, young,
and always highly energized. Their energy is obviously contagious. Such
people can be real sources of personal inspiration and motivation to
those around them. H&Q people at several levels have many close contacts with these clients. They deal directly with founders and CEOs. The
relatively small size of most H&Q teams means that even the very junior
people have frequent, direct interactions and relationships with interesting, diverse personalities.

A second important source of energy is the dynamics of the marketplace itself. The new economy comprises fast-paced and dynamic businesses, with plenty of feedback sources, which range from instant stock
price changes to a voracious business press. If nothing else, the news
coverage makes people at H&Q feel as if they are at the center of the new
economy—being in on the buzz about the next great company. The
competition, which on the one hand is fierce and intense, also constitutes a source of energy to many. Winning against the big boys, beating
big-name investment banks in a fight seemingly stacked against you, is

energizing. So is just knowing that H&Q is battling as the last of the true independents.

Finally, H&Q has been energized by its incredibly magnetic leaders, both past and present. Already bigger than life, CEO Dan Case sets a tone for the firm that seems to reek with opportunity: wide participation, much responsibility, ever-expanding roles—and the expectation that you will figure out how to take the initiatives that make new things happen. Frontline professionals have ready access to the kind of top leaders that they respect and aspire to be like. In addition, these leaders seem to have an almost inbred personal interest in people and their development. Cristina Morgan simply could not resist the urge to have us talk to one new associate after another—because she thought it would energize them at least as much as it would inform us.

The emotional energy that H&Q generates is aligned through four complementary approaches within which H&Q strives for distinction: creating widespread opportunity, generating collective energy, showing people their true value, and making purposeful selections. With each, they achieve a dynamic balance between worker fulfillment and enterprise performance that is unique in their field.

Creating Widespread Opportunity. Of course, entrepreneurship is mostly about creating new opportunity, but it seldom works out as well as it does at H&Q. It begins with the genuinely entrepreneurial approach the firm takes in managing and developing its people. Big opportunities are provided very early in people's careers, and individuals are strongly expected to "figure it out for themselves." There are very few boundaries, and the firm expects that risks will be taken and mistakes made. The firm also provides its people with a great platform for playing in the exciting high-tech and high-growth arena, both in and beyond the Silicon Valley. Access is seldom difficult since, as Morgan quaintly puts it, "everybody is willing to show their underwear," and there are many opportunities to personally participate in deals with a greater degree of independence.

Generating Collective Energy. Although you don't see the kind of collective mayhem that characterizes a KFC or Southwest Airlines environment, you do sense the energy in the H&Q working environment. The conviction that the firm has a strategy of being and staying unique in its field, keeping its entrepreneurial roots, and remaining independent as long as possible is very energizing. These beliefs are not only well known, but consistently reiterated by managing directors and partners in all parts of the firm. The collegial spirit and attitude that Case and his colleagues talk about is very real for most people. Everyone seems to share the norm that this part of the culture is important to preserve, despite the change in ownership (H&Q went public in 1996), the ever-present threat of merger, and the relentless onslaught of size. Collaboration and teamwork are evident from the top on down, and informal personal networks invariably take precedence over formal hierarchy. Finally, the H&Q environment is filled with stimulating people who are very smart, capable, diverse, and interesting. The investment-bank mold is definitely broken here and was apparently replaced by genuine, contagious, collective energy values.

Showing People Their True Value.   Leaders at all levels in H&Q value their people and care about them personally. Individuals are treated with respect even under pressure. No one tolerates whiners or screamers, and the firm instinctively rejects the macho image of a New York investment bank. Although people are clearly expected to work hard and put in long hours, there is little evidence of or tolerance for the use of fear and intimidation. High levels of confidence, trust, and goodwill combine to create a strong sense of personal autonomy, latitude, and responsibility. The hierarchy is minimal, and little of it is imposed. Capability and accomplishment are respected as much as or more than formal position, and there is open access to anyone in the organization. "I can walk in to see Dan or Cristina as easily as I can anyone else in the firm" was a typical comment during our interviews. Most people also expressed a sense of working as peers and partners with people they like and respect.

Making Purposeful Selection.   Of course, it helps that lots of the right kinds of people are naturally drawn to work at H&Q. Like Southwest Airlines, The Home Depot, and others that can pick from a wide selection, H&Q emphasizes cultural fit with the firm's core values. Innate intelligence and attitude are more important than degree or pedigree; nor can you bluff your way into this enterprise with arrogance and appearance. Although high-IQ wing nuts may have the advantage, the firm is also focused on wider interests than banking and demands something more than impressive investment-banking credentials. Candidates with the right attitude will be optimists and open admirers of entrepreneurs. They will also reflect a sincere desire to be part of a collegial firm that expects teamwork as much as it respects and rewards individual initiative.

The selection process continues beyond the initial hiring. Staffing is constrained to ensure that opportunity generation stays ahead of resource capacity. The culling of "misfits" occurs largely through compensation differentiation and self-selection by people who recognize early on that they do not fit this entrepreneurial path. The system holds onto those who value the culture, the entrepreneurial exposure, and the equity-building opportunity. It culls out self-centered, short-term motivated, and high-maintenance people.

These four alignment approaches deliver the critical balance between workforce fulfillment and enterprise performance. H&Q's higher-performing workforce is critical to its performance as an institution. Its underlying employee value proposition offers new-economy excitement and rewards in return for individual initiative, hard work, and collaborative effort.

BMC: SEGMENTED ENTREPRENEURSHIP

Had BMC, a unique software company founded in 1979, been located in Silicon Valley, it might well have been financed by H&Q! Its first product was the 3270 Super Optimizer, a utility that dramatically improved terminal input and output operations of IBM's popular mainframe computer 3270. According to some current employees, "that group of developers was smarter and knew more about IBM products' technical details than IBM's engineers themselves."

BMC's initial offerings turned out to be *killer products*—big ideas that met the high-value-customer needs far better than any competitive offering. Hence, the company didn't have to worry much about its workforce performance beyond those who created the product offering. Specifically, BMC was able to offer high value to IBM's customers by allowing them to squeeze more performance out of IBM's database products and mainframe computers. Because of this unique value offered by BMC's products, the company was able to sell them using a telephone sales approach. Telesales was particularly effective because the potential customers were narrowly defined, namely, the companies who were large and sophisticated users of IBM database products, and because the product was so well designed that its users did not need any hand-holding from BMC.

It is clear that BMC was able to obtain peak performance from two key segments of its workforce: product designers and experienced account representatives. As a result, the company can claim one of the highest productivity records in the software industry. Its average gross profit per employee (based on 1993–1995 average numbers) is $275,000, which compares very favorably to a peer-company average of $110,000— and Microsoft's of $265,000. BMC also maintains the leading market share in its category, and its market capitalization at the time of our research is the fourth largest in the software industry, behind Microsoft, Oracle, and Computer Associates.

BMC's organizational approach is based on a segmented, highly entrepreneurial workforce. It hard-wires individual incentives by linking them tightly with the organization's objectives. In this construct, it is easy to hire experienced people from outside since there is not much of a "culture" to learn, and the implicit ways in which the organization operates become crystal clear early on. The hardwired financial incentives quickly align a new hire to the organization's objectives.

Interestingly, this approach does not depend on the existence of an overall goal or mission to focus the workforce or on a magnetic leader to motivate people (although Max Watson, the current CEO, meets that criterion). Rather, it relies on a focused business strategy plus a carefully integrated business system that energizes individual employees or employee groups to make meaningful contributions of different kinds. The model clearly segments the workforce and thereby allows management to focus its energy alignment approaches and tools on two groups: *product authors* (or designers) and experienced telesales professionals.

We encountered a unique example of how pride of ownership in the specific work product is reinforced with direct, tangible rewards for the product's value. Anouar Jamoussi is a young, energetic, enthusiastic, and very thoughtful person. He joined BMC several years ago, fresh out of school. He had just finished graduate work at a French engineering school and was doing postdoctoral work at the University of Houston. A common friend referred him to John Moores, the original founder and then CEO of BMC. After a ten-minute discussion with Moores and three additional interviews, Anouar was offered an entry-level position at BMC in the Software Quality Assurance Group, which he accepted.

Anouar progressed very well, and he is now what BMC calls a *product author* (a person who conceives new products and spearheads their development). He described what he really likes about BMC: "If you deliver and if you perform, then BMC takes good care of you." Of course, he likes the incentive rewards that the company gives, and he values the stock options as much or more than the cash awards. The options offer him tangible ownership in the company—what he refers to as "skin in the game." He eloquently praised what he views as a unique system at BMC of paying salary plus commission to even the research and development (R&D) employees.

Product authors like Anouar receive 5 percent of their product's revenue in the first year. This percentage declines to 2 percent by the third year. He believes that "everybody in R&D has a desire to become a product author, because it is not only financially very rewarding but also prestigious at BMC."

Anouar was proud to be a product author himself. His driving goal on a day-to-day basis is to achieve market success for his product. He views it as his own business situation. As a result, he is prompt and eager to help sales people in any way he can to ensure success of his product. For example, he and other product authors frequently take time to talk to prospective customers to explain technical details of their products. Success for them is not simply the invention of the product—it is inventing a product that achieves significant business success in the marketplace.

Anouar emphasized his belief that a product's market success is more important than any technical accomplishment. He pointed to a patent plaque hanging on his office wall and commented, "Patents are not particularly important at BMC. And I didn't care for it too, but now that I have a patent, I do feel good about it. It does provide some personal and professional satisfaction." But clearly what makes his eyes twinkle and energy level rise is the discussion of his products' market need and success.

Why the ES Path Makes Sense

Somewhat like the situation at H&Q, the Entrepreneurial Spirit path emerged naturally for BMC from its new-venture origins as the best way to achieve peak performance among the two most critical segments of its workforce. However, BMC's performance priorities, marketplace dynamics, workforce fulfillment needs, and other cultural factors are unique to its own situation.

Performance Priorities.   Like any start-up situation, survival was the name of the game in the beginning. The company required a clear focus on establishing a foothold in the rapidly emerging software market by capturing a few key customers quickly. Hence came the emphasis on inventing killer products to meet the needs of large users of IBM databases and mainframe products to further exploit their mainframe situation. Once the company was established, however, the performance priorities progressed. These priorities included the continuation of big ideas for a few large, sophisticated customers that BMC expected to engage through its highly efficient telesales approach.

Marketplace Dynamics.   Creating high-value software to fit specific customer needs that can be sold to others by telephone is simple to describe, but difficult to accomplish. It requires creative systems designers plus astute customer-needs assessments. Max Watson describes the business and marketplace priorities:

> *Your customers determine your business success, and you must change to meet and anticipate their needs. Your people will determine your customers' value which, in turn, determines shareholders' value. Thus, the individual person in the critical slot—not the process that defines the slot—is critical to our business success.*

Workforce Fulfillment Needs.   From the beginning, BMC leaders instinctively segmented the company's workforce into two critical components: the unique designers, and the experienced sales representatives, who could secure, retain, and nourish the customer relationships over the telephone. The sales representatives are attracted, energized, and aligned by the high earnings opportunity of serving key accounts right. The product authors have some additional fulfillment needs, however. On the one hand, the satisfaction of "inventing" is important to them; on the other, the business success in the marketplace is also important. Money matters, but so does creativity and ownership—not to mention the individual freedom to do one's own thing.

Cultural Factors. When we first visited BMC and Max Watson, we were almost led astray by outward appearances. The exterior of the building is gray and simple looking, almost nondescript. Max later explained that he would rather spend money on creative decor within the building, where employees would benefit. The cafeteria walls are painted in a spectacular wall-to-wall-to-ceiling mural that depicts BMC employees in all stages of work. Every conceivable employee service need—from banking to laundry and car wash—is available on the premises to minimize the need for anyone to leave the building during the heat of battle, so to speak. No doubt that BMC is an open and energized workplace—but it's not because of the accoutrements. It's the entrepreneurial money opportunity!

Energy Sources and Alignment Approaches

The company's primary source of energy is unquestionably the high growth that fuels both the financial gains and the opportunity expectations of its product authors and sales representatives. As the company grows in size and moves into other segments in the distributed systems environment, however, it may need to consider other sources. For now, however, growth plus Watson's enthusiasm and relaxed determination are more than adequate sources of energy for the company's peak-performance workforce segments.

The entrepreneurial path at BMC is similar to that of Hambrecht & Quist in its sources of energy, but BMC pursues distinctiveness and balance with a somewhat different set of alignment approaches. The approaches will be discussed in the following sections.

Making Purposeful Selection. BMC attracts top-notch people in specific skill areas with a demonstrable success record. The company's business success and its position of market leadership attract people much as H&Q's success and market leadership do. In addition, the company offers the potential of significantly higher financial rewards than do its competitors. Most importantly, BMC knows precisely what attitudes and characteristics it is looking for in the two critical areas of its workforce. Doug Erwin, a former executive vice president and chief operating officer, describes it this way:

The whole R&D stuff starts with the authors. These guys are super, super bright. Many are very uncomfortable in a large-company social environment. . . . These were the guys working at our customers who were always pushing us by saying, "Damn it why don't you fix this problem, and this is how to fix it." So we'd say, "Why don't you come over (with BMC), help us fix it, write this code, we'll sell it to others—and by the way, we'll pay you a commission."

Clearly, the company hires experienced people who are significantly above average in specific areas of knowledge or skills and have high integrity. BMC knows exactly what it is looking for within the critical segments of its workforce, and it makes sure to get what it wants. Dale Peterson, sales recruiting manager, sums it up well:

Finding and keeping these "perfect hires" is a real challenge in a business where competition for top people is fierce and salespeople are always ready to jump ship if they see a better deal in another company.

[On the other hand] BMC is fundamentally a great place to work. . . . It has the feel of a start-up—everyone here feels like an entrepreneur—but it's big enough that you know it's not going to fail. It's a friendly environment, and you're selling excellent products. And (he adds with a laugh), you can make a lot of money here—commissions are uncapped, and there are salespeople here making more than the CEO!

Distributing Leadership Broadly. The company creates just enough of a system to ensure that people's efforts are sharply focused, well aligned, and maximally leveraged. Top management provides very clear guidelines that help pinpoint and ensure a focus on opportunities that represent a compelling value proposition to the customer. Beyond that, both product authors and key account representatives are expected to take whatever initiative is appropriate for success in their product or account areas. In addition, the company has designed a rigorous system for product testing before release and technical support after release. As one product author sees it: "We basically create little businesses. . . . We have concentrated on a very small niche . . . market space of really hard customer problems."

Articulating What Matters Most. BMC has developed telesales as a dominant way of selling. Although that approach is more efficient than the more conventional traveling salesperson model, it is also more demanding. To sell this technically sophisticated product requires sharp individuals who know what matters most to their accounts. The telesales approach also poses tough requirements for BMC's product development people—to design a product so compelling in value and so easy to use and install that it can be sold and supported over the phone.

Providing Meaningful Recognition and Rewards. Employees' entrepreneurial spirit is energized when their rewards are linked tightly to their output. BMC uses a commission-driven incentive system for the key functions—R&D and sales—which are responsible for the company's success. Employees expect to earn significantly more than the competition, and they do when their results exceed customer expectations. For example, the product authors receive a direct percentage of the total sales of their product, and the leading sales account people can and do earn more than the president. As Erwin says:

> *We pay our people very well. . . .Our compensation for our software people is pretty unique—[maybe] a couple of companies now follow us, but we've been unique for seventeen years.*
>
> *. . . Three years ago, Max [Watson, the CEO] was only the seventh highest paid employee in the company. We had three salesmen make more money than he did, and three authors make more money than he did. We're halfway through this year, and we're probably going to have five salesmen make more money than he does this year.*
>
> *We're talking big money. . . . One of these authors spends his Saturday mornings driving his two little daughters down to Hobby Airport [in Houston] and taking a Lear jet to fly them to Vail for a ski lesson—almost every week!*

In short, BMC gets peak performance from critical segments in its workforce by a combination of purposeful hiring and strong entrepreneurial incentives within an astute business system. The business system has been designed to exploit entrepreneurialism, to leverage the people performance in critical sales and product development skill segments, and to concretely align people incentives with the overall organization's objectives. This allows BMC to ensure people's professional and personal satisfaction in the segments of the workforce most critical to its competitive advantage.

CLEARLY A SEDUCTIVE PATH

It is no accident that most large companies openly aspire to creating a true entrepreneurial environment within their organization. It is also no accident that few succeed, and the larger the organization, the more difficult it seems to be. Developing a cadre of frontline entrepreneurs is not for everyone.

The cases in this chapter highlight some characteristics that make the Entrepreneurial Spirit path appealing. That is, the entrepreneurial path focuses on the customer, relies on individual initiative to deliver results, and is largely self-policing. At the same time, the path presumes an abundance of high-reward and high-risk opportunities—each of which promises significant "ownership" potential for individuals in the workforce. This invariably means a growing and dynamic marketplace. It is also important that the leadership philosophy at the top be compatible with the needs of people who are attracted to this path. These people need a high degree of independence and control over their own destiny. They also require, and are energized by, the opportunity to grow and develop their business development skills and customer relationships. Although some people are more naturally predisposed to behave as entrepreneurs, many others can choose and learn the required attitudes, skills, and behavior patterns.

Magnetic leaders, impossible dreams, and unrelenting customers constitute the primary sources of energy along this path. People who enjoy this path take and manage risks, but they are intelligent risk takers rather than impulsive gamblers. Both Hambrecht & Quist and BMC give their people great latitude to build their piece of the business and earn whatever that business permits them to earn. In return, the companies expect them to stay within the mission-and-business purpose of the enterprise. When a company's business environment is characterized by constant change along multiple dimensions (customers, products, competitors, etc.)—and when growth is an integral part of the equation—the Entrepreneurial Spirit path is indeed an attractive option for creating a higher-performing workforce.

6 ✦ The Individual Achievement Path

America was built on the principle of individual initiative; most Americans still savor stories of rugged individualists who have followed their own instincts to accomplish great things. The Horatio Alger rags-to-riches legend still captures the essence of the American dream: If you work hard enough on the right things, you will become successful, wealthy, and happy.

Such images are now part of our shared understanding of the way things should be. Nonetheless, most companies are still searching for ways that will lead employees, on their own, to identify and make changes that are mostly in the best interests of the total enterprise. The hope is that somewhere between the traditional lunchroom suggestion box, town-hall meetings, frontline total-quality teams, and the "free-flowing exchange around rough models" (described in Tom Peters's *Circle of Innovation*)[1] lies the secret to unleashing individual initiative.

What our research suggests—not surprisingly—is that the Individual Achievement (IA) path is less about the tools and trappings of empowerment. It is more about creating a pervasive personal achievement mindset that says, "This enterprise offers opportunities that allow me to take the kinds of initiatives I like; I expect to be judged and rewarded largely based upon my own achievements."

So why doesn't every talented worker want to be on an IA path? The simple answer is that it requires a lot of hard work and unpredictable hours. Individual performance shortfalls are jarringly obvious (if not painful), personal anxieties run high, and the peer pressures on underperformers can be very intense. Although the financial earnings opportunities may be attractive, there are higher earnings opportunities in more entrepreneurial situations.

The attributes and conditions that differentiate the IA path derive from people's inherent need to stand out as individuals, to influence their own destiny, and to advance and grow personally. These fundamental human needs receive a much higher priority in the IA path relative to people's other fulfillment needs, for example, to be part of a group or to share in collective performance results. The primary focus of the IA path is on personal initiative, achievement, growth, and responsibility.

There is no question that IA organizations are deeply committed to developing their people. They tend to spend significant sums of money and even greater amounts of senior leadership time on training, coaching, and evaluating performance as well as other professional development efforts. Often they cannot even calculate the total amount of this investment. They believe in each person's ability to make a significant contribution to the overall corporate mission. As a result, they define individual roles broadly and invest in equipping each individual with the knowledge and skills required to fill these roles—and to move beyond them. These investments in people often carry over from the professional domain to the personal domain. An IA organization, for example, often goes to extraordinary lengths to help an employee confronting a family emergency. This chapter focuses on and compares two very different enterprises that pursue the IA path with diligence and distinctive results: The Home Depot and McKinsey & Company, Inc.

THE HOME DEPOT:
UNPRECEDENTED CUSTOMER SERVICE

A local hardware chain becomes one of the leading companies in the world? Clearly, this is someone's fantasy. Yet, in less than twenty years, The Home Depot rose from relative obscurity to become one of America's best-known and most successful entrepreneurial undertakings. It is the largest retailer in its category, with nearly 700 stores, as of the end of the second quarter fiscal 1998, in the United States and Canada and total sales topping $24 billion.

Fortune magazine has named The Home Depot "America's most admired retailer" for five years running, and the retailer's financial performance has been virtually spectacular by any measure. Its average annual return to shareholders over the last ten years has been a whopping 39 percent compared to the industry average of 8 percent. Most recently, The Home Depot posted record sales and earnings for 1998, up 25 percent and 32 percent, respectively, over 1997; and, according to the company's annual reports, this is only the beginning. The Home Depot plans to operate well over a thousand stores by the year 2000, and it launched an international effort with its first store outside North America opening recently in Santiago, Chile. It has also started expanding into the home design business through its EXPO Design Centers, now located in Atlanta, Dallas, Miami, San Diego, and Westbury, New York.

If you ask the leaders of The Home Depot how they do it, they tell you without equivocation that their secret is their employees (called associates). Until very recently, the leaders were quite reluctant to permit outsiders to study what they see as their secret weapon.

Historical Perspective: Perpetuating Ownership Values

The Home Depot was founded in 1978 by two unlikely mavericks who had just been fired from Handy Dan's, a local hardware chain in the Los Angeles area. These two castoffs from the establishment, Bernard Marcus and Arthur Blank, set out in pursuit of a dream that has been literally revolutionizing the home improvement industry. Their simple dream was to combine a level of customer service unprecedented in the industry with the product breadth, ready access, and low prices of a warehouse store. Without the benefit of hindsight, this idea would surely have struck most graduates of major business schools (MBAs) as naive if not impossible. How can you deliver the lowest-cost products through a business system saddled with the high costs implicit in a superior customer-service approach? The mind-set reflected in this statement is precisely why Marcus and Blank reserve the term *MBA* for those "factual, by-the-numbers" people who would surely "send The Home Depot into a downward cycle" if they were ever allowed to take the helm.

There's no doubt, however, that The Home Depot has found a way to make its seemingly incompatible priorities work. Bernie and Arthur, as they are fondly known by their employees, found their first believer in Ken Langone, a Handy Dan investor who helped raise the pair's first $2 million. They were soon joined by Pat Farrah, and this small team quickly honed in on the southeastern United States for its growth potential. Then Blank learned that J. C. Penney was closing four stores in the Atlanta metro area and was looking to lease the space. Six weeks later, they had signed a contract and The Home Depot was up and running. The first stores opened their doors in 1979.

From the beginning, the founders believed strongly that the performance of their total workforce was critical to their success. The retail distribution of home improvement supplies and services has historically been a highly competitive, segmented market—with the needs of professional builders seen as different from the needs of homeowners and repair contractors. To serve all segments well was once regarded as a virtual impossibility. Marcus and Blank, however, decided that more was better and that they would go after a broad mix of customers.

For Marcus, The Home Depot's success is all about ownership—he wants every associate in every store to feel as he does about the company. "I always play a game with the new store managers," he said smiling to himself as if he'd just come up with the idea for the first time. To paraphrase his more lengthy description, Bernie's game is to sit down with store managers and ask them if they would be interested in buying their store if he and Arthur were to franchise the operation. Most managers instantly respond positively, but pause to reflect when Bernie reminds them that they will have to come up with $25 million or $35 million—which, of course, they do not have. He then helps them think through how they might get family members to borrow against homes and savings to help raise the initial investment. In short, he wants them to feel the individual responsibility of ownership. Bernie says , "[I tell my managers] 'I'm giving you the keys to the store. . . . Would you operate it the same way? . . . Would you have [the] same people working for you now with your parents' future on the line? . . . What about the [operating] systems? Would you do the same things?'"

From the answers to these kinds of questions, both Bernie and the managers discover where the store has suboptimal staffing and systems. More importantly, the interchange fires up the critical sense of individual responsibility (ownership) that The Home Depot seeks from every associate.

When asked about the biggest challenge in creating and maintaining this sense of ownership, he answers, "listening and letting people win." Then Bernie smiles again, because he still spends over fifty days a year in the stores—just listening. Typically, he walks into a store, picks out fifteen people at random, pulls them into a break room, and closes the door. Within a few minutes, they are telling him all the ins and outs, pluses and minuses of their operation. He has apparently developed a unique persona—part hero, part next-door neighbor, and part mascot. "When I walk in a store, they hug and kiss me. They come sign my shirt, my hat. They're not afraid to call me Bernie, and there's a real love there."

Marcus and Blank have developed a passionate commitment to decentralized decision making, but it did not come naturally to them at first. By their own admission, they started The Home Depot with more of a benevolent dictator's mentality. "Up until we had our twenty-fourth store, we knew every single person in every store. . . . We were involved in every single decision . . . who got fired, and who really moved up the ladder."

Growth and size changed all that. Increasingly, when Bernie walked into new stores he no longer knew half of the people, much less the key store issues. The balance of marketplace knowledge shifted to "the people in the stores—the district managers, the managers, the assistant managers—who really knew something." Along with this development came the important realization that he couldn't know everything. Bernie began to realize that if one person made all the decisions, he or she would destroy everyone else around. "If people can't win," he explained, "they don't ever try to win. . . . People have to be able to make mistakes. Mistakes are the best teaching tool."

Clearly, The Home Depot gives people equally abundant opportunities to win and to make mistakes. The number of high-impact decisions that Home Depot associates have to make each day is striking, when compared with the number at other retailers. Store managers, for example, are individually responsible for decisions that most retailers usually make centrally. These decisions include identifying the products to be sold in the store, hiring the people, deciding what to pay them, and setting appropriate inventory levels. As Steve Messana, senior vice president for Human Resources, put it, they are playing in "a very large sandbox."

The Store: Where the Dream Comes Together

Jim Wargo was the store manager for The Home Depot in Kennesaw, Georgia, about forty-five minutes outside of Atlanta. With 240 employees and over $50 million in sales, the store is just a little larger than the average Home Depot store, but there is nothing average about Jim Wargo or "his" Home Depot. Jim is a big, athletic guy, about six foot two, and 220 pounds. As soon as he started speaking, we realized the force of his personality was even more powerful than his imposing physical presence. With a huge smile on his face and a booming voice, he filled the room with an almost palpable optimism and energy. When Jim retires from The Home Depot, he might easily make it as a motivational speaker. Much of his story is best told in his words.

Before joining The Home Depot, Jim lived in Pennsylvania, where he was studying engineering and working at Busy Beaver, a local hardware store. He and a friend decided to move to Orlando, Florida, to work for a new Home Depot that was opening there. "I was going . . . back to school the next semester, but when I got to The Home Depot something just happened. I found out that by working hard, learning, and just pushing on my own, I could move up. You don't see that at [most] other companies."

With what he described as a little bit of experience in lumber and gardening, he started as a green associate in the lumber department. A short five months later, he was promoted to department supervisor for lumber and lawn. After running the department for about a year, Jim approached Larry Mercer, executive vice president of operations, and said, "I think I'm ready to be an assistant manager or take on a bigger department." Mercer was one of the first operations managers at The Home Depot, starting out as an assistant manager like Jim, and working his way up to his present dual role as executive vice president of operations and group president for three of the core divisions.

A few days after Jim's request, Larry offered him a chance to move to the store in Daytona Beach. Soon he was promoted to assistant manager in Jacksonville. From Jacksonville, he went to Connecticut to help open the second store in the northeast. Then he moved to Long Island, and then to New Jersey. Jim's next stop was Ben Salem, Pennsylvania, for his first stint as a store manager. While many would have found this type of continual relocation draining, Jim thrived on the challenge: "I didn't mind all the moving. . . . I figured wherever the company needs [me], I'm there!"

One of Jim's biggest challenges was opening a new Home Depot in Harrisburg, Pennsylvania.

I was out in the middle of nowhere. . . . All I had were the fourteen experienced associates . . . and eight weeks to train the rest, none of whom had ever even heard of The Home Depot. I had to teach everybody what was in my heart and put it into theirs.

So, we'd start every day with a fifteen-minute meeting to talk about . . . what was going on that day. Then we'd do jumping jacks and run around the building. We were out there cheering and having a good time. There were people who thought we were nuts, but it was a great experience.

Jim ran the Harrisburg store for two years before he was asked to move to the Atlanta area and take over the Kennesaw store—his eleventh store situation in thirteen years! Although The Home Depot was born in Atlanta and has long dominated the market, a new challenge loomed on the horizon—an arch competitor (well financed and very aggressive), Lowe's, was coming to town. The Home Depot was mobilizing for battle to defend its home turf. Jim had faced Lowe's in other markets and was undaunted by the state-of-the-art Lowe's store opening six miles away. But Jim believes that the competition is not really the issue as long as you get your people fired up to "just take care of the customer" no matter what. It is that individual sense of responsibility to customers that makes the difference in Jim's view. "Lowe's is like a palace. The Home Depot is like a church. Anybody can put up a building and put stuff in it, but you can't copy our culture, spirit, and our customer service. That's what brings people back."

Despite his relatively short tenure in the Kennesaw store, Jim's words and attitude leave no doubt that The Home Depot is already his church: "The Home Depot lets you be your own businessperson. It's exciting. I am so proud of running a $50-million-a-year business and having 240 employees. It's all mine."

Not surprisingly, Jim sees his most important store-manager role as firing up each associate to feel and act like an owner of his or her part of the business, be it a department, an aisle, or a merchandise display. Moreover, the emphasis is on individual achievement, job enhancement, and broadened personal responsibility—not W-2 earnings or personal wealth creation.

Why the IA Path Makes Sense

Clearly, The Home Depot excels at more than one balanced path. Although we have chosen to describe the company's pursuit of the

Individual Achievement path, it also pursues a Mission, Values, and Pride path with diligence and distinction. Moreover, these paths doubtlessly overlap with the Entrepreneurial Spirit path described in the preceding chapter. The key difference, of course, is that the entrepreneurial approach involves much higher personal risk and earnings potential—and was much more of a factor during The Home Depot's early days. Nonetheless, The Home Depot's two current paths lead to passionate testimonials, derive their meaning from a rich and growing body of stories of individuals going to extreme measures, and guide daily decisions on the front line.

For example, you can ask virtually every associate at The Home Depot what is most important and get the same answer—serving the customer. Even more telling is that The Home Depot associates can describe in exacting detail what serving the customer means to them on a daily basis, and these descriptions are remarkably consistent across the organization. It's more than a commitment to customer service that drives the organization, it's an *obsession* with customer service that is inextricably linked to a belief in the power of individuals and individual contributions. The resulting mind-set is what The Home Depot associates refer to as *orange blood,* an affectionate reference to the store's main color scheme. Home Depot associates take great pride in being orange blooded. It takes a core group of orange-blooded people to start a new store, a group of associates told us during our study, and if a store manager is struggling, he or she will probably go to Atlanta for "an orange transfusion."

The components of the IA path complement and support the components required for the MVP path both in terms of sources of extra energy and in balancing worker fulfillment with enterprise performance. Integrating these two paths, which constitute a powerful and demanding combination, makes sense in terms of business performance priorities, marketplace dynamics, workforce fulfillment needs, and internal cultural factors.

Performance Priorities. The company's primary priority is to deliver to customers unprecedented service that results in their loyalty over time. To accomplish this, The Home Depot provides a unique mix and range of quality products and services through a warehouse store that offers important customer access, availability, and price advantages.

The Home Depot goes to extreme measures to care for customers. Arthur Blank strikes a very different image from that of his longtime partner and friend, Bernie Marcus: Blank is less effusive, more meticulous in appearance and demeanor, and on the surface, perhaps more what we might expect the leader of a top U.S. company to be like. Yet, like Bernie, he is passionately focused on the intangibles that he believes are at the core of The Home Depot's success:

> *Anybody can . . . see what merchandise we carry, who our vendors are, and what our prices are. . . . What goes on inside the minds of our associates is really what is very hard to copy. It's our whole orientation: take care of the customer, the customer is always first, do whatever you have to do, go to extreme measures.*
>
> *. . . We have replaced entire kitchens, entire bathrooms, where we knew customers were wrong. . . . They took home the products and they mismeasured and they put them up improperly and they this-that-and-the-other-thing, but when people shop at The Home Depot, they're in safe harbor.*

This same message comes through loud and clear to The Home Depot associates. As Sally, an associate in the Kennesaw store, put it,

> *We are . . . given no limits . . . in terms of satisfying the customer. . . . I don't need my immediate superior's permission, and I certainly don't need to call Bernie and Arthur to do that. I'm mandated to do it, and that gives me a great sense of confidence in the company.*
>
> *[Sure], you have to decide at some point whether making the customer happy is best for the company or just best for the customer. . . . Every customer will test your limits [to see] how far . . . you're willing to go.*
>
> *But . . . [management] feels they can trust me with the decision. I can make it on my own or I can bring someone in to help me.*

The energy created by what Arthur calls this blind passion around customer service cannot be underestimated. The company shares a mind-set that taking care of the customer is absolutely the most important thing. As a result, like Marriott, the U.S. Marines, and Southwest Airlines, The Home Depot creates a *virtuous cycle*. The cycle starts with the associates' going to extreme measures to take care of the customer. As a result, the customer receives service that far exceeds his or her expectations. The cycle completes with the satisfaction that the associates get from their positive interaction with the customer, and that heightens their motivation and their commitment to wow the next customer.

Marketplace Dynamics and Realities. The marketplace is increasingly competitive as others attempt to duplicate The Home Depot's approach. To sustain customer loyalty against the competition requires constant attention to service, value, product mix, and display. This means people dedicated to developing the skills and product/service knowledge to anticipate and exceed customer expectations. To that end, the company seeks people at all levels whose attitudes, values, and personalities are uniquely suited to meeting their customers' needs. The Home Depot attracts these types of people by offering a more vibrant, enjoyable workplace environment and culture, as well as attractive earnings opportunity.

This aspiration to an unprecedented level of customer service implied more than a low-cost, high-service warehouse store approach, however. It meant developing a loyal cadre of frontline workers who would be truly energized by serving the public and eager and able to master the expanding dimensions of complex product offerings. Moreover, to meet the needs of professional contractors, the stores also had to be a certain size and capable of growth to capitalize on the buying and logistical economies. Most importantly, the goal of unprecedented customer service required that every person take individual responsibility for serving customers in a special way, for improving product mix and value offerings, and for maintaining rigorous cost and service disciplines. The Home Depot's efforts have virtually revolutionized the home improvement industry in ways that would not have been possible without a higher performing workforce being a top priority.

The company will do whatever it takes to delight the customers, and individuals at all levels constantly generate new ideas to that end. To repeat what Steve Messana emphasizes in chapter 1, "We encourage all of our people to come up with their own ideas to capture the customers' attention, and to try them out—there's no need for approval here. Sure, we get some lousy ideas along the way that we would rather not have had, but that's the price we are willing pay for the widespread individual initiative that makes this place unique."

With The Home Depot, you are never too young to be a customer. Being at one of its stores on a weekend is almost like being at a county fair, and in the heat of an Atlanta summer, it's probably the better option. The stores are giving away everything from hot dogs to popcorn to balloons, while running their Kids' Workshops. This idea apparently originated in one store, where the associates decided to help kids make a few birdhouses while the youngsters waited for their parents to complete their shopping. The idea quickly spread to other stores and to other projects beyond birdhouses. The Kids' Workshops, held in most stores, now offer free classes every Saturday morning for children ages four to twelve.

Undeniably, growth has been a key factor in marketplace energy. By any measure, The Home Depot's growth during the nearly two decades since the company's inception has been spectacular. Growth has translated directly into opportunity and wealth for The Home Depot associates because of the company's commitment to promoting from within (70 percent of assistant store managers and 100 percent of store managers come from the inside) and its stock purchase plan. Since growth is all this company has known, it's impossible to predict how the company would function without it. At the same time, growth is certainly not the only source of energy on which The Home Depot relies in keeping its workforce fired up.

Workforce Fulfillment Needs.   Associates in all parts of the company derive a special satisfaction from customer interaction. It helps give them a real sense of ownership in what they do, since the feedback is immediate and direct. They also need to be recognized for their accomplishments through rapid advancement and expanded scope of responsibility. They are always looking for new challenges, new roles, and new ways to create value for, and have impact on, their customers—and they need to build their skills to that end. "Training is everywhere, and skill building is everybody's job" is not an idle comment. Finally, the employees also have a sense of belonging to a special group of fun, hardworking people.

Moreover, the company could never attract the kind of people who make up its workforce without recognizing that attitude, values, and personality are more important than education, intellect, or experience. The fulfillment needs for this kind of workforce assume "irrational" investments in hiring, developing, and motivating people. The Home Depot's leaders also assume that associates will take ownership of whatever area of the business they are working in, and exert the initiative required to make it successful. Because of the need for growth and size as well as low cost in this equation, the Individual Achievement path makes more sense than the Entrepreneurial Spirit path, although the founders would not make that distinction.

The IA path also pays off in an employee value proposition that meets the fulfillment needs of the workforce. Bernie Marcus still has the storyteller's style and fascination with human nature that must have fueled his first career as a comedian in the Catskill Mountains:

> *A new employee called me today. . . . I picked up the phone, and he said, ". . . Is this really you?" Then he . . . tells me what was going wrong in his particular store, and what we needed to do about it. He's not afraid of me. He knows his career is here. It's not a job to him. If it's just a job, that's when you're dead in the water.*

Cultural Factors. The company's twenty-year history has created a strong ownership culture that affects people at all levels. The leadership philosophy is based on the assumption of rapid growth, continuous improvement, and change. Leaders encourage individual initiative and responsibility early on—and they expect and accept mistakes that they regard as essential to personal development.

In short, the company is creating a living legacy of providing unprecedented levels of customer service with a group of leaders dedicated to finding and sharing new opportunities. It results in a uniquely widespread sense of individual ownership and initiative, which requires a lot more than providing stock ownership opportunity.

Energy Sources and Alignment Approaches

Two primary sources of extra energy provide the necessary fuel for both of The Home Depot's balanced paths: an incredibly magnetic top leadership duo and a relentless set of marketplace dynamics fueled consistently by the constant, direct customer contact. As noted earlier, what matters most at The Home Depot is pleasing the customer. This message was at the heart of Bernie and Arthur's original vision, and it remains at the heart of The Home Depot's culture. It reaches the employee through a myriad of reinforcing mechanisms. These range from a new-associate orientation session to the informal coaching that associates get from their department and store managers, from the laudatory customer letters read at Sunday morning store meetings to regular store walkthroughs by the district manager and periodically by Bernie, Arthur, Bill Hamlin (executive vice president of merchandising), and other members of the senior leadership group. As Hamlin explains, "When we walk stores, we wear our jeans and our sneakers and we put on our orange aprons. That way the customer doesn't know us from anybody else, and we can break off and help them when we need to."

Certainly, The Home Depot's cofounders, Bernie and Arthur, continue to be a powerful presence across the organization, both in person and in spirit. Each man still spends the lion's share of his time interacting with frontline associates, whether it's in the context of a formal training program, a manager's meeting, or a store walk-through. Moreover, even those who have not met Bernie and Arthur refer to them on a first-name basis, quote them, and feel a strong sense of personal attachment and affection for them. People use them as benchmarks for their daily decisions. As one associate told us, "I often think to myself, 'What would Bernie or Arthur do?'"

As important and instrumental as Bernie and Arthur have been in the formation and development of the company, the primary source of energy in the future will increasingly be the marketplace and the "customer obsession" that the founders have established. The company capitalizes on three energizing facets of its marketplace: demanding customers, aggressive competitors, and growth.

Obviously, the watchwords at The Home Depot are "taking unprecedented care of customers" and "investing irrationally in people." These phrases define the company's fundamental beliefs. Customers provide the sources of extra energy, and people investments produce the mechanisms for aligning that energy. It all balances out in terms of worker fulfillment and enterprise performance. Four alignment approaches ensure that balance over time.

Showing People Their True Value. The Home Depot is perhaps the gold standard on the theme of showing people their true value. The company communicates the value that it places on each associate through its investments in training, through the level of responsibility each associate is given, and through its emphasis on caring for each other on and off the job. The associates can also see the value they are creating in the smiles on their customers' faces and in the item-by-item sales reports available to all employees on a weekly basis. More than one associate reminded us that the best way to judge their store's success is to compare the number of smiles on the faces of the customers in their parking lot to those in the competitor's lot across the street.

Creating Widespread Opportunity. Opportunity abounds at The Home Depot, both for those who choose to climb the ladder and for those who don't. Most senior positions are filled internally, and people willing to relocate in pursuit of the next opportunity can move from an entry-level position to a management position very quickly. At the same time, those who lack the ability or desire to move up have a broad range of opportunities to innovate and excel on a daily basis, whether it's by redesigning a product display or starting a new home improvement class on Saturday mornings.

Distributing Leadership Broadly. Leadership responsibility at The Home Depot is distributed broadly both in store operations and in merchandising. On the store operations side, individual store managers make a much larger portion of decisions than they do at most other retailers. Similarly, frontline associates are encouraged to make the decisions required to meet customer needs, even if it means breaking the rules, and to take the initiative to increase sales, even if it means making some mistakes. On the merchandising side, The Home Depot distributes responsibility across twelve offices, admittedly sacrificing some efficiency in favor of greater focus on local market needs. Moreover, managers at all levels emphasized that they err on the side of letting their people try things, because the pluses of distributed leadership (as evidenced in increased energy, creativity, and productivity levels) far outweigh the costs of a few bad decisions.

Enhancing the Work Itself. Like any organization with a peak-performance workforce, The Home Depot operates at a pace that makes being an employee very hard work. Yet people love being there and seem to end their shift or their week even more energized than when they started. What accounts for this apparent paradox? It's the nature of the jobs and the environment that The Home Depot has created. The jobs are more exciting than typical retail positions because they are more broadly defined and varied in their content. People are encouraged and expected to innovate in responding to customers. Where else would you find someone even thinking of deep-fat frying turkey to lure customers away from a competitor's store?

The Home Depot environment is both highly charged and highly comfortable. It's charged by the intense stream of customer interactions and customer needs to be addressed. At the same time, it's comfortable because taking risks and making mistakes are okay, especially within the store's familial culture.

Summing Up The Home Depot

Among the enterprises that we have studied, The Home Depot is one of the best examples of a company that excels along an Individual Achievement path. The company provides an environment of unlimited opportunity, where associates call themselves the presidents of their aisles and use weekly sales reports to track their achievements. Lot loaders can and do become store managers by trying new ideas and making things happen for the customer and the company, even if that means making some mistakes along the way. Moreover, once they become store managers, they are virtual CEOs. As Jim Wargo stated earlier, "This is my $50 million business."

The clarity around the corporate mission serves as a powerful coordinating mechanism for Jim Wargo and his people. It enables thousands of associates across the organization to function in a highly autonomous yet synchronized fashion. In other words, The Home Depot associates are playing in very large sandboxes, but they are all playing by the same rules. This stems from a leadership philosophy that focuses on enabling individual achievement at every level. This philosophy was perhaps best articulated by Steve Messana, The Home Depot's top human resource executive: "We believe our people are an investment, not a cost; that belief is at the heart of our customer-centered strategy."

When we asked Steve somewhat skeptically if most companies didn't believe that, he responded, "In fact, a lot of marginal performing companies claim people to be their 'most important asset' in one form or another." We asked him if that wasn't the same as believing in the value of investing in people. "Maybe so," Steve replied, "but even if they do believe what they say, it sure doesn't appear to drive their decisions and actions in the same way that it does around here."

Clearly, The Home Depot's entire history, vision, and leadership philosophy has been grounded in their "core ideology" (to use a phrase from James Collins's and Jerry Porras's *Built to Last*): driving a customer-centered business concept by sustaining (investing more in) a higher-performing workforce than any competitor can hope to match.[2] Such seemingly disproportionate investments are always hard to justify to those not truly dedicated to out-compete, no matter what. As Messana puts it: "Other companies can probably copy most of our management strategies, techniques and approaches, but few if any can match the strength of these beliefs."

Steve's degree of personal conviction on this topic belies his relatively short (five-year) tenure with The Home Depot. You would expect to find that kind of conviction from the founders, but not from a relative newcomer. He served most of his fourteen-year apprenticeship within the much emulated and admired "people system" at Pepsi. There, he became intimately familiar with Andrall Pearson's well-documented approach to muscle-building the organization. And while Steve clearly respects Pepsi's process, he sees The Home Depot's approach as very different—much simpler and more focused. He also believes that it is the key to the superior quality and performance of The Home Depot workforce.

We asked Steve if his managers had become virtual zealots about investing in people—did they have something perhaps more like a religious fervor? He quickly dismissed the idea:

> *The phrase "religious zealot" . . . misses the main point. . . . Our twenty-year [performance] record cannot be attributed to anything but our investment in our people. It has paid off handsomely in hard dollar value for shareholders and customers alike.*
>
> *We recruit better people, pay them more, provide them greater opportunity, teach them more effectively, and retain a larger proportion than any other comparable retailer you can name. . . . Put all of this to a numbers test, and it shows that we get a higher return on this investment—look at the growth record of both sales and profitability, and our leadership position in the markets that we serve. That is quite different than "religious zealotry"—and it is virtually unshakable.*

Clearly, Steve Messana has a point.

MCKINSEY: "CREATE YOUR OWN MCKINSEY"

Despite the obvious differences between a home improvement retail chain and a top management consulting firm, both The Home Depot and McKinsey & Company, Inc., are pursuing the Individual Achievement path to a higher-performing workforce. For McKinsey & Company, however, that workforce is limited to the consulting segment of its total employee base.

I remember speaking to an incoming class of McKinsey associates several years ago and making a point that I had made many times before. "This is a team sport," I said with fervor and conviction, "and success here will be a function of how well you master your team skills." But I was wrong. It has always been difficult to find real teams within McKinsey. The firm is fundamentally an individual achievement environment that operates under intense time pressures that strongly favor individual performance and single-leader working groups over real teams.

In many ways, the IA path that McKinsey follows is similar to that of The Home Depot. For example, McKinsey also pursues a Mission, Values, and Pride path that complements and reinforces its IA path. Its primary source of energy comes from its clients, which the firm reveres as much as The Home Depot reveres its customers. And for close to half a century, McKinsey has also drawn energy from the unique leadership of a truly remarkable leader, Marvin Bower, who last inspired the partners at a leadership conference in 1998 at age ninety-four! Bower arguably revolutionized the profession by introducing the concept of top management consulting. Prior to Bower, most firms were focused on time- and motion-efficiency work, market research projects, and compensation systems.

McKinsey's workforce performance is impressive by almost any measure. The quality of its clientele is the envy of the profession and directly reflects the impact of its people. Its "graduates" populate the executive ranks of hundreds of companies and include the CEOs of IBM, American Express, Delta Air Lines, NBC, and Enron, to name a few. Because McKinsey is privately owned by the partners, the firm's earnings are not public knowledge, but it probably has the largest group of multimillion-dollar partners of any professional service organization in the world. Its number of published works exceeds that of any major business school, and its reputation has persisted for almost seventy years.

Furthermore, the firm also supports more pro-bono community and public service work than does any other consulting organization in the world.

Historical Perspective: Creating a Brand New Profession

McKinsey's roots go back to the 1920s, when James O. McKinsey, a professor of accounting at the University of Chicago, achieved a modest reputation from a book on management accounting and started his own firm. He was soon joined by Marvin Bower, a successful corporate lawyer with Jones, Day in Cleveland. Together they shaped a dream of an essentially brand new profession: top management consulting. Bower, in particular, was convinced that there was a market for a truly professional group (modeled after a set of principles practiced by the best law firms) that could provide unique counsel on management to the leaders of large corporations. That simple notion has propelled McKinsey to the top of a profession that has now become prolific throughout the world, with advisors of all shapes and sizes professing to be top management consultants.

Bower assumed the leadership of the firm in 1950, when McKinsey left to become CEO of Marshall Field in Chicago. McKinsey died just a few months later. Bower was a uniquely magnetic leader in his devotion to his dream and his dedication to a set of professional values that still constitute the standard for the consulting industry. McKinsey also set the pace for others in its hiring of top-tier MBAs, its global expansiveness, and the quality of its client portfolio. Few today would question the firm's leadership in the field, and even fewer would argue that the talent and energy of its consultants is less than the very best.

A Two-Tier Situation

The firm contends with business priorities, marketplace conditions, and staff fulfillment needs that differ from those of The Home Depot, although McKinsey also pursues a challenging dual mission: to help its clients make lasting improvements in their performance and to build a great institution that attracts and excites exceptional people. What motivates and energizes the broad base of McKinsey associates, however, is somewhat different from what explains the commitment of the partners. Simply put, the partner group is much more moved by the history, aspirations, and values of the firm than are the associates, who know that the odds of an associate's remaining with the institution beyond five years are low. Hence, the IA path becomes the dominant eye for engaging the associates' emotional commitment.

Performance Priorities.   At the top of the priority list is the firm's dedication to earning privileged relationships with clients by delivering substantial performance impact over time. To that end, the partners recently adopted a slogan of "100 percent cubed"—bringing 100 percent of the firm's capabilities to 100 percent of its clients 100 percent of the time—hardly a trivial aspiration, given the firm's global presence and reach. The firm aspires to develop new knowledge, insights, and expertise about issues that its clients are facing in both industry and functional areas. It also seeks to cultivate a true spirit of partnership among an increasingly broad and diverse international complement of partners.

Marketplace Dynamics and Realities.   The marketplace is overflowing with large and small firms that compete with McKinsey in a variety of ways. Such firms range from highly specialized boutiques like Stern, Simmons (economic value specialists) to full-service firms like the Boston Consulting Group. Literally hundreds of qualified consultants compete not only for clients, but also for the better people. The most aggressive competition in the consulting industry is usually at the top graduate schools, where starting offers can exceed six figures and can include special signing bonuses and job-hunting help for spouses. This competition for people has already spread well beyond the top graduate schools and includes aggressive searches beyond the campus for more experienced candidates from the commercial and public sectors of the economy.

Workforce Fulfillment Needs.   Most associates' fulfillment needs are largely centered on recognition of individual achievement, freedom of choice, and personal growth and development. The realists among them seek to build a set of enviable credentials as much as they seek to advance into the partnership. Many associates openly view a job with McKinsey as a kind of advanced graduate school that will simply prepare them for a more prestigious executive career in the non-consulting world.

In David Maister's seminal work on professional service firms, he describes a churning model that has certainly been an appropriate description of McKinsey's approach in the past.

> *One or more firms . . . have clearly chosen a high target rate of turnover. Partners . . . can routinely earn a surplus value from the juniors without having to "repay" them in the form of promotion. This . . . also allows a significant degree of screening so that only the "best" stay in the organization.*
>
> *Not surprisingly, firms following this strategy tend to be among the most prestigious in their industry. . . . Individuals continue to join these organizations, knowing that the odds of "making it" are very low [because they perceive value in] the experience, training, and association with the prestigious firms in the industry.[3]*

Cultural Factors. Despite its size (over four thousand professionals), the firm remains tightly patterned after Marvin Bower's concept of a top management firm with professional values borrowed from the best legal firms. Its core values include placing client interests first, building unique capabilities in all areas of management, and demanding the highest personal and professional integrity of its people. These values, plus the firm's reputation for delivering superior client service, create an environment that thrives on individual initiatives and achievement. McKinsey hires the best and expects the best of each person they hire. Given the competition, however, it will be a real challenge to maintain a staff quality advantage going forward.

A final challenge that the firm faces affects both client performance and workforce fulfillment. That challenge is the increasing need for real team performance capability, not only in the client service arena, as suggested by the 100-percent-cubed priority, but also in the internal leadership and management system of the firm. Increasingly, partner groups need to function as real teams, as do important senior leadership councils of the firm. Until recently, the strength of the firm's Individual Achievement path has actually inhibited team performance. This would certainly argue in favor of the renewed attention being given to the Mission, Values, and Pride path.

New associates at McKinsey accept a value proposition that promises truly unique individual learning, growth, earnings, and achievement potential. In return, the firm demands dedicated adherence to the firm's core values and a willingness to deal with a lot of pressure, extensive travel, and long hours. The value proposition is currently supported by two unique sources of energy and four alignment themes that ensure a dynamic balance between client impact and consultant fulfillment. The firm, however, is at an important watershed in its development. Several current leaders recognize the need to pay attention to other energy sources and alignment themes as Bower's leadership and values drop further from the natural interests and values of what is basically a young person's environment.

Energy Sources and Alignment Approaches

The primary, overriding source of emotional energy comes from McKinsey's clients, who are especially demanding and expect more because of the firm's reputation and high fees. In addition, members of the partnership continually focus everyone's attention on client impact, which is rigorously assessed in the evaluation of partner performance. Client impact is much more important than client billings, and a partner's compensation seldom correlates with his or her individual billings. Both the portfolio of clients as well as the kinds of issues the firm aspires to address are exciting to employees at all levels. At partner conferences, for example, the participants commonly show video clips of client executives commenting directly on key aspects of being served by McKinsey. The best way to ensure receptivity and credibility for new practice areas is to cite client success stories and reactions.

For much of its history, the firm drew heavily upon an incredibly magnetic leader for inspiration, guidance, and energy. Marvin Bower's larger-than-life image has yet to be equaled by subsequent leaders, even though most have been excellent leaders in their own right. Bower has always been seen as the personification of the values that the partners believe set the firm apart in the eyes of both clients and staff candidates. Several partners still claim to resolve difficult professional issues by asking themselves, "What would Marvin do in this situation?" even though he has not held any formal leadership role in the firm for over twenty-five years.

This source of energy, however, has become less effective as fewer and fewer associates can relate personally to the Bower role model. As this source disappears, the firm faces a need to draw more on its history and legacy than it does today. To that end, the firm's Dallas office recently launched a special history project aimed precisely at filling that need.

Because of the churning model, it is particularly difficult for McKinsey to maintain a balance of enterprise performance and worker fulfillment. The entire associate body turns over every six or seven years, as one in five is elected and the rest leave (as a result of a strongly enforced up-or-out policy). Partners can be relatively inaccessible as they strive to leverage themselves across larger and larger numbers of people in higher-impact client situations. As a result, the firm must continue to be distinctive in executing along the alignment approaches discussed below.

Creating Widespread Opportunity.   The firm goes to great lengths to create a wealth of opportunities for its associates. During the first two years with the firm, associates are encouraged to work on client projects in different industry sectors and different functional areas. During that period, they are also urged to "find a home" wherein they can develop their expertise and become *spikey integrators,* the firm's term for people who become the best at something that matters to important clients. Many consultants, however, often pursue more than one area of expertise, thereby expanding the client opportunities available to them.

In addition to client work, associates are offered dozens of nonclient opportunities to work on knowledge development projects and people development issues, as well as office and firm management processes. Jon Zagrodsky, an associate in Texas, who recently spent over a year working on a special nonclient project to reshape the firm's strategy, describes the undertaking as "a once-in-a-lifetime experience for me." The firm often offers this kind of opportunity to its people at all levels.

Making Purposeful Selection.   The selection of candidates at McKinsey is a two-way process that emphasizes self-selection as much as firm selection. It begins with a rigorously executed recruiting approach in which candidates are screened mercilessly against one another's resume accomplishments and then put through intense interviews and discussions that test their intellectual capabilities, emotional intelligence, and personal values. Most MBAs from all leading business schools will tell you that a job offer from McKinsey is a prize plum.

The selection process extends well beyond hiring, however. Every six months, each associate is evaluated against a set of well-honed criteria that focus on the balance of skills required for different levels of consulting capability. As associates fall behind their peers in this transparent process, the pressure to relocate increases.

The election of partners at McKinsey is particularly rigorous and fact-based. Firmwide committees screen the records of the candidates, conduct extensive interviews with all who have worked with the candidate, and work through a series of open-group dialogues to ensure global consistency in the election of both principals (junior partners) and directors (senior partners). These personnel committees and processes are staffed with the best partners in the firm and consume several person-weeks each year. This world-class selection approach has few equals anywhere in the world.

Articulating What Matters Most. The partner-evaluation process is both comprehensive and transparent. As such, it enables associates to know exactly where they stand in their career development and permits the firm to differentiate rewards based on individual potential as well as achievement.

Associates must pass through six levels, from junior associate to senior engagement manager, to qualify for election to the partnership. Each level has a clear set of consulting skill and client impact criteria, and associates are well aware of one another's relative position on the track to election. Although compensation specifics are not made public, the relative value of each level on the advancement track is well known within the associate body.

Starting with the recruiting dialogues and continuing throughout one's career, the firm's aspirations, core values, and performance standards are made crystal clear to associates. A multimillion-dollar training program contains many modules, each of which clearly articulates what matters to the firm and what an associate must do to succeed in its uniquely value-driven culture.

Countless documents, both formal and informal, are circulated annually to reinforce firm values, aspirations, and performance expectations. Every associate receives an annual review that includes discussions with mentors and formal group leaders, whose job it is to make clear the development needs for the individual if he or she is to advance within the firm.

When asked about the firm's core aspirations and values, virtually any associate will give a clear and consistent articulation of what matters most at McKinsey. Most associates will also tell you frankly where they think the firm is falling short and needs improvement. Like the Marines, the associates and partners at McKinsey are openly (usually constructively) critical of anything less than what their core values imply.

Providing Meaningful Recognition and Rewards. Money matters at McKinsey, perhaps more than it should. It is not, however, a culture of "show me the money." Both associates and partners of the firm certainly have high career earnings expectations, the result of the attractive options that most of them have, and the intensifying competition for the talent they represent to other enterprises. Hence, the firm scrutinizes its compensation levels and adjusts them frequently to maintain clearly competitive levels.

At the same time, the firm does not attempt to compete on this dimension with the high-end investment bankers and entrepreneurs. McKinsey devotes at least as much attention to nonfinancial rewards, which range from rapid-track advancement recognition to early elections and special program assignments. The best performers, obviously, receive more attention than do average or marginal performers. In this respect, the firm is not nearly as distinctive in recognizing the performance and value of the bulk of its workforce as the many other enterprises cited earlier in this book.

The firm is most distinctive, however, in the pace of advancement offered to the higher-potential, fast-track consultants. The emphasis, therefore, is clearly on individual performance and potential. All the firm's personnel processes and criteria are designed to clearly identify and reward the best-performing individuals. In recent years the firm has paid more attention to collective or collaborative contributions, but the recognition and reward system still favors individual achievement. As a result, real team performance remains more of a random occurrence and is particularly difficult to achieve at McKinsey.

INTEGRATING PATHS AT MCKINSEY AND THE HOME DEPOT

Like many of the best energizers of their people, both McKinsey and The Home Depot work along more than one balanced path, namely, the Mission, Values, and Pride path and the Individual Achievement path.

These two paths combine naturally to create a peak-performance work-force that stands out above the competition. The IA path, however, is where both of these unique enterprises best energize their people.

A healthy competitiveness persists among individuals within both companies, although The Home Depot has been able to leverage its collective pride into team performance, whereas McKinsey still has a way to go in this area. Both enterprises have benefited from truly unique leaders in the past and have relied on rapid growth. In the future, however, both may need to turn some attention to cultivating other sources of energy to sustain the emotional commitment of their front line.

The themes of alignment are similar for both companies, though McKinsey relies more on its purposeful recruiting and selection, whereas The Home Depot emphasizes its philosophy of ownership and widely distributed leadership. Both enterprises, however, are classic illustrations of a company's investing in its own people in ways that outsiders might well perceive as irrational. McKinsey's focus, however, is primarily on the professional associate and partner segments of its workforce, whereas The Home Depot targets its entire workforce. Both companies are also incredibly disciplined in the pursuit of their unique sources of extra energy and their well-chosen alignment approaches.

7 ✦ The Recognition and Celebration Path

M*ost good companies sponsor parties* and make a conscious effort to reward and celebrate the accomplishments of their people with other than monetary pay or bonuses. These efforts range from mandatory Christmas parties and company picnics to employee-of-the-month awards, special achievement groups (e.g., million-dollar sales clubs), designated parking spaces, desk and wall plaques, pins, badges, and personal e-mails or handwritten notes from the boss. The list is endless and the practice is widespread.

As gratifying and admirable as this kind of recognition may be, it seldom explains or leads to a peak-performance workforce. In the balanced Recognition and Celebration (R&C) path that this chapter describes, such activities are much more integral to the business purpose of the enterprise, as well as more disciplined about meeting specific fulfillment needs of critical segments of the workforce than are similar efforts in other companies. Since virtually every organization makes some effort at nonfinancial rewards and celebrations, it is important to point out the differences between these normal efforts and what goes on in those few enterprises that are truly distinguished in their execution of the R&C path. Table 7-1 highlights some of the critical differences.

Most important, however, the R&C path seldom stands alone as the primary focal point for a peak-performance workforce. None of the companies we studied rely solely—or even primarily—on the R&C path. On the other hand, this path was an important companion path in two-thirds of the cases and seems to combine particularly well with the

Process and Metrics (P&M) path and the Mission, Values, and Pride (MVP) path. The most notable example of such combinations include KFC and Marriott (both described in this chapter), as well as Southwest Airlines, The Home Depot, Avon, Hill's Pet Nutrition, and the U.S. Marine Corps. This chapter concentrates on how these attributes come into play at KFC, and compares that with the approach taken at Marriott International.

KFC: THE COLONEL'S LEGACY

KFC is the world's leading producer of family chicken dinners. The company was formerly known as Colonel Sander's Kentucky Fried Chicken and is currently part of the newly created Tricon enterprise (a Pepsi spin-off including KFC, Pizza Hut, and Taco Bell). KFC's performance over the

Table 7-1   DIFFERENCES IN RECOGNITION AND
            CELEBRATION APPROACHES

Major Attribute	Typical Company	Company on a Balanced Recognition and Celebration Path
Type of event	Major anniversaries and holidays	Every conceivable excuse to celebrate employee accomplishments
Number of celebrations	Dozens annually	Hundreds annually
Sponsorship	Human Resources Department	Line managers at all levels across all functions plus employees themselves
Employee reaction	"Ho-hum, do we have to do this again?"	"Wow! This is really fun!"
Funding	Company funded only, typically on company time	Often funded by employees themselves, typically on their own time

last ten years has fluctuated, but is most notable for the turnaround achieved since David Novak reinstituted the R&C path in 1994.

KFC has a rich tradition of celebrating its people that dates back to 1955, when the Colonel first began selling franchises for his secret formula from the back of his station wagon. By 1996, the enterprise was generating sales of nearly $8 billion through over five thousand (about one-third company-owned) stores. This level of business requires close to fifty thousand hires per year to support operating needs of forty thousand frontline company employees—reflecting the high turnover endemic to the restaurant segment of the fast-food business. Sustaining peak workforce performance in this kind of high-turnover environment poses a real challenge for any company in this industry, and KFC is no exception.

Historical Perspective: A Secret Formula Survives

Notwithstanding that challenge, however, in the early decades of its existence the company sustained a peak-performance workforce across its franchise operations and its owned stores. After the Colonel's interests were sold and large corporate parents (Heublein, Inc., RJR Nabisco, and PepsiCo, Inc.) took over, performance took a turn for the worse. Well-meaning professional managers imposed priorities, controls, and incentives that undermined employee morale and motivation, particularly among the restaurant general managers (RGMs) and franchise owners. They simply lost the balance between worker fulfillment and enterprise performance.

By the time Pepsi appointed David Novak as the new CEO, KFC was faced with a basic turnaround challenge characterized by five years of declining sales and company store margins falling below 10 percent (compared to 20 percent for franchisees). Novak also had to deal with a loss of all credibility and trust among key franchisees, who had gone through seven long and bitter years of legal battles over territory protection. Workforce performance had clearly taken a back seat to other performance levers that were, in retrospect, inappropriate to this kind of frontline service business. Somewhat surprisingly, since Novak was a product of one of the better packaged-foods "by-the-numbers" systems (PepsiCo), he decided to resurrect the Colonel to restore trust and emotional commitment across the front line.

The late Colonel Harland Sanders remains an icon in Japan and is still legendary in many parts of the United States. Easily one of the best-known brand images in the world, the friendly Southern gentleman in his white suit and classic goatee has symbolized good old home-style fried chicken for about half a century. Both he and his wife have now passed on, but the company owes its continuing vitality to their original product concept and customer-service values that seem destined to survive well into the next century. It is hard to believe that this homespun couple could have created an $8 billion enterprise capable of sustaining a peak-performance workforce among its restaurant managers.

Though the company is still a "work in progress," most people at KFC already believe that they have recreated the kind of higher-performing workforce that made the Colonel a legend in his own time. Management recognizes that its current leadership approach has yet to demonstrate more than five years of turnaround results and has yet to find out what economic hard times will do to its performance. Nonetheless, KFC appears to have the earmarks of another Southwest Airlines in the making, to which Novak unabashedly aspires.

A Trip to the "White House"

KFC's headquarters in Louisville, Kentucky, includes a converted old Southern mansion as part of its corporate complex. Aptly named the White House, the mansion is a symbolic reminder of the rich history and legacy of the Colonel. It also provides a highly visible place to display various individual and group awards and to recognize the current accomplishments of the employees. A technical center and the White House are connected by a colorful underground walkway named the Walk of Leaders. The label conveys the company's conviction that leaders of all kinds are responsible for the realization of KFC's mission. The walkway contains literally dozens of symbolic and motivational displays that characterize KFC's many efforts to energize its people and execute its strategy. The overall atmosphere is one of warm, friendly enthusiasm and energy. People seem to trot rather than walk around, and there is a constant intermingling on the run. A lot goes on in the hallways as people meet, interact, and move on. Even as strangers, we received a friendly greeting from virtually everyone we passed.

Our first discussion was to be with Chuck Rawley, senior vice president of operations and chief operating officer. Chuck is known as the

Bulldog by his troops, reflecting (we later learned) the CEO's playful comment that he "sorta looks like a bulldog." As the discussion proceeded, however, the label seemed to fit his determination more than his appearance. He actually looks much more like the friendly restaurant manager he used to be with the Bo Jangles chain in Louisville, Kentucky.

Chuck joined KFC in 1985 as a "designated program guy." In other words, although the company had no real job assignment for him, whoever hired him believed that something would turn up. Rawley has had the dubious advantage of living through three different eras at KFC, including the present one. The seminal event in his mind was Pepsi's misguided attempt in the late 1980s to change the contract for the franchisee by eliminating the territorial protection formerly provided. To a franchisee, eliminating territorial protection was almost like losing your right to decide who gets to enter your home. As Chuck recalled, the period was marked by a severe loss of trust across the franchise organization, plus a somewhat questionable corporate strategy of acquiring recalcitrant franchisees: "We wanted to own them all!! [The process] was seen by the franchisee as a weapon to put [them] out of business."

In addition, the company undertook several other regrettable actions over a six-year period, from 1988 to 1995. Most of these were seen as evidence of disrespect for the Colonel—and resulted in a costly erosion in the icon and brand image so central to the early development of the company. When David Novak came in as a new CEO in the summer of 1994, a clear message came through from the franchisee group: "You had better be good, boy—or you won't be here for long."

Both Chuck and David describe their change efforts in three stages: strategy, organization, and culture. The strategy was formulated through a highly interactive process that included managers at all levels as well as franchisees. In fact, the strategy formulation process itself coincided with the launching of a new culture characterized by Chuck as "service so good that it drives sales. It all starts with cleanliness, both outside and in—*a dirty store is the unforgivable sin.*"

The watchwords are cleanliness, friendliness, and quality—all at a competitive price. Sounds obvious, but KFC means to adhere to these standards with relentless consistency, an aspiration still to be achieved.

KFC's approach to organization depends heavily on an intensive, two-way communication process that includes several forums and conferences throughout the year. Gregg Dedrick, senior vice president of human resources, sounds more like a sales and marketing zealot than a human-resources professional. Slogans abound, but one of the more compelling ones poses the question "Why would you want to work any-place else?" Gregg is constantly alert for answers to that question that point to problems he can fix. The mind-set at corporate headquarters seems to be to eliminate all possible excuses for changing jobs—and for not achieving performance results. It is a formidable challenge, but it only makes him more determined to make it a reality. As we accompanied Gregg on the Walk of Leaders, he could not contain his enthusiasm for almost every display—ranging from a "doghouse" of Chuck's Bull Dog Awards to videos of several of the more memorable conferences and speeches of the last few years.

Why the R&C Path Makes Sense

David Novak is determined to keep the image of the Colonel alive and well, because he believes that without it the Process and Metrics path would snuff out frontline energy and commitment. Novak neither looks nor talks like the Colonel, but everyone from Mrs. Sanders (before she died) to the franchisees seem to have been completely convinced that the Colonel would definitely approve of David. Novak is also an un-abashed admirer of Herb Kelleher, CEO of Southwest Airlines, and intends to put KFC's people on a pedestal at least equal to that of the customer. "People must believe that you care about them first," says Novak. "Until they do, you have little chance of getting them to go the extra mile for you."

Novak also makes a big deal out of his *shadow leadership* concept—KFC's version of walking the talk. The notion is that people will do what they see their leaders do. That is, the leader casts a shadow that cannot be ignored. And when he uses the word *leader,* he means it in a highly distributed sense—almost to the point of believing that every employee has a leadership role that can and must be played.

His central theme, however, remains that the "RGM [restaurant general manager] is the No. 1 leader"—everything else exists only to support and enhance the results of the RGM. He assumes that a successful RGM will function as a true team leader of his or her restaurant workers. This segment of the KFC workforce—the restaurant team—is the primary focus of Novak's R&C path.

To understand why resurrecting the Colonel made sense, we must look at the situation KFC faced in terms of its business performance priorities, marketplace dynamics and realities, workforce fulfillment needs, and internal cultural factors. These components of the challenges facing KFC are discussed in the following paragraphs.

Performance Priorities. Novak began his turnaround campaign by shaping a new set of aspirations and goals that redefined the central KFC business value proposition (i.e., what benefits will KFC deliver to the consumer at what price), delivering that value with increased rigor and consistency over time, and communicating that value clearly and compellingly to customers and employees alike. This proposition is captured in the following mottoes that were adopted and internalized throughout the organization:

+ *Be the leading kitchen for convenient meals.* An aspiration closely akin to past notions, it tapped into the Colonel's "Sunday dinner" heritage. Consequently, it had a significant, positive impact on the KFC frontline employees as well as the franchise organization workers. The motto also positioned KFC's product and service offering in the customer's eyes as being a dinner rather than a "snackable" fast-food offering.

+ *Feed every family a great-tasting meal at least once a week.* This new aspiration constitutes a significant stretch goal for KFC's entire value chain (product and menu design, marketing, and operations, as well as frontline workers and franchisee behaviors). If the company could get its regular patrons to visit a KFC outlet one additional time per year, the company's existing levels of profitability would increase significantly.

To enforce the importance of these priorities in everyone's mind, several early decision-based actions (as opposed to people-intensive behavioral actions) were effectively mandated. Some of these actions affected the value definition as reflected in menu selection. For example, the original secret recipe was restored and reemphasized, some "loser" products were dropped, and some clear-winner products, such as pot pies and crispy strips, were added. Other actions were directed at delivering the new value proposition. The existing field organization hierarchy was virtually blown up to focus more directly on operations and, in particular, to give a new level of importance to the RGM role. Finally, a distracting franchisee lawsuit was settled, which opened the door to repairing and rebuilding strong relations with franchisees all across the enterprise. These decisions were perceived as very important strategic and structural actions that set the stage for tackling the much tougher, broad-based behavioral changes necessary for higher levels of performance.

The bulk of the behavioral changes concerned how the value proposition would be delivered, for example, in food preparation, order taking, and restaurant conditions and ambiance. The obvious but clearly challenging goal was to provide customers with a great experience with every visit, that is, to "give them the confidence to come back" again and again.

Unfortunately, there were no simple decisions or easy actions for ensuring the behavioral imperatives behind increasing the number of repeat customer visits. The food preparation process (all of which takes place at the outlets) had to ensure uniformly high product quality and availability ("satisfy *all* customers with what they want"). The order taking had to be noticeably rich in customer responsiveness and friendliness ("wow them with service so good it drives sales"). Each restaurant location had to be visibly cleaner and brighter ("eliminate the unforgivable sin of a dirty store") than it had been before.

In short, increasing what the customer would "reward" (pay for) required significantly improved individual and collective performance from virtually all workers—every position in three thousand company-owned restaurants, not to mention those in the over six thousand franchises. It was an awesome workforce performance imperative.

Marketplace Dynamics and Realities. Managing a behavioral turnaround of this kind in the fast-food industry is no easy task; most competitors do not attempt it. For one thing, the industry economics simply cannot support paying high wages to hire superior people or offering big financial rewards for better performance. In fact, financial pressures often result in squeezing the labor line (i.e., minimizing staff) to boost short-term earnings.

In addition, the demographics (age, intelligence, education, work ethic, etc.) of realistic workforce sources, plus low unemployment conditions, make it hard to even find, much less keep, superior or even acceptable employees at rates the marketplace will permit. In short, the competition among fast-food providers for available workers is intense and contributes to the high turnover that characterizes the industry. Given the hot, unpleasant, and demanding nature of the work, high turnover is literally endemic. Nor does it help that many workers are experiencing their first real job and hence are naive about the relative attractiveness of other options.

As a result, most competitors elect to design and work around the workforce through automation, technology, and tight systems controls. They assume that the best they can hope for from the workers is a barely acceptable work ethic and a short-timer mind-set. KFC has chosen a completely different response. The company decided to make people its competitive advantage by the disciplined use of nonmonetary incentives, by investing more in the people it already had, and by creating a teamlike work environment where more people would want to stay (at least a while longer than at the competition). Although it is too soon for KFC to declare victory, the turnover and productivity statistics are moving in the right direction. Restaurant general manager turnover has been reduced from 27 percent to 17 percent.

Workforce Fulfillment Needs. At one level, the fulfillment needs of the workers are easily described; they parallel the generic human needs described early in the book. Every human need can be met in some way in the workplace, as shown in the following list:

+ Direction, structure, and order: a workplace where people feel secure

+ A sense of identity, purpose, and self-worth: a position where what people do really matters to the company as well as themselves

+ A feeling of belonging: being part of a group that they respect and with whom they like to work

+ Having a voice in what happens to them: an influence over their own destiny within the company

+ The chance to develop and improve as a person: the opportunity to take on increasing challenges, learn new skills, and advance over time

At KFC, as at many companies, the importance of these needs varies, depending on the tenure, position, and experience of the employee. For example, the formal job hierarchy from the new kitchen worker up through the position of market coach represents four or five different levels of job responsibility and worker fulfillment needs. The new entrant up through shift supervisory roles is focused on fulfilling his or her basic employment needs (pay and benefits) with some sense that the job will last. Since other parts of the person's life (family, community, etc.) often lack any sense of order, discipline, or direction, the job has to provide it.

As people move into assistant unit manager and restaurant general manager roles, other needs take priority. Many are looking for a group they can feel good about joining, as well as the opportunity to advance despite their lack of formal education and basic business skills. Finally, the better RGMs and market coaches are looking for a chance to lead others, to build something successful, and to have greater influence on their own careers. At every level, however, people are looking for recognition of their value, both as a person and in the job, and they seek affirmation of their ability to succeed along some important dimension.

Cultural Factors. Every company's culture influences what kind of path will lead to a higher-performing workforce. At KFC, that culture underwent numerous stresses, strains, and changes, from the early days of the Colonel's energizing visits by station wagon to the series of acquisitions that finally led to the creation of Tricon in 1997.

The most relevant time to depict the KFC culture is during the early 1990s, when Novak made his dramatic push to shape and integrate a powerful R&C Path with an already entrenched P&M path. At that time, the company's more recent reliance on superior marketing and product innovations to boost sales had completely lost momentum. The company was not a packaged-goods enterprise. Yet typical packaged-goods attitudes prevailed at headquarters. Assuming that market analysts knew best, headquarters issued orders, pushed compliance, measured results, and seriously enforced consequence management.

Unfortunately, the actions that these attitudes produced were simply not working in the marketplace. Sales and profits were well below acceptable levels, good people were leaving, and franchisees were in a near-revolt frame of mind. In some ways, however, this marketplace trauma was an advantage, or at least a "burning platform for change." It had created such a deep level of despair across the enterprise that people were willing to try almost anything.

Fortunately, the new CEO deeply believed in winning through people—particularly people across the baseline of the organization. He seemed to thrive on personal contact in large groups and small, face-to-face discussions with people at all levels, and basically pressing the flesh at every opportunity. Although he certainly did not wear a white suit or sport a groomed mustache and goatee, he began to personify the same values that worked for the Colonel decades before. Moreover, Novak revived the Colonel's traditional commitment to quality and hospitality, a rich tradition apparently "just waiting to be resurrected."

In other words, the primary source of new energy across the organization became a fortuitous combination: the legacy of the Colonel and all that he stood for in people's minds, plus a new leader who saw management's real job as pumping people up, turning them on, and paying lots of attention to even the smallest of accomplishments. As new levels of energy started to emerge from these two sources, it was quickly reinforced and aligned. Today, that energy in aligned actions brings about a dramatically different work environment than what prevailed before Novak resurrected the Colonel's legacy.

KFC'S CHOSEN PATHS

KFC's peak-performance workforce is the result of the integration of two complementary balanced paths (figure 7-1). By itself, the Recognition and Celebration path would probably not have done the job—just as by itself, the strong consequence management, process and metrics approach that had been a Pepsi hallmark did not by itself do the job. By combining the two, however, KFC has made remarkable progress in a relatively short time. The two paths complement one another in a very powerful integrated approach.

Energy Sources and Alignment Approaches

Clearly, KFC draws almost equally heavily on two unique sources of energy: David Novak and Colonel Sanders. Novak is a magnetic leader, and

Sanders is the icon of a rich legacy. It is not coincidental that the two have become seamlessly connected in energizing the organization.

Novak may not be a clone of the Colonel, but he will do until one comes along. He is respected by all for his energy, enthusiasm, and dedication to preserving the Colonel's legacy. Everything, from his endless visits and other interactions with the workforce to his humorously savored rubber-chicken awards and his insistence that "the RGM is No. 1!" connects people to both the future and the past. It is a powerful emotional connection.

Novak had the wisdom to recognize the indelible impression that the Colonel left on the marketplace, the franchisees, and the employees. His dedication to simple rules of quality, customer service, and respect for his people is now immortalized in a brand image that calls to mind that legacy. The current leadership of the company is relentless about using

Figure 7-1 INTEGRATION OF TWO BALANCED PATHS AT KFC

Deliver enterprise performance priorities
- Consistent product quality and availability
- "Wow" customer service and friendliness
- Absolute restaurant cleanliness
- Great experience every time

Address workforce fulfillment needs
- Provide clear structure and direction for how to succeed
- Give recognition beyond people's wildest expectations
- Emphasize career and leadership opportunities
- Emphasize a team environment

Recognition and Celebration

KFC

Process and Metrics

Work within marketplace dynamics and realities
- Make people your advantage and priority
- Use nonmonetary incentives
- Invest in who you have

Leverage and redirect internal cultural forces
- Bring back the Colonel and his values, rules, and guidelines
- Model new people-centered leadership through the CEO
- Invert the organization to focus more directly on the RGMs

that legacy as a constant reminder and source of emotional energy and pride throughout the enterprise.

Clearly, the most challenging aspect of the KFC workforce performance effort is maintaining distinctiveness with a set of complementary alignment approaches that can support two balanced paths. Its R&C path is based on four approaches, the first two of which also support its P&M path. All four approaches are discussed in the following sections.

Showing People Their True Value.   Showing people their true value all starts with the top leader's strong belief that continued company success is impossible without the special efforts of a lot of people. Perhaps the most important element of this approach has been the CEO's unequivocal declaration that the restaurant general manager is the number-one position in the company. Against that focal point, the corporate staff was transformed into a *restaurant support center* entirely focused on serving the RGMs and their frontline teams. The emphasis switched from accepting high turnover as inevitable to concentrating on keeping more people longer. To that end, tenure is now celebrated, and the focus is on turning people around versus the more typical hire–fire–replace syndrome within the industry. It's still a high-turnover game, but most people at KFC are finding it harder and harder to leave an environment that seems to care about them as individuals. The P&M path lends powerful support to this approach as well, by relentlessly measuring and reporting the results of an in-store-climate survey and by pushing for full staffing while insisting on keeping labor cost at budget (never below, however).

Providing Performance Transparency.   A core element for most successful Process and Metrics paths is performance transparency. Providing performance transparency means that the company allows the workers to see how well they and others are performing. KFC also relies heavily on this element to ensure that its recognition efforts and celebrations reinforce performance objectives. And KFC accomplishes this transparency in ways that are not considered overbearing. Every twenty-eight days, the company force-ranks stores on sales, profits, and a "hospitality, quality, service and cleanliness" (HQSC) index. This index provides on-site, real-time evaluation of performance on the "Colonel's Dozen" store guidelines (the same dozen that the Colonel himself introduced decades ago). These guidelines are now an integral part of the biweekly coaching sessions between each RGM and his or her market coach. In addition, KFC uses mystery shoppers to provide HQSC scores for each restaurant twice a month. Obviously, these processes provide important metrics that are the basis for many recognition awards and celebrations throughout the year.

Providing Meaningful Recognition and Rewards.   The company has created a complete recognition culture that rivals the best. It is hard to argue that KFC is not rewriting the book on forms of recognition. Consider, for example, the rubber chickens awarded by the CEO, the bulldogs awarded by the chief operating officer, and the Road-Runner awards from the director of operations and recognition. The recipients of these seemingly silly awards proudly display them wherever they work—on a desk, a restaurant counter top, or a windowsill. It would be literally impossible to list all the special awards and citations along the Walk of Leaders, simply because the awards are constantly being added to and improved. Among management's top priority tasks at all levels are things like "having fun, recognizing people, and pumping them up." Most significantly, perhaps, this cornucopia of recognition is made credible because management deals promptly and fairly with those who do not perform. Like its Southwest Airlines role model, KFC employs few serious skeptics who ignore, complain about, or scoff at these efforts.

Generating Collective Energy.   The R&C path is all about spreading collective energy, and KFC managers pay special attention to the collective, or group, aspects of what they do. It is a clear, distinctive approach that receives top priority. The company builds in lots of hoopla, and trained facilitators (internal and external) are masters at helping groups stimulate their members to feed off of one another's enthusiasm. Things like the "recognition band" (an employee musical group that plays at the drop of a hat) and the unending promotion of friendly competition are intended to keep people's spirits high and synergistic. The clearly perceptible attitude is "We are all in this together, guys."

While this chapter is about the Recognition and Celebration path, it is important to note that KFC's other balanced path (Process and Metrics) is sustained by two other alignment approaches (in addition to the first two described above). The first is that of distributing leadership broadly, as already illustrated by the emphasis on the RGM's role. In that context, the company has developed a common model, language, and tool set for leadership at KFC. It designs and runs a ten-stage cascade or series of off-site workshops and meetings that reach from the CEO to chicken cooks. The purpose is to teach and reinforce the principles of the company's leadership model so that it is always fresh in the minds of leaders and prospective leaders. KFC has shifted the role of area managers to market coaches who support RGMs and work to eliminate excuses for low performance. Moreover, the company has recently reduced the managerial spans (i.e., the number of RGMs covered) of market coaches to give them more time for coaching. Distributed leadership is much more than just a theme at KFC; it's a fundamental element of management philosophy.

The second approach that supports the P&M path is that of clearly articulating what matters most. This started with the Colonel's Dozen operating practices and measures—which were based on the early best practices across the franchisees. It has spread to other areas and is, of course, the mirror image of the critical measures referred to earlier (e.g., providing performance transparency on sales, profit, and turnover trends). In addition, extensive effort is devoted to training and coaching the restaurant staffs in both understanding and using the Colonel's Dozen. For example, the staff is trained in how to use food projections and evaluate labor schedules.

Sustaining the Balance over Time

The critical balance between performance and fulfillment is alive and well at KFC, but it has been far from easy to sustain that balance over time. The chief financial officer reminds us that "this [celebration] stuff is phenomenally expensive" and requires real conviction to pursue. "Try calculating an internal rate of return on a recognition program," he explains. In CEO David Novak's words, "it takes a lot of energy to create a lot of energy." For example, visiting ten stores a day, eating a wing at every stop, talking to every employee, giving out awards, dreaming up new awards, and creating fun as you go—this is not for the faint of heart or the weak of stomach.

Certainly, the company's business performance benefits from non-people factors as well. External trends have been favorable to KFC. For example, chicken has become the protein of choice, and "comfort foods" (a culinary segment in which KFC is very well positioned) are enjoying a comeback. Internal actions that are not workforce dependent have also contributed to KFC's favorable sales, profit, and turnover trends. Examples include new menu winners from franchisees, investments in physically upgrading stores, and the creation of two-in-one Taco Bell combos (which have better value than separate items—and include a drink) to build noontime and nighttime traffic.

In the end, however, the dynamic balance of worker fulfillment and business performance will keep KFC on top of its game. Accordingly, the company has been rigorously integrating its R&C and P&M paths. The combination is proving to be particularly powerful.

MARRIOTT: R&C PATH IN A STRONG SUPPORT ROLE

Much like KFC, Marriott combines its Recognition and Celebration path with a strong Process and Metrics path. And in some ways, the histories of the two companies are similar. Both have a rich tradition that dates back to their origins, and the lasting values of their founders—J. Willard Marriott and Colonel Sanders—who still provide an important source of energy throughout their respective workforces. Although the senior founding Marriott, J. Willard Marriott, did not become personalized into a global brand symbol like the Colonel, his image and vision still prevail and are reinforced through the leadership of his son, J. W. ("Bill") Marriott. The continuity of aspirations and values that father and son promoted across two generations of leadership is remarkable.

In 1993, the original Marriott Corporation split into two separate companies bound together only by a strategic alliance: Host Marriott (which holds and develops the real estate), and Marriott International (which manages the properties). Marriott International, the focus of our case study, operates two divisions, with combined revenues of $10.2 billion and 192,000 employees. The Marriott brand maintains a 10 percent occupancy-rate advantage over its competition and is consistently named one of the top ten family-friendly corporate employers. For this book, we drew primarily from the higher-performing workforce situations at two properties within the Marriott Hotels, Resorts and Suites Division: the Salt Lake City Marriott (a downtown hotel), and the San Antonio Riverwalk and Riverfront Hotels (a downtown convention center complex).

Historical Perspective: A Rich Family Legacy

In 1927, John and Alice Marriott opened a root beer stand in Washington, D.C. From that modest beginning emerged, in a few short years, a regional chain of restaurants called The Hot Shoppes, which by 1967 became the Marriott Corporation. Today, Marriott International is one of the world's leading hotel operators, whose leaders continue to believe that its fundamental strategy is to be the preferred employer in the industry. Started by a unique family, the company makes most of its workers feel part of a family.

Along with Southwest Airlines, Marriott has placed the employee at the top of its value chain, so it is no accident that the hotel operator pursues a peak-performance workforce. To sustain that competitive advantage, the company provides impressive integrated support for its Mission, Values, and Pride path, with strong emphasis on the Process and Metrics path plus the Recognition and Celebration path.

Because Marriott is so distinctive in its pursuit of the MVP and the P&M paths, its emphasis on recognizing and celebrating its people can easily be overlooked. Marriott's R&C path all starts with its strong aspiration to be the employer of choice in the industry, which leads to an unrelenting emphasis on individual praising. "You can't say thank you enough" is a behavioral habit at Marriott. Managers are conditioned to believe that simple thank yous and personal expressions of appreciation to employees are essential in a workplace environment that cannot afford to rely on monetary rewards. This kind of personal attention taps people's insatiable need for recognition, enriches their self-satisfaction from serving guests, and cultivates spontaneous peer recognition.

There are also many celebrations within the company whereby people are conspicuously recognized for their customer service achievements—and people know where they stand on customer feedback, which is also extensively used as a personal reward. For example, Marriott sponsors the Pathways to Independence program, a unique effort to help welfare recipients become productive workers. The program's graduates are presented with a framed certificate, a permanent nameplate, and a job.

The celebration is a profoundly moving moment for the graduates, their families, and their friends—and many tears of joy are shed. These kinds of recognition events are tied directly to the measures and metrics that track and highlight customer-service performance.

Why the R&C Path Makes Sense

The conditions in Marriott's situation that warrant multiple paths are reflected in the business performance priorities, marketplace dynamics, workforce fulfillment needs, and other cultural factors. In the following sections, we discuss how Marriott addresses these aspects to align the hearts and minds of Marriott's employees.

Performance Priorities.   Marriott's business requires dividing the lodging market into several rational segments; it must provide a unique package for each segment. At each hotel, the overriding aspiration is to deliver a great guest experience every time with every guest. This aspiration requires the coordinated efforts of large numbers of associates (employees) across many functions, from engineers to housekeepers. Although many elements of the company's value proposition are either defined at the corporate level or "fixed" by the physical characteristics of the property, it is the frontline workforce that determines a hotel's day-to-day performance.

Marriott's challenge in this respect is perhaps more complex than KFC's, since Marriott has to be concerned with more than one kind of hotel service and more than one kind of restaurant service. Nonetheless, it still faces similar industry circumstances:

- ✦ Industry economics do not support paying high wages or offering large financial rewards for better performance; hence, nonmonetary incentives are very important.

- ✦ Workforce demographics and low unemployment make it very hard to find and attract suitable employees, and competition among competing lodging companies is intense.

- ✦ Many workers are first-level entrants who come from over thirty different ethnic backgrounds; high turnover is always an issue.

Marketplace Dynamics and Realities. The marketplace contains chains and independent competitors of all kinds—each with different economic and market interests; there is no predominant "enemy or single point of attack." Staying competitive on decision-based, nonemployee dimensions is essential, but getting more from the average worker can be a big advantage in both productivity and quality.

At Marriott, associates always know where they stand in terms of customer satisfaction. Customer survey results are distributed to all, and any individual citations as well as complaints are given directly to the associates concerned. Marriott is continually redesigning most jobs in its hotels to place more workers in direct contact with more guests more often. They measure and report on everything from how long it takes guests to go from "curb to closet" (often as little as three minutes in San Antonio, down from over ten with a previous system), to how much time servers in their restaurants spend *not* waiting on tables. Everybody knows how his or her behaviors affect these measures and what good performance is.

Workforce Fulfillment Needs. The fulfillment needs of the Marriott associates closely parallel those of the KFC frontline workers. First and foremost, many simply need a job that provides for basic family needs. Because of the workforce demographics, there is a premium in providing a clear sense of order, discipline, and direction. People need structure for stability and consistency, which will enable them to gain fulfillment in the other parts of their lives.

The family environment that prevails at Marriott speaks directly to the need of most workers to belong to something that not only is relatively stable, but is also composed of people they respect and like, so that they can feel good about being a part of that community. Naturally, the deeply ingrained sense of mission and values adds pride to how workers feel about what they do and whom they work for. This is a powerful fulfillment combination, which works across all levels and segments of the company. For those who lack formal education and training, the company provides opportunities of two kinds: assistance in furthering their education and advancement possibilities not limited by their lack of formal education. Associates looking for a chance to lead and grow into broader managerial roles can find it at Marriott. The majority of Marriott's employees, however, are simply seeking recognition of their value and affirmation of their ability to make a difference. And they find that affirmation at Marriott.

Marriott's associates come from even more difficult and diverse kinds of backgrounds than do Marine recruits. Despite the associates' lack of education, experience, and work ethic, Marriott believes strongly in the potential of each person it selects. In fact, the selection process itself is the first step in showing people their true value. In other words, Marriott conveys to new associates that they were considered to be pretty special people (in attitude, demeanor, and intent) to get the job in the first place. And from that point on, the company takes every opportunity to make its people feel wanted and needed. A *Business Week* article describes an example of Marriott's kind of personal concern that can engender lifelong associate loyalty:

> *"Every day I put on this uniform, just like an NBA player," proudly proclaims Thong Lee, a bartender who has worked 16 years at the Seattle Marriott. Lee has never forgotten that his boss, Sandy Olson, shut down the hotel laundry where he used to work for a day so the entire staff could attend his mother's funeral. The gesture earned Lee's loyalty for life.[1]*

The fulfillment needs of such a diverse workforce run the gamut from structure and security to individual opportunity and group approval. These needs vary by associate level and function. Since members of the workforce at all levels are critical in the Marriott mission, it is as understandable as it is remarkable that the company pursues three balanced paths successfully.

Cultural Factors. The culture reflects the long-standing leadership philosophy of putting people first and never giving up on complete customer satisfaction. The company cares deeply about its people and aspires to sustain a true family-type environment. This is reflected in Bill Marriott's twelve rules for success (table 7-2).

Like KFC, Marriott has chosen to make its frontline people its primary competitive advantage by using nonmonetary incentives, investing in the people it has, securing high performers from unlikely and unskilled sources, and creating a familylike environment where people develop strong loyalties. What is most important, however, is obtaining a higher level of performance from average workers than does the competition.

In return for their better performance, the associates get truly meaningful personal satisfaction from serving guests well, from being trusted to "do whatever it takes," and from being treated with respect by managers at all levels. They work in a friendly, supportive, positive environment with a palpable family feel, and they enjoy job security and career stability if they perform well. Most believe that they can have a long and varied career with the company as well as many little perks and other benefits to supplement reasonable pay. Balancing employee fulfillment and enterprise performance sounds simple enough, but it is truly demanding on both sides—and it works! As Aung Win, director of services, puts it, "It's a very simple culture: We take care of the associates, and the associates take care of the guests. . . . If your people are happy, the guest will be happy." As Aung points out, this philosophy comes straight from the Marriott family and reflects not only Marriott's emphasis on consistently good customer service, but also the deep-seated belief that associates deserve to be treated with sincere respect.

Table 7-2   BILL MARRIOTT'S TWELVE RULES FOR SUCCESS

1. Continually challenge your team to do better.
2. Take good care of your employees and they'll take good care of your customers, and the customers will come back.
3. Celebrate your people's successes, not your own.
4. Know what you're good at, and mine those competencies for all your worth.
5. Do it and do it now. Err on the side of taking action.
6. Communicate. Listen to your customers, associates and competitors.
7. See and be seen. Get out of your office, walk around, make yourself visible and accessible.
8. Success is in the details.
9. It's more important to hire people with the right qualities than with specific experience.
10. Customer needs may vary, but their bias for quality never does.
11. Eliminate the cause of a mistake. Don't just clean it up.
12. View every problem as an opportunity to grow.

Multiple Paths at Marriott

It is Marriott's belief in the value of emotionally committed people that has led the company to be almost as rigorous about its pursuit of the R&C path as it is about pursuing the Mission, Values, and Pride path. Though the company is better known for the latter path, it focuses on the R&C path to help stimulate individual customer service achievements and company loyalty. The R&C path engenders the feeling that "I am an essential part of something worthwhile." The multiple paths at Marriott are uniquely complementary and powerful. Clearly, the MVP path is the "dominant eye" that integrates and is supported by the other two paths (Figure 7-2).

Energy Sources and Alignment Approaches

The Marriott culture is driven by customer reaction, which is measured and reported relentlessly at all levels. The pursuit of satisfied customers is the primary source of energy. At least monthly and sometimes weekly,

Figure 7-2   INTEGRATION OF THREE BALANCED PATHS
AT MARRIOTT

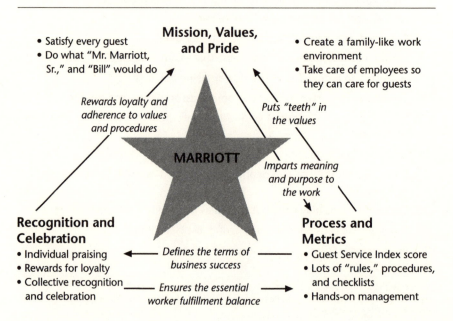

every associate—from housekeeper to residence manager—gets a report on customer feedback. In this way, the associate knows how the customers feel about the service that was provided, both individually and collectively. The various Marriott hotels are ranked against these reactions, and any negative trends demand and receive immediate attention.

There is an intense focus on this report—the guest service index (GSI). It is a monthly measure based on direct customer reactions and feedback and is a primary source of energy and motivation at all levels. Additionally, a balanced scorecard measures three sets of parameters: the P&L (profit-and-loss earnings statements), the associate satisfaction survey, and the GSI. Of the three, however, *GSI is king!* The guest service index is more important to the workforce than any financial indicator. As Betsy Gates, front desk supervisor at the Salt Lake City Marriott, says, "The GSI is a 'big deal,' because if the front desk looks good, then I look good."

A key second source of energy for the company, of course, still emanates from two generations of Marriott family leadership. The image and values of the founder, J. W. Marriott Sr., remain at the heart of the culture, and few associates do not still relate to that legacy and take pride in perpetuating it. Bill Marriott Jr. is perhaps an ideal leader to carry on his father's tradition, not only because of the family ties, but because his personal contributions reinforce the need for every associate to pay attention to every detail of customer service. His walk-through visits to the various hotels have become legendary as people remember for years how he noticed, commented on, and captured the attention of others over such details as frayed carpeting, imperfectly presented meals, and improper dress. In addition to relentless quizzing of management on the GSI scores, he also uses the visit to get feedback directly from frontline employees. The message to the workforce is very clear: "If Mr. Marriott notices these kinds of things, we'd better make darn sure the customers don't get a chance to see them." And as Marriott himself has said, "More than half of this [the visits] is about morale. If the workers can see me, it helps them personalize the company. And in the end, good morale means good productivity."

The complementary alignment approaches that support the many events, awards, mechanisms, and other forms of recognition and celebration at Marriott are the best way to show how the company effectively integrates its actions along multiple balanced paths. The alignment approaches with which the company is truly distinctive are summarized below, and they serve to reinforce all three paths.

Showing People Their True Value. As in so many of the best peak-performance situations, it all starts from a deep-seated leadership belief that every associate matters. Virtually all associates are convinced that their efforts are highly valued, both individually and collectively—and that they matter to the company as individuals. At Marriott, this alignment approach is reflected in the familylike care and loyalty values, the amount of personal time frontline leaders spend with their people, and the personal relationships that they develop. As Larry Lyons, engineering supervisor, told us:

> *The world needs ditch diggers. You have to love 'em and hug 'em. You need to keep them informed and loyal. You need to recognize them. You cannot leave them out. . . . The world goes around because of people who put in their forty hours. They don't want to put in extra time to learn about budgets and [they] don't have big aspirations to move up in the organization.*

Despite their modest aspirations, these average workers are the ones responsible for much of the extra performance in the Marriott workplace. Because the company aspires to sustain the kind of emotional commitment that leads to peak performance, its leaders know that such workers need to be recognized and celebrated for who they are as well as what they contribute.

Articulating What Matters Most. In this regard, Marriott leaves nothing to chance. The "Marriott Way" to guest satisfaction is clearly embedded in many principles, lists, rules, and mnemonics. It is inculcated in new hires through an intensive ninety-day orientation and is constantly reinforced with associates in their day-to-day work—by peers and customers as well as management. What is more important, the Marriott Way is ingrained in managers and supervisors throughout their careers and is therefore nearly cultlike in its effect. Although the Marriott Way is clearly at the heart of the P&M path, it also determines exactly what must be recognized, rewarded, and celebrated—more often than not in nonmonetary ways. Marnie Harvey, restaurant manager, knows he could make more money elsewhere. He looked seriously at managing another restaurant, where he could have made several thousand dollars more annually, but he didn't like the way it was run or the management style. He chose to stay with Marriott simply because "it feels more like family here. I feel more ownership . . . [but] my mother thinks I must be in some sort of cult the way I talk about family and am willing to work for less."

No doubt Marriott fails to attract, and loses, some people for monetary reasons. Most associates, however, derive real fulfillment from the company's clear articulation of what matters—particularly when they are recognized for their part in taking care of the customers "the way Mr. Marriott would want me to." And that is exactly what their immediate leaders are devoted to ensuring.

Providing Performance Transparency. Marriott's periodic measurements of employee satisfaction correlate closely with the guest service index (GSI). This is hardly surprising, since the GSI ratings are frequently reported (monthly), widely known, and visibly recognized throughout the workforce. The GSI breaks down guest experiences into discrete elements directly related to the work performance of individuals and groups. It is the focal point for corrective action and continuous improvement activities.

This performance transparency not only makes it clear to everyone how the customers think Marriott associates are doing, but it also makes the various recognitions, rewards, and celebrations highly credible. In fact, in and of itself, the distribution and transparency of these ratings is the primary mechanism for recognizing the better performers. People know what the survey results mean, and they also know that they will be recognized for what counts in the Marriott Way. They take real pride in moving the GSI in the right direction.

Making Purposeful Selection. The labor market dynamics pose a huge challenge for Marriott as well as others in this industry. Low wages predominate, turnover is endemic (typically 80 to 100 percent for housekeepers and food servers), and tardiness and absenteeism are major problems. It is a tough labor pool. As a result, the hiring and selection criteria are very clear and focused on what one bell captain describes as finding the true "hospitality animals"—people who can easily relate to and respond to all kinds of guests and who enjoy doing it. They look for a positive attitude, a warm and friendly personality, a sense of humor, and a desire to make people smile. These are hard characteristics to test for, but Marriott has developed criteria, questions, and processes that reveal what they need to know. Moreover, as the company changes its guest service systems, it changes the people requirements as well. One human resources manager reports, "We used to hire people who were good at the keyboard, good at processing information. Now we want associates who can look you in the eye, carry on a conversation, and work under stress."[2]

This selection process is highly disciplined, placing as much emphasis on self-selection as it does on company selection. Moreover, it continues well beyond the initial hiring decision in ways that ensure that misfits are quickly identified and appropriately dealt with.

Providing Meaningful Recognition and Rewards. Marriott works hard at making recognition and rewards meaningful, even though it is constrained by what it can pay within its business economics. The most often cited element of this effort is the individual coaching, praising, and teaching that occur in all parts of the organization. The Marriott motto holds true: "You can't say thank you enough." Nor can you spend too much time with individual workers making sure they understand the "why" of what they do.

The company emphasizes, recognizes, and rewards loyalty and performance over time. "You have to develop your Marriott backbone," one supervisor said, which means people get credit for paying their dues and can expect very good compensation over the long haul. Virtually all promotions are from within, and transfers and special assignments go to those who have clearly earned them with their consistent performance in serving the guest's interests.

The various perks, benefits, and compensation are awarded to those who consistently demonstrate a "guest obsession." Tuition reimbursements are used to attract the best workers; good health benefits are aimed at attracting and keeping those with families; and dozens of timely small perks are used to add to the personal thank yous, which leaders at all levels make a point of giving.

Creating Widespread Opportunity. A big part of the Marriott R&C path is based on providing a wide variety of opportunities for all associates. These opportunities constitute tangible recognition for those whose performance consistently makes a difference in serving the guests. The most important opportunity is that of a long-term career, which in today's volatile labor situation is of increasing value. The company makes good on its promise to "take eager young people, give them opportunities, and help them build a career at Marriott." This promise includes promotions from within, mobility across properties, and mobility across functions.

In addition, distributing leadership broadly is another facet of creating widespread opportunity. However, the concept of encouraging workforce initiative at Marriott is more than just another approach. It is a fundamental element of the company's leadership philosophy. It demands and usually results in great bosses up and down the line within a fairly traditional hierarchy. Many associates made unsolicited comments like "My boss is just a great individual—I really appreciate working with her." *Boss* is really a misnomer at Marriott because of the emphasis on caring for and developing the associate's full potential. Supervisors and managers at all levels are seen as caring, down-to-earth people; self-serving "phonies" do not last long in the management ranks. The personal role models and mentors are abundant, if not pervasive. Moreover, the standard of hands-on management is strongly enforced. Leaders have to get directly involved with their people. They cannot be above the work if they expect to foster real team levels of performance.

The frontline supervision is perhaps the most highly valued level within the organization. In one manager's words, "You can't cheat [i.e., skimp] on frontline supervisors." Building a focus (obsession) within associates for satisfying guests requires a great deal of daily coaching and working with associates by frontline supervisors. It can't be done at arm's length. As one supervisor observed, "Making sure you have plenty of exchanges with associates through the day helps keep their focus on guest service sharp, provides them with personal interactions to break up the day, and demonstrates that management is equally committed to guest service."

Highly credible role models, hands-on supervisors, and the individual attention these leaders give to the workers is at the heart of Marriott's emotionally committed associates. These capable leaders are the primary source of the recognition and rewards that workers thrive on, and they are also the critical drivers of the process and metrics effort. Without the leaders' efforts, neither the R&C path nor the P&M path would be as distinctive as it is. We chose to end our examples with Marriott, not only because it excels at the R&C path, but because of its unique ability to integrate three different paths.

THE CRITICAL SUPPORT PATH

It is clear from our research on Marriott, KFC, and others that the Recognition and Celebration path is essentially a supporting path. By itself, it seldom leads to a peak-performance workforce. In some ways, this is contrary to popular belief, and widespread programs to inject more "hoopla" into an organization can prove both disappointing and expensive. As indicated at the outset of this chapter, we found no examples of institutions with higher-performing workforces relying entirely or even primarily on the R&C path. Notable standouts on this path—SWA, The Home Depot, KFC, and Marriott—all integrate their recognition and celebration efforts with one or two other paths.

As an integrated support path, however, the R&C path offers unusual balancing power, particularly with respect to the P&M path. Since most organizations focus primary attention on some kind of process and metrics effort, the potential value of adding the R&C path is great indeed. We saw the value of just that kind of integration at KFC—and believe it was at the heart of the company's recent turnaround in performance. With Marriott's long, rich history, its primary path has been that of Mission, Values, and Pride. The MVP path has always been supported and reinforced by a rigorous Process and Metrics path. The essential balance, however, requires Marriott to be disciplined and distinctive along the Recognition and Celebration path as well.

Enterprises that find themselves out of balance with respect to worker fulfillment needs and that already have a finely honed process and metrics approach should consider adding and integrating R&C mechanisms to readjust their balance. Moreover, companies with a history that naturally leads to a Mission, Values, and Pride path might also benefit from adopting a more rigorous R&C path to reinforce their primary path and help ensure a dynamic balance over time.

III ✦ APPLYING THE LESSONS LEARNED

Figure III-1   DISTINGUISHING FACTORS FOR PURSUING A BALANCED PATH

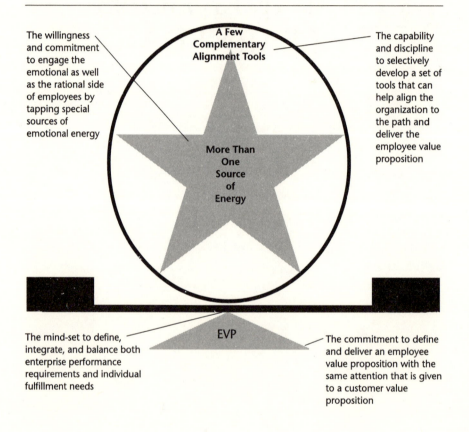

The willingness and commitment to engage the emotional as well as the rational side of employees by tapping special sources of emotional energy

A Few Complementary Alignment Tools

The capability and discipline to selectively develop a set of tools that can help align the organization to the path and deliver the employee value proposition

More Than One Source of Energy

The mind-set to define, integrate, and balance both enterprise performance requirements and individual fulfillment needs

EVP

The commitment to define and deliver an employee value proposition with the same attention that is given to a customer value proposition

Not *every enterprise needs or wants* the kinds of higher-performing workforces illustrated in part II. Many successful enterprises can sustain a competitive advantage by applying the principles of consequence management based on average workforce performance. Many others, however, will see a lasting value in the pursuit of strong emotional commitment within critical segments of their workforce. Obviously, it is important to make that determination before embarking on any of the five paths described herein.

Part III of this book summarizes the lessons learned about sustaining a balanced path and will help those who see the value in finding the right path for their situation. While business conditions strongly influence that choice, so do the fundamental characteristics of the enterprise culture and leadership philosophy. The most critical factor, no matter which path(s) you follow, is a relentless determination to balance enterprise performance with worker fulfillment. Achieving that balance requires more than one source of emotional energy, plus the discipline to channel that energy into performance results consistently over time.

Obviously, it is important to choose sources of energy that can work in your situation and to be selective and disciplined in applying a set of complementary alignment tools that allow you to have a distinctive impact on the workforce (figure III-1). Although none of the paths pose easy choices, those who choose wisely can expect results that are rewarding to shareholders, customers, and employees alike.

The previous parts of this book illustrate how various enterprises have tapped different sources of energy and applied different tools and alignment approaches to excel along five integrated paths. Part III summarizes the options from all five paths and compares them directly to help you make your own choices in considering different combinations.

8 ✦ *Generating and Aligning the Energy*

*B*oth *the U.S. Marines* and Southwest Airlines are outspoken proponents of sustaining a warrior spirit throughout their institutions. Many other high-performing workforces demonstrate that same kind of energy, courage, and dedication. The term *warrior spirit* implies a deep emotional commitment that causes important segments of a workforce to emerge as the enterprise's primary competitive advantage. Engendering that spirit demands resurgent sources of emotional energy and clear channels, or management approaches, for aligning that energy. This chapter summarizes how those two essential underpinnings of all five paths happen.

GENERATING THE ENERGY

Most people are familiar with George Lucas's *Star Wars* trilogy, which has captivated two generations of moviegoers. Luke Skywalker, Obi-wan Kanobi, and Darth Vader wave their mysterious wands and attempt to summon the "Force" to win impossible battles and thwart the efforts of dozens of enemies, not to mention each other. The Force is a mysterious source of special power and energy that only the Jedi master, Yoda, an ancient and shriveled up but cuddly wizard apparently in the 899th year of his life, can convey to young Luke Skywalker. The power of the Force is strong in Yoda, who teaches Luke that the secret of the Force is in doing, not trying. Unless Luke masters this challenge and learns to draw upon the Force for good, he cannot survive to lead the good guys to victory over "the dark side" (which, unfortunately, can also draw upon the Force for special evil powers).[1] I find this highly entertaining and imaginative story of intrigue and space adventure strangely analogous to what a company must do to generate the extra energy that a peak-performance workforce demands. Tapping into powerful sources of energy—consciously and regularly—is clearly what companies that sustain higher-performing workforces do. These sources of energy are not quite as intangible or mysterious as the Force in *Star Wars*. But they are nonetheless powerful in producing the cohesion, commitment, and extra effort of large numbers of employees. Without such sources of energy, the workforce would seldom be the determinant of a company's competitive advantage.

The most evident characteristic of any peak-performance workforce is the energy level that it exudes. Walking into the workplace, you feel its energy, which is noticeably different from that of any average-performing workplace. Activity levels are more intense, attitudes are more positive, interactions are less constrained, and formal positions are less evident. People work hard, but they have fun at work and take full advantage of a widespread sense of humor. This implies a quotient of extra individual and collective energy well beyond the norm. The following three categories represent the more compelling sources of energy that we observed:

1. Magnetic leaders with impossible dreams (larger-than-life individuals who capture the imagination of multitudes)

2. Dynamic marketplaces (unpredictable conditions created by aggressive competitors and demanding customers)

3. Remarkable histories and legacies of accomplishment (perpetuating legends, heroes, and martyrs)

Although these three categories are not intended to be comprehensive or all-inclusive, they encompass the vast majority of energy sources that we observed and illustrated in part II. Such sources are mostly outside the realm of what the current leadership of an enterprise can create or mandate. However, they become powerful potential sources of energy when management consciously and consistently taps into them over time. Unfortunately, they come into play only when they are fully recognized for their unique energizing potential and are consciously drawn on for that purpose by current leaders at all levels.

Seldom is a company in a position to utilize all of its possible sources at the same time. Yet, none of the higher-performing workforce situations that we have explored in depth has been content to rely on only one—particularly in the long term. The most prevalent pattern is to draw on two over time in a way that reflects the changing external and internal conditions the company faces.

Magnetic Leaders with Impossible Dreams

It is no secret that a larger-than-life leader can be truly energizing for large numbers of people. Unfortunately, if a company doesn't already have such a magnetic personality at the top, it's pretty tough to "beam one up from below," to paraphrase Captain Kirk of *Star Trek* fame. Leaders like J. Willard Marriott (Marriott International), David Packard (Hewlett-Packard), General Al Gray (U.S. Marine Corps), Marvin Bower (McKinsey & Company), and Bernard Marcus (The Home Depot) not only draw crowds wherever they go, they move these crowds emotionally. They also weave a spell around memorable and inspirational stories to which everyone can relate. Hence, they constitute a powerful source of energy.

In his seminal work, *Leading Minds: An Anatomy of Leadership,* Howard Gardner takes his readers through an intriguing exploration of the leadership approaches of a few truly great leaders from all walks of life (e.g., Margaret Mead, J. Robert Oppenheimer, Alfred P. Sloan, George C. Marshall, Eleanor Roosevelt, and Martin Luther King, Jr.). He has chosen his sample to meet a leadership definition that centers on influencing large numbers of people, that is, "persons who, by word and/or personal example, markedly influence the behaviors, thoughts, and/or feelings of significant numbers of their fellow human beings." The most compelling characteristic of these people is captured in Gardner's introductory observation that such "leaders achieve their effectiveness chiefly through the stories they relate."[2] While few corporate leaders would pass Gardner's screen (the single exception in his book is Alfred Sloan of General Motors), the magnetic leaders that we found to be a primary energy source in a few peak-performance workforces used stories in a similar way. Kelleher of Southwest Airlines (SWA) continually tells stories about his people living their values; Gray of the Marines told stories of his "warriors" (Medal of Honor winners); and Marcus of The Home Depot was a former stand-up comedian in the Catskills, where storytelling is a life-support system.

Instinctively, of course, when we think about a large body of energized workers, we see it as a function of something that emanates from leadership at the top. In some cases this is true. However, in *Built to Last,* James Collins and Jerry Porras provide convincing evidence that their so-called visionary companies were seldom dependent on any single magnetic leader or even a small band of such leaders at the top. Instead, a broad-based leadership and organizational system was much more important over time than any small group at the top: "A charismatic visionary leader is absolutely not required for a visionary company and, in fact, can be detrimental to a company's long-term prospects."[3]

This is not to say that when such a leader does exist, he or she is not sometimes a powerful source of energy for a higher-performing workforce. We found, however, that such a leader was never the sole or even primary source of extra energy for very long. Sooner or later, other sources of energy must come into play. In *Nuts!* (the story of SWA's amazing revolutionary impact on the airline industry), Kevin and Jackie Freiberg aptly portray Herb Kelleher's unique energizing effect on the company. He created "the cause" that SWA pursues, he personifies the vision and values that people believe in so strongly, and he symbolizes the love and caring for the employees that define SWA culture. Yet, we found very few at SWA who believe that Herb needs to be SWA's future primary source of energy—or even that he needs to be "cloned" to sustain the enterprise going forward.

The company's model of broad-based, collaborative effort and leadership already draws more heavily on other powerful energy sources, such as its increasingly compelling legacy and a fierce group of competitors in a dynamic marketplace. Besides, even when Herb and his alter ego, Colleen Barrett, executive vice president, are no longer there in person, they will likely still be there in spirit and symbolism. SWA's broad-based leadership system will likely continue to use Herb's and Colleen's memorable images (already larger than life) well beyond their active SWA careers to help sustain the company's uniquely committed workforce.

Such images of bygone heroes, when cultivated and kept alive, become lasting symbols. The heroes and their "impossible dreams" remain in the hearts of others, who persist in their commitment to build something that lasts. The following sections illustrate this phenomenon.

Leadership Symbols That Continue to Motivate. Consider the case of Colonel Sanders at KFC. In the beginning, the Colonel—Harland E. Sanders—was an unlikely magnetic leader source of energy. Armed with his special secret formula for fried chicken (which the company still jealously guards), Sanders opened and franchised hundreds of outlets across the country. He traveled from city to city in his car, while his wife, Claudia, was back home working out of their garage filling orders for the seasoned flour mix. His many face-to-face contacts were focused on helping and encouraging the franchisees to follow a few simple rules and values. As a result, the Colonel remains a lasting symbol of hospitality, quality, and value. His image still persists as a larger-than-life symbol of what the company was about and continues to be about: a simple, affordable chicken meal for all the family—provided by a warm, familiar friend of the family.

For a time after the Colonel sold the company to larger, more professionally managed companies (RJR Nabisco and Pepsi), his legacy was lost. Hard-nosed new management decided that there were more efficient ways to get fried chicken to the masses. As understandable and businesslike as their efforts might have been, however, they nearly lost the support of their best people and franchises and almost destroyed the company. Fortunately, when Pepsi put David Novak in charge, he was wise enough to resurrect the Colonel (now deceased) and restore his image to its proper place as a symbol of quality food, friendly service, and convenient dining. Novak drew heavily upon the Colonel's legacy as a powerful source of energy for his new inverted leadership focus, the restaurant general managers (RGMs), be they franchisees or KFC employees. Novak even brought back the bucket, which had been dropped as too old-fashioned, cumbersome, and caloric looking for the more health-conscious crowd. Now the bucket is embraced as a symbol of great value, family eating, and good times with friends.

When current KFC leaders trumpet the slogan "RGMs are No. 1!" they mean that the restaurant general manager role is the number-one KFC leadership role responsible for building a great restaurant team. The

RGM team is clearly "on point" to fulfill the Colonel's commitment to quality and hospitality for customers. Thus, the Colonel's symbolic power is not simply that of a revered icon from the past; he is the model for every RGM today.

Impossible Dreams That Persist. Magnetic leaders often have or spawn impossible dreams, which can capture the imagination of many. Consider two examples from a list of many: Malcolm McLean's stubborn persistence in using a regional trucking company to transform three global industries (railroads, trucking, and ocean shipping) by creating Sea-Land Service (the father of containerized shipping, better known as *piggybacking*), or Michael Dell's presumptuous daring in believing that he could bypass the entire dealer channel through which personal computers were sold. Entrepreneurial dreamers know no bounds and are unencumbered by the naysayers reminding them of the obvious impossibility of what they are attempting. But impossible dreams are not solely the province of a few hearty and courageous entrepreneurs. Some military leaders, politicians, scientists, and artists pursue equally unbelievable fantasies. It is the relentless pursuit of a dream—not the dream itself—that generates the energy. People are mysteriously attracted to those Don Quixotes who do not know when to quit tilting against their windmills.

Creating an impossible dream is not something that logical thinkers and professional executives do on purpose. If they are perceptive, however, they will recognize a dream when they see it rising from the embers of marketplace upheavals and survival debris. Herb Kelleher did not start out with the dream of opening the skies to everyone within reach of his airline's routes—but he has certainly ended up there, largely based on what SWA had to do to survive its price wars. General Al Gray, former commandant of the Marine Corps, didn't create his warrior-spirit dream out of logical analysis; it was born of necessity in the emotional aftermath of the Vietnam War, which had eroded standards, weakened values, and damaged discipline.

Something That Lasts. Most of us experience, at one time or another, a strong desire to create something of lasting value in what we do and how we do it—the desire to leave our mark and to control our own destiny. The whole idea of entrepreneurship is based on rewarding people directly in proportion to how they apply that desire to deliver value to their constituents. Moreover, one of the most powerful incentives of true entrepreneurs is the lure of building successful enterprises and lasting institutions—which usually supersedes any desire they may have to make a lot of money. This invariably sounds like an impossible dream to outsiders.

"Something of lasting value" is a catch phrase easier to articulate than to create. Virtually every entrepreneurial venture has leaders who dare to dream that their idea will be the rare exception that not only survives the start-up swamp, but also rules whatever commercial seas they choose to navigate.

Not surprisingly, the people in start-up ventures work at very high levels of intensity and energy. They are owners in a very tangible sense, not only because they have invested heavily in the venture, but also because they seriously dream of creating a new enterprise that lasts. They are as motivated by their dream as they are by the potential financial prospects. No question that the promise of building something of lasting value can constitute a powerful source of energy whenever it starts to become a reality in people's minds. Companies within memory range of their start-up days can readily convert the memory into extra energy—particularly when the people who struggled and lived through those early days are still around. Several companies that we researched (namely, Southwest Airlines, The Home Depot, BMC Software, Hambrecht & Quist, and i2 Technologies) have experienced and continue to draw from that source of energy.

SWA's early struggles against seemingly insurmountable odds resulted in a cohesiveness among its people that is evident even today. Its survival turned into a cause: "Herb Kelleher is a master at turning things into a cause. Anyone who knows Southwest Airlines well understands that its survival is the cause Kelleher has been fighting for since 1971."[4]

One of the better examples of extending the entrepreneurial dream of the founders into the core ideology of the enterprise is The Home Depot. The two founders, Bernie Marcus and Arthur Blank, were entrepreneurs who imbued a special sense of ownership throughout the entire organization. They also converted their enterprise-building dream into somewhat impossible dreams for their people. For example, the spirit of individual ownership is alive and well in every Home Depot store manager. Surprisingly, perhaps, it is also alive and well even below the store manager level because the associates (The Home Depot's term for its employees) believe they are "owners" of things like a plumbing department or even a particular product aisle. Taken literally, these are impossible dreams—but they constitute very motivating aspirations nonetheless.

Dynamic, Chaotic Marketplaces

Unpredictable and explosive marketplace dynamics can also provide compelling sources of energy. In fact, companies whose leaders fall prey to marketplace denial (e.g., "I don't care what you heard—our products are still as good as our competitor's") invariably get left in the dust of those who are always probing for what the customer truly thinks.

A good example of the energizing power of marketplace reality comes from Johnson Controls Automotive Systems Group (JCS), a supplier of automotive seats to original equipment manufacturers. JCS traditionally had viewed its customers as big automakers; its customer contacts were engineers and purchasing agents—not particularly inspiring or energizing. When JCS decided to conduct some research for the first time with the ultimate customers—people who sat in JCS seats—it was a different story. First, JCS got lots of great ideas for improving the product, but equally important, the company was energized by the face-to-face reactions of those who experienced the product improvements firsthand. There is no substitute for a delighted customer.

Simply put, a dynamic marketplace is a powerful source of energy. It creates explosive opportunity at many levels, breeds fierce competition that generates emotional reactions, and encounters unrelenting customers who require unique personal attention.

Explosive Opportunity Growth.   Explosive growth is undeniably energizing in itself. And the prospect of further, faster growth is even more energizing—simply because it implies more opportunities. Companies in an exciting growth situation like Microsoft or Dell have little time or little need to look for other sources of energy to fuel a higher-performing workforce. Dynamic growth continues to be a powerful source of workforce energy at companies like Southwest Airlines, The Home Depot, and Hewlett-Packard.

First USA (FUSA), a very successful and rapidly growing provider of custom credit cards, cultivates a workforce whose sources of energy have been a powerful combination of growth and two strong, charismatic leaders. Catherine West, executive vice president of Cardmember Services, captures the essence of why the FUSA top leadership personal charisma is as energizing for members of its workforce as rapid growth:

> *But when I came and talked to John Tolleson [chairman] and Dick Vague [CEO] at FUSA, . . . they were talking about things that excited me even more.*
>
> *[They were] two of the most committed, charismatic, visionary leaders that I have ever contemplated working with directly. . . . Working directly with them . . . really appealed to me because they were very clear and focused on what they were trying to accomplish. . . . I really liked the idea of working for leaders with a lot of integrity and commitment, and I wanted to tie my star to . . . a company like that.*

The problem comes if and when growth starts to run out. Unfortunately, the energizing effect of any big idea does not last long. Consequently, companies whose peak performance appears to be sustainable by growth alone often must draw upon other sources of energy as well.

Fierce Competition.   Many executives believe that the threat of competition—converted into the natural human instinct to be a winner—is essential in sustaining a competitive advantage. Although less evident today, relative to the other sources of energy at Southwest Airlines, competitive threats were a very powerful source in the airline's early days. At times, the competition appeared to be actively intent on destroying SWA. During an intense price war between the struggling newcomer (SWA) and Braniff Airlines in early 1973, Braniff "struck what appeared to be a lethal blow" by dropping the fare between Dallas and Houston to literally half the existing fare as a "get acquainted with Braniff" ploy. This tactic infuriated Southwest, since it—not Braniff—was the new airline on the block. Moreover, the Dallas–Houston route was Southwest's primary source of income, whereas that route was a minor part of Braniff's operations. Losing that business to Braniff could well have meant the end for Southwest. The threat energized SWA's fighting spirit as little else could have done, leading to one of the most famous ads in Southwest's history: "Nobody's going to shoot Southwest Airlines out of the sky for a lousy thirteen dollars." It also led to fundamental changes in SWA's flight- and plane-turnaround capability (the time it takes to land, unload and reload passengers, and take off again), which continues to be central to its competitive advantage.[5]

Certainly, a real enemy—with a name and an image—makes the adrenaline rise. A lot can be said for the ability to personalize the enemy in exploiting the potential of this source of workforce energy. We see it most clearly in companies in which head-to-head competition—*mano a mano*—dominates the scene, for example, Coca-Cola versus Pepsi; GE Motors versus Emerson Electric; Motorola versus "the Japanese."

Obviously, these examples are unique to their circumstances, but they make an important point nonetheless. An aggressive competitor can provide a compelling sense of urgency—and source of energy for the workforce. An aggressive natural enemy, however, is not always plausible or even possible. If an enterprise does not have one, it may not want to create one. Nor is a fierce competitor essential in energizing a peak-performance workforce.

Unrelenting Customers.   Closely linked to the notion of competitive threats is the notion of customer pressure. Although it is hard to separate the two in practice, it is helpful to consider them separately in understanding the role of each as a potential source of workforce energy. In the peak-performance workforce, the notion of customer satisfaction is often carried to its logical extreme. Workers become literally obsessed with serving the target customers better in every way than anyone else can. Although we see this kind of obsessiveness at companies like Southwest Airlines and Marriott (both of which place the employee ahead of the customer in their value chain), it is even more pronounced in companies like The Home Depot—where a delighted, smiling customer is the primary goal. The Home Depot likes to use the term *unprecedented* when describing its customer-service aspiration.

Similarly, customer obsession is a primary source of energy at Marriott International. We talked with dozens of housekeepers, bellhops, waiters, and kitchen workers, as well as their supervisors and managers, during our visits to both Salt Lake City and San Antonio. Without exception, their focus was on the customer. All communications from customers somehow make the rounds of the employees. When the feedback is positive, faces light up and chests puff out; when the feedback is negative, legs and arms fly into action to somehow correct the situation, if not change the customer's negative impression to a positive one.

Nothing is as motivating to a Marriott frontline worker as a few sincere words of appreciation and praise directly from a customer.

Those who would draw upon the force of the customer in energizing their workforce are well advised to follow Marriott's philosophy of customer obsession. It is a philosophy that clearly characterizes companies like SWA, The Home Depot, Marriott, and KFC—all of which work hard to ensure that the customer remains a primary source of energy for their people.

Truly Compelling Legacies

Pride has always been a powerful energizer, stemming from past accomplishments, current values, and beliefs, as well as future dreams and aspirations. Pride makes athletes strive to extend their individual best. It explains the irrational eagerness of the firefighting troops of the now-legendary Red Adair to follow him into the fierce heat and dangers of oil-field fires. It entices large numbers of people to adhere to the same set of values at Hewlett-Packard. Individual pride is usually closely linked to collective pride within the peak-performance workforce—at both a company level and an individual work-group level. When it remains visible and relevant over time, pride can truly energize a workforce. Although past accomplishments speak for themselves, leaders in higher-performing workforces do not leave it at that. Rather, they make sure that such accomplishments remain visible and relevant and reinforce values and "core ideologies."[6] In addition, they work hard to build pride in what the company and specific work groups are striving to become, based on mission and collective aspirations consistent with a legacy of accomplishment.

Pride in Enterprise Accomplishments. The U.S. Marine Corps, Johnson Space Center in NASA, Marriott, and The Home Depot are enterprises whose present and past heroes provide a powerful source of workforce energy. Those companies consciously and continuously cite the accomplishments of their heroes to perpetuate and encourage other role models.

3M is yet another example of this kind of pride. Founded in Minnesota at the turn of the twentieth century, 3M literally "began life nearly bankrupt as a failed mine."[7] This well-known visionary institution has led competitors and noncompetitors alike in the development and marketing of innovative products that range from radiation-processing and micro-interconnect systems to adhesives and plastic tape—and that path has taken them far afield from their initial fight for survival as a mining enterprise. In early 1996, I was invited by John Mueller, chairman and CEO of 3M-United Kingdom, to address the company's international leadership conference in Spain. While there, I spent time with a number of the company's senior managers and executives. When I told a senior international executive of my interest in understanding what explains different high-performing workforces, he said, "While I don't know what you will find at other places, I am confident that at the core of it all for 3M is a simple, deep-rooted pride in our institutional accomplishments that transcends both time and geography."

Similarly, at the Johnson Space Center (JSC) in Houston, a special display center for outside visitors epitomizes how the organization uses the heroics of the astronauts to energize the rest of the organization. The center was built in the early 1960s as part of the Kennedy administration's drive to put a man on the moon by the end of the decade. Like each of NASA's space centers, JSC focuses on a particular area of excellence—in this case, manned space flight. JSC engineers were responsible for building the Mercury and Apollo crafts that first launched men into space, and JSC was and continues to be the mission control center for all U.S. manned space flights. Today, JSC manages the space shuttle and space station program, as well as a variety of smaller programs and life-science experiments. It was JSC's scientists, working with researchers at Stanford, who made the initial discovery of possible signs of life in a meteorite of Martian origin.

For the Marines, 3M, and NASA, an intrinsically exciting, highly visible, and well-documented set of past accomplishments automatically generates strong feelings of pride that enhance the pride in present accomplishments. Moreover, that pride serves as an added reward and justification for what these groups do. As one manager at the Johnson Space Center commented during an interview:

> At cocktail parties, my wife and I really enjoy being asked where I work. The answer always stimulates positive reactions. Most people remember the moon landings and space walks as times of great national pride. Families

sat together around the TV screen in the early morning hours to witness these once-in-a-lifetime events, and they still remember it. That sense of pride is still an important part of why I am here.

But the pride as a source of continuing energy needs to be regularly re-fueled, stoked up, and tended to if the fire is to stay alive in the hearts and minds of employees.

Pride in Individual and Group Accomplishments.   Clearly meaning-ful legacies motivate and energize workers. An institution, however, need not have pursued such conspicuously noble missions as NASA's space exploration. Plain old commercial enterprises like SWA, The Home Depot, Marriott, and 3M engender equal pride and emotional commit-ment from missions that are strictly business.

The sense of pride at 3M builds on its past accomplishments. It is reflected in what the company is today, as indicated in different kinds of comments from down-the-line people at 3M. For example, John Owens, research specialist and team leader in the fluorochemicals division, first worked at 3M as an intern while in college and joined the company full time after graduating in 1984. He says that growing up in the Twin Cities, he "always wanted to work for 3M," because of its strong and lasting reputation in the community. He had many neighbors who were proud to work for the company and who spoke highly of 3M as a place where researchers are "allowed to pursue their scientific interests" with-out undue interference or micromanagement.

John is also proud of leading a team that sets its own stretch goals and works hard to meet them. He obviously takes as much pride in the accomplishments of his work group as he does in the company's past ac-complishments. Although management has some say in determining timelines and goals for the project, John's team members are primarily responsible for developing their own work plan. Far from padding the project to add in extra time, John says that the team pushes itself to work harder. They are motivated to set these goals by pride in their work and their ability to do a good job. "People take pride in being able to fol-low through on their work. . . . The team members want to do as good a job as they can, and work to the best of their abilities."

In a 1996 interview, 3M's chairman listed one of the four key values as continuing to be "a company employees are proud to be part of."[8]

This pride in the company, however, depends heavily on pride and aspirations that work groups feel down the line, all across the enterprise. A more apparent source of energy and alignment at frontline levels is the extensive team efforts, characterized by clear, demanding collective aspirations and goals. People take great pride in their team achievements and in belonging to real teams that meet and exceed performance expectations. This kind of pride will undoubtedly help sustain the emotional commitment of 3M's workforce during the periods of financial and economic difficulties that it has recently experienced.

Cultivating More than One Source

The energy for a peak-performance workforce requires special, ongoing attention if it is to continue over time. Although there are many sources of such energy in a dynamic organization, the most effective ones reflect attention to one of several well-documented categories of fundamental human needs (see table 2-1 in chapter 2).

It is tempting to believe that one powerful source, such as rapid growth or magnetic leadership, can provide all the needed extra energy for the higher-performing workforce. The companies we explored, however, actively cultivate more than one source in their effort to satisfy as many of these fundamental needs as possible.

At the same time, it is neither necessary nor wise to pursue simultaneously or with equal intensity all the sources of energy described in this chapter. Each higher-performing institution that we explored has selectively focused where it places its emphasis and investment during any period. SWA's history, for example, reveals that the company has cultivated and emphasized different sources at different times. During its early formation stages, when survival was the name of the game, its primary sources of energy consisted of a magnetic leader and a fierce set of natural enemies trying to "take them out." After the survival phase, SWA began to systematically tap into other sources, such as demanding customers and an emerging, impossible dream of air travel affordable for everyone. Today, the emphasis continues to shift away from its magnetic leader as a primary source of energy toward the pervasive and growing sense of pride in the remarkable legacy that the company has built and is still building. Sustaining pride over time can be a moving target, and over the course of its history, SWA has certainly tapped into several different sources of energy—but the emphasis and concentration has varied over time.

Unfortunately, not all companies that can tap such sources of energy succeed in converting it into a higher-performing workforce. Even the most powerful sources of energy are not enough to ensure alignment of people's actions and decisions. Energy sources generate extra effort, but they do not necessarily align or focus that effort adequately to ensure peak performance. As a result, companies achieving higher levels of performance place as much importance on alignment approaches and mechanisms as on their sources of energy. Consequently, the approaches and mechanisms for alignment described in this chapter deserve as much attention as do the sources of energy in constructing the appropriate balanced paths for any company.

ALIGNMENT APPROACHES AND TOOLS

Finding a source for or generating emotional energy is only half the battle. The energy must also be channeled in ways that align workforce behaviors with the performance imperatives of a successful enterprise. Too often, well-intended efforts to align behaviors can also discourage workers, weaken their commitment, and undermine their energy. Aligning emotional energy is easier said than done.

The remainder of this chapter summarizes the primary alignment approaches of the over two dozen situations that we explored in depth. We found that each approach or set of mechanisms reinforced both the needs of the workforce (fulfillment) and the needs of the company (performance) which relies on the workforce. At the same time, balancing performance and fulfillment appears to require a well-integrated combination of alignment mechanisms to ensure the right balance is sustained in the long term.

As simple as this notion seems, it is at the core of why—and how—paying disciplined attention to a few tools or mechanisms can lead to a higher-performing workforce. The route to pursue, however, is definitely not to seek a score of "10" on all the tools summarized herein. While the tools are common to more than one company, only a few can be executed distinctively by any one company. Moreover, the integrated set of tools that are used to align behaviors and decisions in each of our cases were specific to each company's business, marketplace, and culture situations. Thus, the relative emphasis placed on any particular approach varies to produce different successful combinations.

The various mechanisms and tools that we observed can be loosely grouped into three basic alignment approaches, namely, building the personal self-image and confidence of employees, sustaining a clear focus on performance, and opening up attractive options and opportunities for employees. These three approaches are detailed in the following sections.

Building Personal Self-Image

No doubt the institutions with peak-performance workforces place a priority on designing a more fulfilling organization and work environment for their employees. This fulfillment not only makes people feel better about their work opportunity, but builds their personal self-image and self-confidence as well. They are reminded repeatedly that what they and their work group do really matters both to the company and to its customers, that they are individuals whose well-being is important to the enterprise, and that they can influence their own destiny in positive ways. They are made to feel special, no matter how menial or routine their formal job may be. Although other companies often describe similar intentions, the peak-performance workforce company differs in emphasis on worker self-image. These companies pursued this priority more rigorously and specifically than companies that are content with only average workforce performance. The enterprises we explored simply went to much greater lengths to pay attention to how employees feel about themselves, their co-workers, and their jobs.

Showing People Their True Value. The notion of showing people their true value is a fundamental underpinning of a positive self-image. It means that the company demonstrates clearly and consistently to its employees that they are respected as individuals and that their personal well-being is a primary concern of their leaders. As a result, all workers truly believe that their work is valued and that they are entrusted and encouraged to act on their own. While mistakes are not encouraged, they are understood and accepted, and well-intended personal initiative is rewarded. As a result, the prevailing attitude across the workforce is "I make a difference here, my efforts are noticed and appreciated, and I need not fear making honest mistakes."

Perpetuating this attitude requires (1) showing respect for all individuals at all times, (2) placing importance on every job, and (3) engendering feelings of mutual trust and confidence to act. These attributes are much easier to describe than to accomplish and invariably imply a willingness to invest heavily (somewhat irrationally, perhaps) in training, development, and the creation of opportunity. In essence, the company is more willing to take risks on its people.

Job titles and work relationships minimize the importance of organizational levels. The U.S. Marine Corps expects and insists that the front-line Marines receive top-priority attention. Marines think of themselves as a family, and that feeling permeates all levels of the organization. The biggest concern of graduates of the Marine Officer Candidate School is "How will I earn the respect of my (enlisted) men?" The Marines are perhaps the "gold standard" when it comes to believing in the value of their people. The amount of two-way respect and genuine caring that exists between officers and enlisted men and women is impressive. As more than one recruit remarked, "The colonel and his wife treat me like family."

Merely paying lip service to the value of people or asserting that "people are our most important asset" is not the same as treating employees "as family." The companies that sustain a peak-performance workforce insist that the theme of showing people their true value reflects accurately the top leaders' sincere beliefs. It cannot happen any other way.

Creating and Sharing Bigger Pictures. All employees in companies using this approach have a complete picture of the context in which they work, where they fit in, and what they can do to make a difference. This contributes to their self-image because it demonstrates that the company trusts them and wants them to be an integral part of the big picture that determines their company's success. When employees are part of the big picture, they understand the internal and external environment, which is clarified and updated regularly through mechanisms such as "town meetings," competitor tracking, and direct customer contact. For companies that emphasize the approach, there is a remarkable transparency with respect to both internal and external elements of the business and an unusually extensive set of informal networks and communication vehicles. For example:

+ At NASA, regular exposure to astronauts—past and present—is provided throughout the organization; the energizing effect on employees at all levels is notable.

+ At General Electric's Motors and Industrial Control Systems business, regular town-hall-like meetings are held in each plant, and a regular Monday morning telephone conference is convened to share the latest customer and competitor information across the system.

+ Southwest Airlines continually reminds its people of the bigger pictures at the heart of its mission and values. People are proud that SWA's presence in the market results in air transportation's becoming affordable for a lot more would-be travelers. SWA people may not believe that they are "replacing the automobile," but they certainly use the phrase freely.

Generating Collective Energy.   The most obvious indication of a peak-performance workforce is its collective energy. You can literally feel the energy difference if you compare the atmosphere to that of most organizations. Individuals and small groups move beyond the bounds of their self-interests and individual capabilities because their work environment involves them in something bigger than themselves. This involvement contributes to individual self-image because the positive feelings become contagious, and people constantly try to make others feel positive. Companies that emphasize this approach invariably attract a great deal of outside attention as well.

The essence of generating collective energy is a collaborative effort produced by broad-based teamwork, multiple real teams, widespread mutual support and assistance, plus formal and informal incentives to help others and to make others feel good about what they do. This kind of effort is usually driven by a very strong sense of purpose that emanates from a compelling and often-reiterated mission, a set of shared values, and a common desire to build something truly lasting and great.

Employees often express a sense of personal identity with their natural work group or a larger entity, or both, if not the entire institution.

The collective pride that results becomes evident across large numbers of people. The uniqueness of the work is legitimately emphasized and reinforced with fun activities both on and off the job. The company history is well known, and people take personal responsibility for perpetuating the legacy that the history implies.

Sustaining the Focus on Performance

If the workforce has a clear understanding of what matters for enterprise performance, then that performance is more likely to result. Companies that maintain a sharp focus on performance do so by ensuring consistency across different functions and levels as well as providing clear specificity for each job. There is also a significant difference in the ability of these companies to translate job and performance clarity into worker fulfillment—usually by creating pride in the accomplishment of "what matters." Interestingly, it all starts with the recruiting and hiring process and continues throughout the evaluation, recognition, and reward processes. The leadership system of the enterprise is finely tuned to communicate both directly and indirectly with the following four tools—in ways that workers instinctively understand.

Making Purposeful Selection. Institutions that use this approach to sustain higher-performing workforces treat the determination of who becomes a permanent part of the organization as a critical decision; determining where they work within the organization over time is considered equally important. These companies go to great lengths to ensure that they get "the best of the right kind of people." They are both rigorous and careful about matching up personalities and values with skills, attitudes, and experience. There is a widely and commonly held sense of what kind of person will fit well there.

Leaders are very clear about "our kind of person." They are equally clear about their recruiting strategies, hiring/development choices, and the skills and attitude required for the job. Both the search and the selection are more rigorous than at most other companies. The effort is primarily driven by line rather than staff managers and benefits from active employee referrals and multiple coordinated interviews. In fact, the hiring decision is a uniquely two-way decision. Self-selection is a vital, often inseparable, component of the process both during and after the initial hiring effort.

A philosophy of continuous rehiring prevails and implies that employees expect and are expected to maintain a market-level skill capability. Gary Marino, executive vice president of marketing and credit at First USA, voices perhaps an extreme version of purposeful selection: "We seek world-class capability in all of our key positions and will replace [with world-class hires] those who do not maintain that level. In fact, CEO Richard Vague never gives up." Pursued by Vague for nearly two years before coming aboard, Marino describes the CEO's intense approach to recruitment:

> *Dick is truly remarkable in his commitment to recruiting. We have all learned from his example. He will literally do anything, go anywhere to get a key hire. He opens up his home, changes his personal schedule at the last minute, sends flowers to the wives, buys toys for the kids, and flies candidates here in his private jet. There are no lengths to which he will not go to get the right person.*

In fact, Vague is actually most challenged by and interested in those who are openly and honestly negative. As he told us, "The only people you should have are probably those who don't really want to come. . . . Really great people are usually well liked as well as happy and content where they are. . . . They are not out looking for jobs. . . . I am immediately suspicious of someone who wants it." Hence, he treats the unsolicited resumes that come across his desk "as though they were radioactive"—he avoids them.

Articulating What Matters Most.   It stands to reason that when members of the workforce have a common and clear understanding of what matters most to the company, the decisions and behaviors of its people will be more closely aligned. And the top management of most companies certainly attempts to ensure that its employees have that understanding. In companies that use this tool to sustain a peak-performance workforce, virtually all employees clearly and consistently understand what really matters for company performance in terms of both what they do and how they do it. That understanding translates into pragmatic and actionable activities for every worker.

It starts with clear points of performance focus. At all levels, people can answer the critical and tough *which* questions, that is, which customers and which product and service attributes are the principal concern of which workers; which numbers need to be closely watched (and which actions taken to optimize or correct) by which people; and which nonnumeric indicators need to be monitored by which people. Daily priorities are evident at every level, and there is little question as to what comes first.

People demonstrate a common understanding of how to work in the organization. Only new hires are in doubt as to "how we do things around here," and that doubt is short-lived. Not only are values made clear, but they are described in terms that bring them to life for different levels and types of workers. Role models and mentors are liberally sprinkled throughout the company and are easily accessible. The company history is widely told and enjoyed time and again. People take personal pride in maintaining the legacy. Multiple sources provide a consistent, almost boring, repetition about what matters. This communication begins during recruitment and selection and continues through the new-hire orientations, annual performance appraisals, job and skill training efforts, and formal and informal communications.

Different organizations find different definitions of what matters most, and use different means of reinforcing. For example:

+ At NASA, there is an intense drive to achieve the mission, which includes bringing crews safely home; everyone is passionate about crew safety.

+ At Marriott, what counts is the reaction of the guests, and nothing is more closely monitored than their comments and complaints.

+ At Avon's Chicago plant, "thou shalt not short" is the first thing a new employee learns. Employees relish stories of heroic efforts made to avoid a *short* (a customer order that is either incompletely filled or not delivered on time).

Providing Performance Transparency. Performance transparency means that employees clearly understand how performance is measured and what current performance is for them, their work unit or team, their business, and the overall company. Of course, this understanding starts with a set of clear performance measures and objectives for the overall company. Increasingly, the better companies are attempting to measure three dimensions of corporate performance: shareholder gain, customer satisfaction, and employee well-being. This kind of balanced-performance concept or aspiration recognizes the near-equal importance of all three constituencies. It also complicates the measurement challenge, since customer satisfaction and employee well-being are less subject to regularly generated measures or indicators.

To achieve performance transparency, a company must take a few focused measures that can then be disaggregated for different levels and categories of workers. Another important attribute of this alignment approach is clear, quick, and direct feedback. A variety of mechanisms are employed for that purpose, including disciplined feedback cycles, the highly visible posting of results, and meaningful evaluations based on multiple observations and evaluators. Competitive benchmarking and 360-degree evaluations (i.e., a person is evaluated by all who work with him or her, be they superiors, subordinates, or colleagues) are typical mechanisms. Although there is a heavy emphasis on hard facts (a "facts are friendly" philosophy prevails) and clear accountabilities, the evaluation process often includes several creative intangibles.

General Electric Motors and Industrial Control Systems, for example, measures the immeasurable. Jim Rogers (former CEO) developed a simple quarterly survey of employee opinions and reactions to the workplace and their role in it. The results allowed him to assess the "satisfaction" ratio of the workforce in each business unit and functional department. In other words, he compared the number who believe that "the sun is shining, I love my job, and this is a great place to work" versus those who believe that "it's always raining, I hate my job, and this is a lousy place to work." For a manager in this setting, the ratio must be improving, or the financial and operating numbers don't count. The use of the ratio was Rogers' way of implementing the well-known GE philosophy that "the numbers no longer protect you."

Making Recognition and Rewards Meaningful. Everybody knows that recognizing and rewarding performance works. The difference in a higher-performing workforce is simply that recognition and reward levels clearly differentiate the higher-performing workers from the average, and every conceivable method and mechanism for recognizing excellent performance is explored, if not applied.

Typically, something of value is put at stake, which can mean anything from coveted artifacts (e.g., David Novak's rubber chicken award at KFC) to equity-based compensation. Group achievements are rewarded with the same rigor, fairness, and performance distinctions as individual achievements. The company makes a real effort to tailor rewards and recognition to fit the natural motivations of the workers in different role and job situations.

The Vail Resorts Ski School is an example of a monetary reward system that has a clear sense of cause and effect in its recognition efforts. The criteria are clear, simple, and easy to measure, and the feedback is direct and immediate. Ski instructors are given incentives that encourage them to behave like entrepreneurs. They become experts at the "soft sell" and develop a list of loyal clientele whom they may see several times a season, for several seasons in a row. Each instructor acts independently and is free to earn as much or as little as he or she wants within a fairly broad range. In addition, they are paid for referrals to other instructors, which emphasizes the importance of repeat business for the school as well as the individual instructor.

It is no accident that the Vail Ski School, which excels along the Entrepreneurial Spirit path, is also a classic example of performance transparency at its best. Over 1,400 ski instructors operate at industry leadership productivity rates in a system based on creating individual entrepreneurs at the teaching level. The instructors are crystal clear about their performance goals (number of return students and number of referrals), and they receive daily, if not hourly, feedback on how well they are doing directly from their students and peers, as well as their supervisors. Performance transparency and meaningful recognition and rewards invariably go hand in hand. Ultimately, the role of nonmonetary rewards and recognition seems far more significant than monetary ones in creating the peak-performance workforce.

Opening Up Options and Opportunities

The approaches in this category are aimed directly at giving the workers a sense of personal challenge and an abundance of opportunity to increase and develop their capabilities. Again, while every company claims to do this, the difference with those in the sample that excel here was fairly dramatic. They are not content, for example, to let "growth" take care of motivating workers. Nor are they content to make "climbing the hierarchical ladder" the primary determinant of employee opportunity. Instead, they seek all kinds of opportunities to both expand existing jobs and to provide options outside normal job and advancement tracks. Dick Vague at First USA places the emphasis on *effective delegation,* plain and simple. He believes that those who learn to delegate effectively will not only create new leadership options and capacity among those below, but also open up capacity whereby those who delegate will reach out for new challenges.

Creating Widespread Opportunity. In peak-performance situations where this approach prevails, the company creates the opportunities and provides the support for tapping the hidden reserve of skill, insight, and experience within its workforce. High-growth situations, of course, automatically create more than enough opportunities to go around. We even tend to assume that growth situations are always more attractive and motivating to workers than nongrowth situations. At both The Home Depot and SWA, where growth has exceeded 20 percent a year for over two decades, there has been no shortage of opportunity. In a maturing or low-growth situation, however, the challenge becomes greater. The U.S. Marine Corps, for example, has been stable or shrinking in size since the end of World War II, so the Corps must exploit every conceivable opportunity. From the time recruits are officially designated Marines at the end of their three-month ordeal at Parris Island, every formal advancement or informal skill accomplishment is recognized and celebrated. The Marines appear to make more opportunity out of their situation than do most other institutions.

Companies that emphasize this approach are purposeful and innovative about opening up alternatives for greater involvement. Such alternatives occur both within the job scope and beyond. Some of the best examples of multiple roles came from Hill's Pet Nutrition, the industry leader in dietary pet foods. For example, Scott Lacey's work on the canned food packaging lines sounds much like a typical, monotonous manufacturing job, but his official job description does not begin to capture all the roles he plays in the plant:

✦ *Maintenance mechanic.* He provides maintenance for the packaging machines—and fixes whatever breaks.

✦ *Budget owner, purchasing agent,* and *inventory keeper.* Lacey is responsible for maintaining and purchasing all the oils, greases, and lubricants used on his machinery; as a result, he is in contact with all kinds of people all across the plant. Furthermore, he maintains and purchases the various solvents and chemicals used in his area—a $234,000-a-year responsibility.

✦ *Diet owner.* For one of the forty-plus pet nutrition formulations, Lacey samples the line; inspects for color, smell, and viscosity; decides on releasing the batch; and fixes any problems.

✦ *Tour guide.* Lacey gives tours for the dozens of groups that come through the plant to see how it operates. The groups range from Colgate executives to local school classes.

Enriching the range of advancement opportunities is another way that companies emphasize the opportunity-creating theme. When institutions focus on people development, their efforts usually emphasize job advancement, that is, moving up the ladder. Peak-performance companies, however, also provide a wealth of career and personal development options that include lateral opportunities, stretching part-time assignments, career self-management guidance, and talent and opportunity inventories. The management is constantly seeking innovative ways to change and enhance people's situations.

A final element of the opportunity-creating approach is encouraging individual initiative and personal risk taking. Most companies bemoan the shortage of true initiators and risk takers throughout the organization. Yet risk taking is a characteristic of the venture-capital world that gets stifled in established organizations. In many peak-performance workforces, however, we found conspicuous efforts to bring individual initiative back to the forefront of organizational behaviors.

Distributing Leadership Broadly. Most organization theorists today argue that a distributed leadership system is fundamental to the organization of the future. Certainly, our exploration of the peak-performance workforces would support that argument. However, the most valuable leadership in a broadly distributed system is apparently closest to—or in most direct contact with—the workers themselves.

Distributing the leadership means that many people at many levels in the organization effectively play leadership roles as needed. Consequently, the leverage of effective leadership in "getting more" from the workforce is large and widely available. Organizations that rely on a distributed-leadership approach reflect a common understanding of what leadership means within the organization, and leaders from top to bottom consistently practice that model. This creates a leadership presence that is greater than the sum of individual leaders and results in subordinates stepping into leadership roles. Widely distributed leadership also helps "followers" understand the position and perspective of leadership in the organization. A common statement from the top of such institutions is "We assume everybody can lead in some important way." In other words, most people in situations that reflect their abilities can and do initiate action that others will follow.

In short, learning to lead isn't just for the higher-ups. It is everybody's responsibility and opportunity. As a result, leadership development opportunities are pushed far down into the organization, and people at all levels are expected to rise to the occasion. At KFC, distributed leadership permeates the organization. The following comment from a senior manager addressing a group of restaurant general managers is indicative of KFC's philosophy: "Good leaders don't grow on trees. That's why we're trying to develop you to become better leaders, so that you can go back to your restaurants and develop our future leaders, so that we keep this chain growing."

The role of market coach is to provide direct coaching. To enable more effective coaching, KFC consciously reduced the number of RGMs (sometimes as many as thirteen) for whom each market coach was responsible. The following comments from KFC marketing coaches illustrate the attention they pay to the widespread development and presence of people who can lead others:

The first thing you do with an RGM is convince them that you are there to help them succeed.

Now there is time to really coach and "show how." There is also time to just sit with an RGM over a cup of coffee and talk about how things are going personally and how the family is doing.

They wear the same kind of shoes that we wear, I know these people, I've seen these people walk in and say "Hi, how are you doing?"

Before, a call from the boss meant trouble. Now it's great. It feels like they are there to help and they have some genuine concern for you as a person.

Enhancing the Work Itself.   Enhancing the work means that much attention is paid to ensuring that the specific job or work activities—in and of themselves—are enjoyable, meaningful, and satisfying. People work hard at what they do because they get great personal satisfaction out of the work itself. This happens when a company selects people whose interests and skills fit well with the tasks required and when management does whatever it can to increase the intrinsic satisfaction of the work.

The work-enhancement approach conspicuously values fundamental skills and experience. In many cases, hands-on work is cherished at all levels, and managers expect to do—and enjoy doing—real work that affects products and customers directly. Marine officers, for example, take great pride in being able to field-strip a rifle, well beyond the point in their career when they need this skill. And numerous engineers at NASA were gratified when a reduction in subcontracted work resulted in an increase in the amount of hands-on engineering work for many of them. As one engineer remarked, "Doing the hands-on design work is much more satisfying than delegating, directing, or deciding."

The heart of the matter is creating a genuine sense of personal ownership and pride in the individual's actual work product. Often this is aided by making sure that individuals participate in the whole work assignment (i.e., from start to finish) and that the products of each person's work are both visible and valued. Pride of ownership also results when direct customer contact is encouraged and provided for throughout the organization. At companies like Marriott International and The Home Depot, few pronouncements are as convincing or meaningful to the worker as a customer's direct comments about his or her efforts.

DISTINCTIVENESS DEMANDS SELECTIVITY

It is hardly surprising to find a focused set of energy sources and alignment approaches in organizations sustaining a higher-performing workforce. By emphasizing a few clear and meaningful sources and approaches, however, an institution can focus, reinforce, and align the activities and decisions of large numbers of people. Often, the fundamental difference between average and peak performance is determined by "a few things that workers must start doing, plus a few things they must stop doing." Simple tools provide a way of communicating throughout the workforce those few critical dos and don'ts. Similar repeated approaches also clarify what the organization is trying to achieve, why the achievement is important, and how "we do things around here."

Although some tools or mechanisms more typically emphasize worker fulfillment over performance (and vice versa), both dimensions are often present to varying degrees in each alignment approach. In fact, one of the most useful insights of our research is that a well-executed alignment mechanism will invariably stimulate improvement in both worker performance and fulfillment. At the same time, however, each higher-performing workforce uses a combination of tools and mechanisms to ensure that it gets a balanced emphasis over time. At one point, we thought that some tools received high priority in all of the two dozen situations that we explored. However, when we applied the very tough criteria of distinctive application and execution, it became clear that was not the case. While some alignment approaches are more common than others, none are mandatory.

Each approach summarized herein, however, does recur in several situations. The critical factor in determining which tool to apply is clearly that of balance. Without a good balance between worker fulfillment and organizational performance, it is impossible to sustain a peak-performance workforce over time. Certainly, you can obtain performance in the short term by approaches that simply replace those people who do not meet certain standards. Unless the supply of able workers is limitless, however, this "hire 'em and fire 'em" philosophy eventually drives the best people into environments where their well-being and job fulfillment receives more attention. Conversely, if empowerment and fulfillment approaches dominate, the performance of the organization will eventually suffer, which is also a nonsustainable condition.

9 ✦ Enforcing Disciplined Behavior

While the sources of energy and alignment approaches may vary, one constant element runs throughout all the institutions we studied: *discipline where it counts.* The reason is, perhaps, intuitively obvious: Enforcing disciplined behavior is the only way that an enterprise can hope to ensure a balance between enterprise performance and worker fulfillment. And as Charles Schwab reminds us, self-discipline is the most important part of the equation: "Most talk about 'super-geniuses' is nonsense. . . . When 'stars' drop out, their departments seldom suffer. And their successors are merely men who have learned by application and self-discipline to get full production from an average, normal brain."[1] Self-discipline, however, seldom occurs in large numbers of people without wise enforcement by top management in a few key areas.

Frankly, we did not expect to find enforced discipline quite so important in higher-performing workforce situations. Some would argue that it is the antithesis of the empowerment notions that dominate the literature on energizing people. And when we observe disciplined behavior in a peak-performance workforce, we usually attribute its benefits more to a strong set of core values (as though that were somehow different from disciplined behavior). Yet, the enterprise with a peak-performance workforce is seldom content to rely solely on its values to ensure disciplined behavior in critical areas.

However, it was not until we saw the fulfillment potential of the disciplined behavior with the Marines at Parris Island that we began to realize how critical discipline was in each of the five balanced paths. The United States Marine Corps has truly mastered the art of using institutionally and peer-enforced discipline to cultivate widespread self-discipline that is both energizing and fulfilling. This triple combination of institution-, peer-, and self-enforced discipline is typical of all the higher-performing workforce situations that we have explored. Without it, management's efforts are too easily dispersed across dozens of good people practices instead of being concentrated on the few approaches that it can execute with distinctiveness.

For those who aspire to an emotionally committed workforce, discipline and empowerment must go hand in hand. This may sound like heresy to some disciples of empowerment, but that is what our research suggests. Webster defines *discipline* as "a set of rules or training that corrects, molds, or perfects." Of course, you would expect disciplined behavior to be a core element of any military organization. Numerous case studies and books have been written about breakdowns in discipline that have led to defeat and disaster in most major wars. There is also the perennial ethical dilemma of when to violate the chain-of-command discipline in pursuit of a higher purpose. Military discipline is a well-understood imperative.

Discipline in the commercial and nonprofit world, however, is not as well recognized or understood. Sometimes it is viewed as an evil bedfellow of command and control. The word itself implies a set of constraints that are demotivating and presumed to limit initiative, innovation, and empowerment. Human resource organizations do not have a Department of Discipline or even a head disciplinarian, nor are they likely to use the term in trying to recruit and motivate talented people. To the extent that disciplined behavior is required, most companies prefer to disguise it within a broader context of "sharing core values" or "adhering to fundamental policies" or "applying the rules of engagement." While these euphemisms may be more comfortable because of their emphasis on beliefs and values, each demands a set of disciplined behaviors.

Disciplined behavior implies a clear set of rules that are enforced. Everyone knows those rules—even if they are not written down. The rules are to be followed without question, unless they conflict with the intent of an overriding shared value or higher authority. Those who break a specific rule expect to be penalized, and those who consistently ignore them are soon separated.

In contrast, a set of shared values implies strong beliefs (usually without explicit rules) that can be applied in several ways. Everyone who subscribes to the values does not need to interpret them in the same way with respect to individual behaviors. Because a shared value (like integrity or caring) seldom has a finite right or wrong point, its violation is usually much less clear than a "broken rule"; consequently, penalties are applied only for extreme or egregious violations. Moreover, within a set of shared values, there can often be conflicts (e.g., worker fulfillment sometimes conflicts with putting customer satisfaction needs first). An institution needs wisdom and judgment to sort through these conflicts. Nonetheless, those who cannot support the values of an institution invariably leave, at least as much by their own choice as by company decision.

Subsuming the need for disciplined behavior under the banner of shared values can result in undisciplined behavior in key areas that hurt the essential balance between worker fulfillment and enterprise performance. Those who sustain a peak-performance workforce simply do not allow that to happen. To illustrate, this chapter recounts how three different institutions—the Marines, Southwest Airlines, and Marriott—go well beyond promulgating their values to ensure disciplined sets of behaviors where they count.

MASTERS OF DISCIPLINE

Obviously, the U.S. Marine Corps demands disciplined behavior. How else can they ensure that difficult orders are followed in battle conditions, when lives are at stake? That they use discipline as much for worker fulfillment as they do for enterprise performance, however, may not be so obvious.

The Yellow Footprints: Where Discipline Begins

As mentioned previously, our research for this book took us to Parris Island, South Carolina, where we could observe the various approaches that the U.S. Marines use to shape their recruits. Our visit to Parris Island began exactly where every recruit begins—getting off the bus at the receiving center and standing in a set of painted yellow footprints on the tarmac. Brigadier Generals James Battaglini and Keith Holcomb, who had arranged this visit, had also decided to give us a good feel for the place, so our tour started in the same kind of bus that the new recruits arrive in. As soon as our bus stopped, a six-foot-five, 210-pound drill instructor (DI) bounded aboard and glared menacingly as he addressed us exactly as he would new recruits. A recruit's first experience in seeing a DI in action is a somewhat daunting one, as we can now attest. He barked sharply, "Exit the vehicle and move quickly to fit your feet into one of the sets of yellow footprints." Only upon exit did we experience the full presence of Staff Sergeant P. Masinto; his height, dark skin, proud bearing, and lean, muscular frame cast a powerful shadow on us "new recruits." Almost without thinking, we found ourselves shouting back the mandatory "Yes, sir!" and "No, sir!" to his ear-piercing questions. Since we had no forewarning of this introduction, it was impressive—primarily because we realized that the minute the recruit sets foot on Parris Island, he or she gets a dramatic wake-up call as to the importance of discipline and good order.

After this five-minute introduction, we were able to revert to our normal civilian mind-sets—but the point was made: At Parris Island, disciplined behavior is required of all recruits. The Parris Island experience is like no other experience the recruits will ever have; they will remember it as long as they live. We were next ushered into a "stage room," where we were given the same indoctrination spiel that recruits receive regarding integrity. On a chart, ten categories were displayed (including education, dependents, medical, prior service, prior convictions, substance abuse—even tattoos), within which all past transgressions must be reported. Those recruits with something to report must stand on the "stage" (a foot-high platform in the front of the room) and tell the truth, or risk being dropped from the program. For the U.S. Marines, when it comes to past violations by their recruits, there is no such thing as "stricken from the record." The attitude is "We don't care what others [civilian authorities] have told you. If you did it, we will get it! But we won't hold it against you unless you try to keep it from us—or do it again."

Of course, it is hard for these recruits to stand up and admit publicly to some of these transgressions in their past. But the DIs know that every group has some past offenders, and they keep at it until someone screws up enough courage to step on the stage and confess a past transgression. After that, others follow suit, creating what General Holcomb calls a "popcorn effect." As many religions contend, "confession is good for the soul." The discipline of telling it like it is begins here.

Graduating Recruits Tell It Like It Was

Next, we met with a group of eight recruits who were approaching their graduation. They had been selected for a discussion with us primarily based on their availability. Four were men who would be in the next day's graduation ceremony and were already officially Marines; they were in their dress uniforms and could use the first-person terminology. The other four were women with two more weeks to go; they wore their working "cammies" (camouflage fatigues) and still had to use the third-person terminology. Throughout their Parris Island tour, recruits cannot refer to themselves in the first person: "There is no *I* (or *me*) in *team.*" This group of eight was picked somewhat at random based on whether they had family members visiting that day. As we were about to enter the room, General Battaglini whispered to me, "This may be a little confusing for them, since half can say 'I' now, and the other half may feel compelled to use 'this recruit.' We've told them not to worry about it for this meeting, so it will be interesting to see what happens."

Battaglini need not have worried. With one exception, self-discipline prevailed. The men had already adopted their newly earned right to use the first person, whereas the women remained with the mandatory third-person "this recruit" as though it were part of their native tongue. The only exception was an intelligent Hispanic woman from Arizona who was on a special assignment and would return to finish college after the program. She occasionally lapsed into the "I" (first-person) mode. Though the other recruits were not noticeably bothered by her lapses, General Holcomb was quick to point out after the meeting that her DI would have disciplined her on the spot. The language discipline at Parris Island is rigorously enforced.

The group snapped to attention as we entered the room and remained so until Battaglini put them at ease and told them to speak freely, openly, and candidly. At first I thought, "Sure—with two generals and four strange civilians in the room, these kids will be hard pressed to get beyond a *Yes Sir! No Sir!* vocabulary."

My first question, "Why did you join the Marines?" belied that thought. Each told us of his or her personal background and the circumstances leading to enlistment. Reasons ranged from "My father was a Marine" to "I wanted to get out of a poor environment." Recruit Ramirez from the Dominican Republic was particularly articulate and emotional in describing how he had always believed the Marines were the best—and he simply wanted to be with the best. You could see the emotional pride engulf his entire face.

The recruits all described significant changes in themselves as a person. The changes varied but all shared an element of personal achievement or team pride, as these quotes imply:

developing self-confidence for the first time in my life . . .

learning what team discipline really means, and getting rid of the "I" in my attitude . . .

losing forty pounds and feeling great about myself physically, mentally, and emotionally . . .

finding commitment—I never really finished anything before . . .

When asked about what was best and worst about the program, they were equally articulate:

The crucible . . . In the crucible, everyone got to step up and show what they got.

This recruit loves the tests—being put to the test every day.

This recruit likes the close order drills . . . [which] taught this recruit discipline, and our DI made the entire platoon love it.

This recruit [a woman] thinks that the female DI should be much harder and harsher . . . Women need to be more challenged, just like the guys.

It was the best and the worst three months of my life.

The Gas Chamber was really tough. . . . It made this recruit so proud that she could do it when she was so terrified.

You are motivated to put out a lot for your DI.

Again the skeptic may suspect that we were listening to a stacked deck. After all, these recruits had been handpicked before the meeting, and two generals were in the room. As a writer and researcher, however,

I've been exposed to lots of stacked decks. You learn to spot them, no matter how well camouflaged they are—and this was not a stacked deck. These recruits answered from the heart—disclosing personal feelings that most people would not disclose. They were free with their criticism as well as their praise.

Moreover, the comments of this group of recruits were mirrored in the comments of the dozens of recruits with whom we talked at random throughout our visit. We were always encouraged to talk with anyone about anything—with or without officers present. And we did. To their credit, the U.S. Marine Corps believes in openness and honesty about what they do. They are relentlessly self-critical, as any reader of the *Marine Corps Gazette* can easily verify. They might resent the criticism of naive outsiders like myself, but they expect, encourage—and pay attention to—constructive criticism from their own.

HIDDEN DISCIPLINES AT SOUTHWEST AIRLINES

We decided to leave twenty minutes earlier than necessary for our appointment with Libby Sartain and Rita Bailey at SWA; we did not want to be late. When I had talked with Libby earlier in the week about the session, she made it clear that promptness mattered. Like the Marines, SWA people are well disciplined about being on time, and they don't have to spell it out for you to get it.

Though we signed in at 8:15 A.M., Libby's assistant did not come out to get us until 8:30 A.M.—on the nose. Promptness works both ways at Southwest. It is a by-product of the disciplined set of behaviors required to turn the planes around in eighteen minutes (most other airlines cannot do it in less than thirty). It is also reflected in an ability to deliver all checked baggage items to the claim carousels within ten minutes of a plane's arrival—which is about as fast as most deplaning customers can walk to the carousels. Such behaviors help SWA to serve 2,400 customers per employee (nearest competitor serves 1,200) and to fly its planes 11.5 hours per day (versus industry average of 8.6). The discipline that produces these results also produces pride and energy among the employees who apply the discipline to get those kinds of results.

While waiting, we could not help but notice the dozens and dozens of plaques, photographs, mementos, and letters of commendation hanging on the walls. These tributes are tangible symbols of the accomplishments of SWA people, past and present. Of course, this was no surprise. It reminded us of the entrances and offices of every Marine Corps installation we visited; the Walk of Leaders at KFC; and The Home Depot's statue of "Homer," the home-improvement mascot of the company. And as we followed Kathy Rickard, Sartain's executive assistant, through the corridors, we were never without visual reminders of the importance and value of people at SWA.

What we didn't recognize until after our discussion with Sartain and Bailey, however, is how many of these symbols actually highlight and remind people of the key disciplines within SWA. For example, the discipline of low cost is captured in the innovative events and awards, all done on "low or no budget." In fact, the employees self-fund most of their major celebrations. The discipline of customer service is highlighted in pictures of employees going the extra mile, posted letters from customers, as well as the triple-crown awards for best on-time service, best baggage handling, and fewest customer complaints in the airline industry. SWA has now received this award for five years in a row. Nonetheless, the casual visitor could easily assume that it's all about empowerment and miss the rigorous disciplines that underlie the aspirations and values of the company. In addition to low cost, there are three other areas in which disciplined behaviors are noteworthy: customer service, recruiting and training, and common language.

Cost Discipline

The drive to SWA headquarters was our first exposure to the relentless low-or-no-cost discipline that permeates the organization. The headquarters is near Love Field, outside of Dallas, Texas, the origin and center of the airline's operations. As we drove past the main entrance, reconstruction efforts were much in evidence, reflecting nearly a decade of renovations to the airline itself. SWA can't seem to catch up with its growth. Denton Drive, which leads to SWA, takes you along the west side of Love Field past a strange array of ramshackle housing and business structures like Gerados Supermarket, the Mona Lisa Club, a Speaco Foods warehouse, and the Pupuseria Bar. It is a dog's-breakfast collection of small businesses, poorly maintained storage buildings, and low-cost industrial sites—not exactly a high-rent district.

Low cost is central to SWA's aspiration of bringing affordable air transportation to the masses. It is central to the company strategy of providing *the* lowest-cost service in the industry. Low cost is the center-piece of SWA's brand identity. Although this strategy has undoubtedly caused much consternation among its competitors, it has also materi-ally increased the overall size of the air travel market on the routes that Southwest flies. Sartain likes to refer to this as "the Southwest effect." In other words, because SWA causes other airlines to drop their fares, many more people can now afford to fly!

Low cost is also the result of a set of disciplined behaviors that every employee must follow. These disciplines are both enterprise- and peer-enforced as well as self-imposed. SWA's people are masterful penny-pinchers. Some call this a core value; others, the key element in their strategy. Whatever the name, keeping costs low requires a rigorously en-forced set of disciplined behaviors. SWA does not simply leave it to peo-ple's sense of what's right. People who consistently ignore the guidelines for ensuring low-cost behavior do not remain with SWA for long. As Rita Bailey puts it: "We tell our people, 'You are free to try any and all ideas you can think of—as long as they don't cost much!' In fact, nothing we do costs much money."

If necessity is the mother of invention, then Southwest is the living proof of the old adage. Libby and Rita explained that the company's ap-parent discovery of the value of discipline—on which SWA is now highly dependent—grew out of plain old business necessity. The com-pany learned to turn the planes around in eighteen minutes because it had to; it was short of aircraft.

Customer Service Disciplines

The set of disciplined behaviors to keep costs down at SWA are paral-leled by an equally clear set of customer service disciplines, which go well beyond the shared value of customer service. Everyone knows the importance of customer service at SWA. Although Herb Kelleher (CEO) and Colleen Barrett (executive vice president—customers) constantly emphasize that employees come first, SWA employees know that the customer is a very close second. Everyone's fundamental commitment to "positively outrageous customer service" does not deter SWA from also establishing a clear-cut set of disciplined behaviors to ensure its achievement. The company sets clear standards on how customer service issues will be handled, as well as for other important elements of customer service (e.g., checked-baggage delivery time to the carousel). Of course, the "value aspects" of customer service take it beyond the standards in many ways—but the standards are rigorously enforced nonetheless.

Recruiting and Training Disciplines

People come first—but SWA doesn't hire just anyone. In 1997, for example, it received approximately 105,000 applicants for 3,000 openings. SWA can afford to be selective—and it is. To ensure that it gets the best from this rich pool, SWA spells out the standards clearly, and the screening process for each candidate is very disciplined. Since attitude is the most important hiring criterion, SWA recruiters are explicit about what that means and how to determine a person's attitude. Warm and friendly, positive, straightforward, and fun are attributes they know how to determine and document. *Fast Company* magazine quoted one of SWA's leading recruiters, José Colmenares, on what he's looking for in a candidate: "A genuineness—a sense of what it takes to be one of us." To get at that elusive quality, candidates are asked to read aloud a personal "coat of arms"—a questionnaire on which candidates complete statements like "One time my sense of humor helped was," "A time I reached my peak performance was," and "My personal motto is."

While most answers tend to be unremarkable, a few stand out and help to pinpoint the candidates that SWA seeks. For example, one woman described herself as "zippy"—a term that fellow applicants found hilarious, but that Colmenares found intriguing.[2] SWA is equally disciplined about the behaviors required during its initial training programs. Candidates for flight attendants, for example, not only must go through the training without pay, but must also follow explicit rules about dress, appearance, and promptness. Show up late for the classes, and you are dropped from the program. Ignore proper grooming, and you are gone. Sounds more than a little Marine-like, right? Sartain emphasized, however, "We really never use the word *rule* at SWA; we prefer *guidelines* and *standards*. Please, do not use *rules* and *SWA* in the same sentence!" (Henceforth, we will respect that request.)

For pilot slots, an acceptable candidate must have passed the 737-type rating, which requires a \$5,000 to \$10,000 personal investment that SWA does not underwrite. The guidelines and standards for pilots are equally clear and rigorously enforced (as is the case in any major airline), but SWA also includes clear guidelines for customer interaction and service that are more explicit and extensive than most. Safety is at the top of every major airline's list of imperatives. At Southwest, however, the normal standards of safety are only the beginning. For example, "attitude" standards and guidelines are every bit as important to pilots as they are to the flight attendants. One of my colleague's wives is a regular SWA passenger. She tells the story of how a male flight attendant became a little flustered during a flight delay and was a bit brusque with her. When she jokingly said, "You've got an attitude problem, buster," his face went white. After landing, he sought her out to find out exactly what she meant and to apologize. He was not about to take the chance that even a passing facetious comment might suggest a violation of the guidelines intended to ensure a friendly interaction discipline.

There are standards and guidelines for customer service agents, ramp attendants, baggage handlers, maintenance people—even cleaners. Again, such rules are not uncommon among other airlines, but the rigorous discipline with which they are enforced at SWA—by employees almost more than by managers—is. Moreover, a great many jobs have a probationary period during which a trainee must demonstrate that he or she can meet the standards and follow the disciplines required for the job. For flight attendants, for example, that period is six months. If the guidelines are violated at any time during the probationary period, it is a strong indication that the trainee cannot fit into the culture. A second chance is possible, of course, but only if the rationale for violating the standard is convincing. Sartain argues, "We don't give up too early," but as soon as they conclude that someone is a cultural "misfit," that person is gone. Southwest Airlines is well known for its philosophy of encouraging its people to take initiatives, be innovative, and come up with new ideas—but only after they follow the guidelines for disciplined behavior in the critical areas.

Most SWA people see the standards, guidelines, and the culture as uplifting rather than constraining or demotivating. Moreover, the values, disciplines, and other elements of the culture are made very clear during the recruiting process. The company wants to give every candidate the opportunity to decide to join on the basis of wanting to be a part of this kind of culture. Obviously, it is not for everyone, but most who try it sincerely believe that it helps them to be a better person.

What is perhaps most important, companies like SWA and The Home Depot often reward employees who break the rules when it is the right thing to do. SWA can be very forgiving of well-intentioned mistakes, particularly when they reflect the kind of innovation, creativity, and self-discipline that SWA expects from its workforce. The cost discipline at SWA has a material impact on innovation and creativity. Since people can't spend much money, they become highly innovative in thinking about how to attack new problems and opportunities. For example, seven years ago the company established a Culture Committee to make sure that the individual freedom of employees does not inadvertently erode as the company gets larger. According to Sartain, the mission of the committee is as follows:

> to help create the Southwest spirit and culture where needed; to enrich it and make it better where it already exists; and to liven it up in places where it might be floundering . . . This group is to do "whatever it takes" to create, enhance, and enrich the special Southwest spirit and culture that has made this such a wonderful company/family.

The committee has established a subteam called the Freedom Fighters. Its purpose is to raise the awareness level of all SWA employees as to the many special freedoms they all enjoy (e.g., casual dress, job security, an overabundance of "can-do" people to work with, lots of opportunity to be yourself and have fun at work). The Freedom Fighters also seek to raise the awareness of each person's responsibility and accountability for helping to preserve these kinds of freedoms. The group has launched a "freedom tour" to bring these messages to the forefront of people's minds throughout the company.

The Discipline of Common Language

Every strong culture has a language of its own, and Southwest is no exception. Like the Marines, however, the application of certain elements of this language constitutes a discipline that is enforced, probably more indirectly than directly. The language simply grew up alongside the airline, but certain aspects are consistently and relentlessly reinforced by people at all levels. In itself, the SWA language constitutes a discipline that creates the behaviors that count for both performance and fulfillment.

First, some terms, like *rules* and *formal strategic planning,* are purposefully avoided if not forbidden. The latter is a pet peeve of "Our Fearless Leader and Sometime Elvis Impersonator" (CEO Herb Kelleher), who says, "Reality is chaotic; planning is ordered and logical. The two don't square with one another. . . . The meticulous nit-picking that goes on in most strategic planning processes creates a mental straitjacket."[3]

Virtually every special effort is given a unique name or label, for example, Quest, Re-Quest, Tool Time, Freedom Fighters, and Walk a Mile in My Shoes. Labels like Big Hearts, Winning Spirit, and SWA Family have special meanings to SWA people. Titles like the People Department and the University for People emphasize what matters most at SWA. Acronyms like POS (positively outrageous service) and purposeful misspellings like LUV create images that lead to disciplined behaviors of great importance to the company. Simple phrases that are both meaningful and memorable permeate the language: "color outside the lines," "hire for spirit, spunk, and enthusiasm," "follow the Golden Rule," "customers come second," and "the warrior mentality." Colleen Barrett illustrates why the last phrase has deep roots that are surprisingly parallel to the warrior spirit at the heart of the USMC's leadership system: "The warrior mentality, the very fight to survive, is truly what created our culture."[4]

A common language invariably supports a disciplined effort in peak-performance workforces. Virtually all of the organizations that we explored use a set of terms, phrases, and acronyms that have a special meaning for the workforce and that remind them of disciplined behaviors key to their performance and fulfillment. The power of disciplined language and behavior is evident in SWA's peak-performance workforce, which is the key to the company's remarkable success and was summed up well by authors Kevin and Jackie Freiberg: "The real secret to Southwest's success is having one of the most highly motivated and productive workforces in the world. They are motivated by a sense of fairness that says, 'We want your well-being to be tied to the company's well-being because, after all, you are the company.'"[5]

THE MARRIOTT DISCIPLINES

When we arrived at the San Antonio Rivercenter/Riverwalk complex, it was easy to see why the Rivercenter ranked so high among Marriott properties. The weather was a balmy seventy-five degrees, the hotel was located on the colorful San Antonio River, and the facility was well designed to handle large and small conferences alike. The decor was tastefully "modern Marriott," and the bellhops and check-in crew were neatly attired, well groomed, and smiling. The entire effect was inviting if not irresistible, and I privately resolved to bring my wife for a weekend.

While we were waiting to meet Robert Graymer-Jones at the executive offices, we could not help but notice the many award plaques on the walls. Although the awards were a bit more formal and tastefully grouped than those at SWA, this place was also clearly a winner. Among the citations on the walls were the Pinnacle Magazine Award (based on a readers' poll of successful meetings), the Award of Excellence, the Gold Key award, the M&D Medical Meetings award, and the Four Diamond Award. Whatever the customer service award, this hotel has probably won it—at one time or another in the past five years.

Nonetheless, since our visit accidentally coincided with a scheduled visit by CEO Bill Marriott, we expected to encounter a frenetic staff rushing to get things ready for "the Chief." Nothing could have been further from the truth. While we heard a few light-hearted references to the big-wigs, everyone was completely relaxed, pleasant, and accommodating. "Whatever you need, please ask. We'd like to make your inquiry as useful as possible." We had been set up, right? You might think so, except that Marriott expects every guest to receive that kind of attention— and we were free to talk with any and all associates and managers about anything. It was a no-holds-barred set of interviews and discussions. Certainly, Mr. Marriott would have wanted it no other way.

The Seamless Check-in Discipline

Tom Turcotte has been bell captain at the Rivercenter for over seven years. Originally from Providence, Rhode Island, he started his Marriott career fifteen years ago as a summer bellhop in Fort Lauderdale, Florida. As he says, "I just fell into the job right out of high school—and never wanted to leave."

He is responsible for a staff of thirty-five people, including the bell-hops, the concierge staff, and all transportation people. This team ranks as the number two bell-stand staff within the entire Marriott chain, based upon a Guest Service Index that reports customer feedback monthly. The turnover among his total staff is less than 5 percent because, as Tom says, "The job pays very well, the benefits are great, and the work environment is terrific. It's a lot of fun interacting with the friendly customers we get here. . . . I love this city!!"

Though Tom makes it sound fun, it is still hard work. Since Marriott believes that the most important aspect of a guest's stay is the first ten minutes, Tom and his group are very disciplined about making sure that the ten minutes are hassle-free. To begin with, there are the "cardinal rules" that cannot be broken for any reason without immediate conse-quences: honesty above all, cleanliness, good grooming, no sexual ha-rassment, and no customer insults. Following these rules not only re-sults in satisfied customers, but also results in emotionally energized workers who take great pride in meeting the standards that generate cus-tomer praise. The triple combination—enterprise-imposed disciplines enforced by peers and then converted to self-discipline—is at work again, which results in pride of accomplishment and worker fulfillment.

The "seamless arrival process" itself requires a set of disciplined be-haviors. The bellhop who takes your bag at the entrance also checks you in, gets your messages, and delivers you to your room. He or she goes through a precise procedure designed to get the guests happily into their rooms as expeditiously as possible. All bellhops are thus also trained in front desk check-in and mail procedures and computer systems. Further-more, job applicants are carefully screened for the skills and attitudes required.

Recruiting and Training Disciplines

The hiring process is also based on a set of disciplined behaviors. It starts with an explicit set of well-known criteria, including dress (what consti-tutes acceptable casual wear), grooming (neatly trimmed hair), concise-ness (say what you mean), friendliness (speak in a warm and friendly manner), and local knowledge (what's what on the riverfront).

The first test of these criteria is a group interview with several appli-cants, followed by individual interviews with several different people (typically four or five). The interviewer follows a scripted-interview procedure designed to help assess the intrinsic aspects of attitude, demeanor, and behavior.

Later, the candidates participate in an SRI (Stanford Research Institute) test, an assessment conducted by phone (from Gallup, the polling people). Marriott describes it as an assessment of personality traits (ego, pride, diversity) or personal tendencies. It provides value in screening for people who are a good fit relative to the actual work required of them. It also helps determine "how long people are likely to stay with the job," according to Walter Kennedy, resident manager. This assessment is an important step in the hiring process, but is used more as a threshold test than as a way of making final decisions. A low score will eliminate you, but a high score doesn't necessarily guarantee a job offer. On the positive side, it helps identify the clearly gregarious, outgoing self-starters—who are very likely to become highly self-disciplined about satisfying the guests.

In essence, Marriott is looking for the friendly and honest candidates who, as Tom says, are "hospitality animals who [will] really have their heart in satisfying our guests." Early on, every hire must learn and adhere to Marriott's basic principles of hospitality. Consistent with "Bill Marriott's Twelve Rules for Success" in chapter 7, all employees are given a wallet card to remind them of six disciplined behaviors not to be violated:

1. Smile and greet every guest.

2. Speak to the guest in a warm, friendly, courteous manner.

3. Display genuine and enthusiastic interest.

4. Anticipate guest needs and be flexible in responding to them.

5. Be knowledgeable about your job.

6. Learn to take ownership of guest problems and resolve them.

The sixth point above is particularly important. Marriott has expanded the point to define the actual steps that associates should take to resolve the problem to the guest's satisfaction. The steps are simple: listen, empathize, apologize, react to resolve or compensate for the problem, and notify the appropriate person to make sure the problem does not occur again. The steps are not so simple to enforce without widespread understanding and commitment. Tom says that those who violate these simple rules are always given the benefit of the doubt—but "three strikes and you are out."

Training is equally disciplined. New hires go through an intensive two days of exposure to Marriott history, rules and regulations, the ten commandments (a list of cardinal rules), and the fundamental values and principles. The training that includes this indoctrination covers about four weeks. The week after indoctrination is focused on guest response topics and includes familiarizing each associate with the computer systems they will need to use. The next week covers the front-desk procedures and the concierge process. The final weeks are with certified trainers for on-the-job exposures to different situations they will encounter. There is a great deal of cross-training at the desks, and the on-the-job efforts are long enough to ensure "buy-in."

The Restaurant Disciplines

Melissa Escanulia provided us with a similar exposure to some of the disciplined behaviors required of the associates who work in the restaurants. An attractive, dark-haired woman from the border town of Eagle Pass, Texas, Melissa has been with Marriott for about fourteen years. Her first job was with Pizza Hut, but she left after three and a half years because of a cost squeeze that she remembers all too well: "Marriott would never treat its people that way."

She worked her first four years as a cashier before becoming a restaurant supervisor, where she now has responsibility for the coffee bar and J. W.'s Steak House (the main dining room). She works with three other managers who report to the director of restaurant services. She is also a TIP-certified trainer (how to handle intoxicated guests). In addition, she takes full advantage of Marriott's employee education policy and is working toward her business management degree at St. Phillips Community College in San Antonio. Of course, she also works the "normal" fifty-five-hour week at Marriott (five eleven-hour days), and her education efforts (the company pays the first two thousand dollars) are on her own time. She believes that getting her degree will enhance her career prospects at Marriott; she has no desire to leave.

The Rivercenter facility restaurants employ between fifty and sixty restaurant associates who are cross-trained in every position, including cashier, hostess, bus person, server, and kitchen support. Even though few will actually fill all these positions, Marriott believes that a cross-trained staff is the best way to ensure cohesive service from the guest's point of view. The same rules of hospitality and guest problem resolution that Tom Turcotte enumerated must be learned by the new restaurant hires.

Every morning at 6:15 A.M. and every afternoon at 3:45 P.M. the oncoming shifts gather for what Melissa calls "the line-up." In this fifteen-minute briefing about what is going on at the hotel that might affect the restaurant, any issues are discussed and resolved if possible. Issues left on the list (which is posted) for a week are usually positioned for group solution. Melissa says, "It's a very good way for people to get their frustrations out." Other departments (housekeeping and front desk) use a similar approach.

Although Melissa generally supports these rules, she has concerns about the point system used by Marriott. Apparently, this system is somewhat like the demerits system at military academies, which determines when someone can be discharged for cause. For example, those who are late for work or absent without permission receive points or demerits. Even marginal workers cannot be terminated, however, until they have accumulated ten points for infractions (during the initial ninety-day probationary period for all employees, they are only allowed five points). The discipline works both ways. Melissa realizes that the system is designed to ensure fair treatment, but she believes it is far too easy for a few irresponsible people to "work the system" to their advantage. As a result, she has had to keep some obvious misfits too long.

Nonetheless, when rules are violated, people are terminated. In one of our focus group discussions, we learned of a recent termination that illustrates that fact. One of the experienced chefs, Ronnie Ortiz, had a verbal altercation with a co-worker the week before. The heated argument resulted in Ronnie's being physically pushed by the other person. This incident went all the way to the general manager, Steven Lundgren, for resolution. Lundgren explained the dilemma he faced:

> I really wanted to find a way to keep this guy, but any kind of physical encounter is simply not permitted. We had to let him go. Ronnie was actually a friend of his, so I wanted to make sure it didn't harm their relationship. Unfortunately, that's the best I could do and still maintain the discipline.

Walter Kennedy, the resident manager for both the Marriott Riverwalk and Rivercenter, elaborated further on the role of discipline in the system. Overall turnover rates at both Marriotts are about 40 percent (industry range is 30 to 65 percent), but Kennedy believes that a lot of it is "more voluntary than involuntary . . . It's pretty much discipline driven. . . . We don't terminate that many people for poor job performance. . . . The progressive disciplining process is mostly for the marginals—it doesn't really affect the normal and high performers at all."

The Importance of Self-Discipline

We met with a group of associates from Lundgren's ACE program (Associates Committed to Excellence), which includes some of the best informal leaders among the associates. These men and women have been specially designated to help enforce the key disciplines and ensure that people live by the values and principles at Marriott. Several of the following quotes illustrate how the basic sets of disciplined behaviors established by Marriott have led to a strong sense of self-discipline reflected by this group. The comments also reflect their sense of pride and fulfillment.

You come to Marriott, and we will treat you like "this is our house."

We try never to use the words "we cannot do it."

You are not an employee here—you are an associate! That means something to me.

We can do whatever it takes to solve a customer's problem.

Being number one is not good enough—we are never satisfied.

People will weed themselves out when they see what is required here.

We run this hotel. . . . We make it what it is.

We don't spend money carelessly here—but we do spend it on the associates. We believe that money spent on the associates is well spent.

Although the ACE folks are special, they are not unique. They challenged us to talk to anyone at random to see if their views hold true. We did—and the views hold true. In fact, one of the roles of the ACE group is to be sure that they consistently tap into the rest of the workforce and that the ACE people understand the issues, feelings, and concerns of the entire workforce. They are extremely disciplined about their "tapping in" responsibility.

The Pathways Program

Melissa also encouraged us to look into the relatively new Pathways to Independence program, which is designed especially for people on welfare and has received national recognition for its quality and success. Basically, the program takes people off the welfare rolls and puts them through a special six-week training program (without pay) that teaches them self-discipline and self-respect as well as the other Marriott disciplines. Launched in 1991, the program teaches disciplined behaviors for such things as how to clean a hotel room in under twenty-four minutes and what standards of personal grooming apply. The training pays off in retention rates. In the Washington, D.C., area, for example, the percentage of new associates remaining on the job longer than one year was 10 percent better than for comparable workers in that area who had not had the training. It also pays off in worker fulfillment—big time! As Melissa says, "These people are very committed. . . . At graduation many of them have tears in their eyes" when they realize that they have been enabled to "pull themselves up by their bootstraps" and develop a sense of purpose and self-discipline that they did not have before.

BOTH KINDS OF DISCIPLINE MATTER

On all the many lists of how to energize employees, discipline rarely appears. Yet, when all is said and done, you cannot get there without it. Among our case studies, no higher-performing workforce situation has not required disciplined behavior of its workers in certain key areas. Moreover, the discipline is of two distinct kinds: clear rules of behavior enforced by management and a strong sense of self-discipline imposed by the workers themselves. One without the other is not enough to sustain a peak-performance workforce.

Perhaps the importance of discipline is obvious; in retrospect it certainly seems so. You cannot turn airplanes around in eighteen minutes without discipline; you cannot convert welfare recipients to productive hotel workers without it; and you cannot sustain battlefield composure and order without it. Nor can you expect the kind of pride, positive self-image, and worker fulfillment that result from self-discipline successfully applied. The presumption that a strong set of values takes the place of disciplined sets of behavior doesn't hold true in practice. Those who would rely only on the values have few precedents to point to. No peak-performance workforce situation is without its disciplined behaviors—and they are enforced by more than a strong set of shared values.

On the other hand, disciplined behaviors alone—whether enforced or self-imposed—do not replace the need for values or other sources of energy and approaches for focusing that energy. Nonetheless, disciplined behaviors in a few critical areas both complement and help sustain a dynamic balance between enterprise performance and worker fulfillment. As companies approach that balance point, they can rely less on imposed discipline and more on self-discipline—but they cannot do without both. Such disciplined behaviors are a fundamental underpinning of every higher-performing workforce that we have explored.

10 ✦ *Choosing the Best Path(s) for You*

"*Mr. Kelleher*, Sir, *I'd like to* shake your hand. Anyone who runs a company that cares as deeply about its people as Southwest Airlines deserves my sincere respect."

This unexpected testimonial came straight from the heart of Gunnery Sergeant Troy Ricks, a battle-hardened Marine with nineteen years in the Corps. Ricks was a member of a panel discussion among six leaders (three each from SWA and the U.S. Marine Corps) who had recently participated with three dozen of their compatriots in a joint workshop on leadership development challenges. Turns out this unlikely grouping had a lot more in common on the topic than either organization anticipated. As a result, the subsequent panel had been convened by SWA's top management to encapsulate the results of the workshop for roughly one hundred senior leaders of SWA, including CEO Herbert Kelleher.

Ricks, the first speaker on the panel, is a "Marine's Marine" by any measure. Standing just over six feet tall, his slender, muscular frame showcased in his tightly fitted dress blue uniform, he personifies the honor, courage, and commitment that all Marines stand for. You want him on your side.

From Amityville, Arkansas, Ricks speaks in a way that reflects those origins—blunt, deliberate, and unmistakably Southern. One had only to watch him march briskly to the podium to sense that his audience would listen closely to whatever he had to say. He had opened his comments with a sharply commanding "Good afternoon, Southwest Airlines"—so surprising to his audience that it left them all momentarily speechless, an unusual state for any group of SWA folks. Ricks, however, didn't allow them to remain speechless for long, as he repeated his greeting again, only louder and more commandingly.

This time they responded with an enthusiastic *"Good afternoon, Sergeant!"* At this point, Ricks looked out across the audience briefly and then inquired, "Is Mr. Herbert Kelleher in the audience?" From the back of the room, an all-too-familiar gray head (you couldn't miss it in a blizzard) nodded and slowly raised his hand. Ricks instantly executed a flawless Marine right-face and marched briskly off the podium and all the way around the audience to the back of the room, where he shook Kelleher's hand as he spoke clearly the opening quote of this chapter. Kelleher, along with all the rest of us in the room, knew that Ricks meant exactly what he said. In fact, when the panel discussion ended, Kelleher took the Marine participants up to his office for a private toast of Wild Turkey, his infamous celebratory elixir.

In that two-minute episode, Ricks not only captivated his audience, but captured the essence of what the leaders in peak-performance workforces instinctively know: You have to really care about each worker, and you have to honestly believe that he or she matters to the performance of your enterprise. Otherwise, none of the five paths described is worth the effort.

The U.S. Marines and SWA were able to learn from one another, despite their dramatic differences. This is the same kind of learning opportunity awaiting any leadership group that believes in the unique value of the individual worker and wants to shape a path to emotional commitment throughout critical segments of its workforce. The paths described represent powerful alternatives to simply "treating people better"—perhaps not the only ones, but by far the most prevalent ones. The sources of energy and complementary alignment approaches suggest a variety of tools and mechanisms that can help most companies achieve the right balance between fulfillment and performance. The important thing is to shape a path that fits your circumstances and that you can execute with distinction. While you may choose not to follow any of the five, you ignore them at your peril if you are seeking peak performance from key segments of your workforce. These five patterns have proven effective in over twenty of the best-performing enterprises in the world.

Finding the right path to peak workforce performance, however, requires much more than following in someone else's footsteps. Each enterprise presents a different and changing set of circumstances that determine both the potential value of its workforce and the best way to energize that workforce. So how can the leadership of any enterprise determine if it is worthwhile to shift some emphasis from the bottom line to the front line? To some extent, it is a matter of the personal convictions of the leaders. Many executives simply do not believe they need more than good compliance within their workforce to achieve their business aspirations—nor do they believe it is worth the investment required to seek more. For others, however, the opportunity for a peak-performance workforce is attractive but perplexing. When should an enterprise invest in developing a truly energized, higher-performing workforce? How can leaders decide between the various options and combinations? What will ensure an ultimately successful effort? Although the answers are implicit from the experiences described earlier, this chapter postulates a diagnostic methodology in two phases:

> Phase I: Developing a truly compelling case for where and why. While few enterprises cited in the book consciously "developed" such a case, their journey had clearly produced one. For companies whose journey has not yet done so, however, they must develop one. This phase describes what such a case should contain.

> Phase II: Making the critical choices required for a balanced path(s). Every successful path that we have explored was based on very clear choices, rather than a random application of "good people practices." Hence, the book concludes by summarizing those choices and what is required to make them wisely.

Several analyses and assessments described in this chapter are commonplace in the best-managed companies. Some aspects of these assessments, however, take on slightly different—and critical—dimensions with respect to the challenge of achieving a higher-performing workforce.

PHASE I: DEVELOPING A COMPELLING CASE

In short, a compelling case for a peak-performance workforce answers the following questions: Where is an emotionally committed workforce needed? What will it cost to build such a workforce? Finally, what might the workforce be worth to other stakeholders? Like any other significant investment decision, this one should begin with a rigorous assessment of the fundamental determinants of enterprise performance, namely, performance aspirations and business strategies, worker fulfillment expectations, and internal cultural imperatives. The overall objective is to place the performance of the workforce in its proper context, that is, which segments of the workforce matter the most, and how much do they matter relative to other determinants of enterprise success? The question is simple enough, but getting a fact-based answer may require some insightful analyses and managerial judgment that consider different workforce scenarios.

Like the leaders of several enterprises that we explored, you may instinctively know the answer to the aforementioned questions—or have already determined the answer, based on earlier trial and error. If not, however, you must consider what kind of situation analysis is required to make intelligent choices with respect to workforce performance. That analysis is analogous to what is required to make intelligent choices with respect to enterprise performance. A key difference, however, is that it must provide a rationale that is equally compelling to workers as well as management.

Performance Aspirations and Business Strategies

Increasingly, we see that the best companies consider performance aspirations and strategies with respect to customers and employees as well as shareholders. Key questions to be asked include the following:

+ What are your performance aspirations with respect to each of three constituencies: customers, shareholders, and employees? How can you quantify them so that the workforce receives appropriate attention?

+ How important is your workforce relative to other determinants of enterprise performance? How does this vary within different areas of your business? Where and why do competitors have a workforce advantage of significance?

+ Which segments of the workforce are most critical to sustaining a competitive advantage over time in each major part of the business?

Virtually all commercial enterprises today are fairly rigorous about spelling out aspirations with respect to the expected financial returns to owners and investors. Customer performance measures are nearly as well developed and diligently pursued as financial performance measures among the best companies. Not surprisingly, the workforce has assumed increasing importance as customer situations have become more demanding and competitive offerings more discriminating.

In fact, a higher-performing workforce, more often than not, is necessary precisely because of what the customer situation requires. Hence, the more effectively an enterprise can segment, analyze, and comprehend changing customer needs, the more wisely it can determine which parts of its workforce are most critical to meeting those needs and the value of cultivating a superior workforce in those areas.

Consequently, enterprises that rely on a peak-performance workforce devote just as much rigorous attention to their key employee constituencies as they do to their customers and shareholders. In a few cases (most notably, Southwest Airlines and Marriott International), the employee constituency is actually placed at the top of the aspiration triumvirate, at least on a par with the customer and clearly ahead of the shareholder. The case studies suggest that regardless of how an enterprise orders its three constituencies, those who aspire to a higher-performing workforce must be equally rigorous about establishing aspirations, strategies, and metrics for performance relative to that workforce. Compelling rhetoric, good intentions, and anecdotal assessments are not good enough; a company must measure what it is delivering in terms of worker fulfillment.

An enterprise must somehow compare the relative importance of improvements in workforce performance (overall and by segments) with improvements in other factors that determine economic and marketplace results. Investments in technology, for example, may offer a far greater improvement in enterprise performance than do similar-sized investments in energizing the workforce. Investments in brand or market position constitute another example of where the benefits of improving workforce performance might be dwarfed by a significant change in brand image. This situation would be particularly relevant in the packaged-goods business. While these comparisons and trade-offs are important in the diagnosis of the workforce opportunity, they are by no means the only trade-offs.

Workforce segmentation can be as important as market segmentation. The normal value-chain analysis of workforce performance produces one type of workforce segmentation. A rigorous assessment of fulfillment needs may produce another. Such fulfillment-based segments may be determined by many of the same demographic, psychological, and lifestyle variables that drive consumer segmentation. For example, the Salt Lake City Marriott had to consider the fulfillment needs of a wide range of employee groups, namely, college students working their way through school, welfare recipients gaining their first real job experience, professionals with degrees beginning their careers in the hotel industry, and new immigrants orienting themselves to a new environment. For each group, the hotel was seeking to offer the employees a set of tangible and intangible values that would yield a higher level of productivity and customer service. This required meeting both common and segment-specific fulfillment needs.

In many situations, some sort of improved performance is needed from the front line, for example, improved productivity, quality, responsiveness, or efficiency. However, there may be cheaper and faster ways to achieve these ends than pursuing a peak-performance workforce. Productivity has greatly increased in the twentieth century, and not always through improved-workforce approaches. An auto worker on a computer-assisted production line in 1998 may be less motivated and give less of himself or herself to the job than a craftsman who hand-assembled entire autos in 1905—but the 1998 worker is far more productive. Such "non-people-intensive" approaches are very familiar in today's economic life. Other examples include mechanical technology to automate work, information technology to speed work, information technology to control quality, and work redesign and process reengineering to make work flows more efficient and effective.

For many companies, opportunities still exist to improve organizational performance in these non-people-intensive ways. Moreover, these methods tend to be easier and faster to implement because they are essentially design-, equipment-, and decision-based. Investment in an energized workforce is justified only when it represents a better opportunity than these other alternatives.

Worker Fulfillment Expectations

The relative importance of the various elements of worker fulfillment can be diagnosed by answering the following questions:

+ How well does the enterprise meet the basic human needs of job security, family support, and personal safety?

✦ What kind of structure and control do the key segments of the workforce seek and receive? How significant is the gap between what the workforce seeks and what it receives?

✦ When do feelings of identity, self-worth, and purpose become important in key segments? How well are they being met?

✦ Where does a sense of belonging, camaraderie, and trust take on a high priority? How is it provided, and by whom?

✦ How much opportunity is provided for a worker to learn and grow as a person, to take special initiatives, and to try something new?

Assessing potential sources of greater workforce fulfillment is akin to the market research done frequently with customers. Two basic concepts of customer analysis are particularly relevant: needs assessment and segmentation. In the earlier chapters, we discussed a general classification of fulfillment needs that starts with the fundamental need for a job that will at least meet a worker's basic subsistence requirements. Beyond that, workers also need a reasonable amount of order in the workplace (structure and control), some value and purpose in what they do, a sense of belonging to a group they can respect, and the opportunity to progress in their work. Table 2-1 in chapter 2 elaborates on those needs.

This categorization can provide a useful starting point since particular needs will vary in any specific assessment. And like customer needs, some are tangible and some intangible. In fact, many of the fulfillment needs expressed by interviewees in our research were intangible. The tangible needs, namely, compensation and benefits, were typically identified as *threshold* issues: As long as the person felt the monetary rewards were at or near a fair level, they were not great energizing factors. Only if the respondent perceived (rightly or wrongly) that he or she was somehow being treated unfairly did money become an issue.

In assessing fulfillment needs, many of the same tools used in consumer research can be used with the workforce. These tools include interviews, surveys, focus groups, and *conjoint analysis* (surveys that draw statistically valid cross-comparisons of the answers to seemingly different questions). These kinds of analyses can be extended to assess the fulfillment offerings of competitors through such tools as exit interviews with people voluntarily leaving the company and "turndown interviews" with job candidates who turn down the company's offers.

The relative importance of the basic fulfillment needs will often vary by workforce segment and, in particular, by level in the organization. For example, the basic needs for a job and a reasonable amount of structure and control are usually more important at the lower or entry levels, whereas the needs for personal growth and opportunity emerge at higher levels.

Internal Cultural Imperatives

Whether by design or happenstance, an existing internal workforce dynamic in every organization reflects the culture that governs informal attitudes and behaviors. This dynamic is the result of past and current approaches to managing workforces and likely includes factors that can both hinder and support development of a peak-performance workforce. The following questions can provide a realistic assessment of the established internal culture and the "solution space" that it represents for possible workforce performance initiatives.

+ What is the overall history of work relations within the relevant workforce segments?

+ What are the top leadership beliefs, preferences, and overall guiding philosophy with respect to the workforce?

+ What are the roles of various intermediaries such as labor unions, work guilds, and regulatory agencies?

+ What ingrained cultural factors (networks, leadership styles, relative formality/informality patterns, diversity conditions, etc.) influence how and why people become energized?

+ What is the prevailing institutional belief in the potential and character of people, how much they can be trusted on their own, and how they should treat one another?

Any time that an organization decides to embark on a new strategy or make a major change in its executional approach, there is bound to be uncertainty and the potential for wavering commitment. In such cases, everyone involved must be sufficiently on board. The pursuit of higher workforce performance implies that the enterprise has chosen to make a major strategic move and invest heavily in people. Regardless of which path is chosen, this investment must be made. It may be in dollars; it will certainly be in management time and personal leadership.

It is very important that leaders at all levels show genuine respect for the contributions of frontline employees. How leaders at various levels talk about the front line in management meetings and what examples of success they praise can make a huge difference in worker attitudes and energy levels. The focus and attention that leaders give to their people and the importance leaders attach to the contributions of frontline individuals in written and oral communications (internal and external) cannot be overestimated.

Personally modeling the behaviors expected of the front line is also an important part of the peak-performance workforce equation. The Marine drill instructors at Parris Island were unquestionably the best example of "walking the talk" and creating lasting role model impressions for their recruits. However, unless leaders up the line believe in and respect the contributions of their workers, it is unlikely that frontline supervisors will step up to the challenge. To that end, the USMC picks only their very best officers and noncommissioned officers as drill instructors and leaders at their basic training schools.

The preceding section outlines the kind of diagnostic methodology that should help most companies assess the potential value of peak workforce performance, as well as where that performance will matter most. It starts with the establishment of clear aspirations with respect to customers, shareholders, and employees. It follows with strategic analyses of where and how the enterprise intends to compete and extends those analyses to determine which segments of the workforce are most critical. When fact-based analysis creates a truly compelling case for investing in a higher-performing workforce, enterprise leadership must make the key choices that are required for any of the paths to achieve the necessary balance between performance and fulfillment.

PHASE II: MAKING THE CRITICAL CHOICES

The secret to the peak-performance workforce boils down to making the key choices explicitly and wisely. And as author Jim Collins reminds us in his speeches, it is at least as important to choose *what not to do* as it is to keep extensive *to-do* lists. Those who have succeeded in sustaining a higher-performing workforce over time have become masters of where and how to spend their time by making discrete choices with respect to four fundamental questions:

1. What tangible and intangible values will individuals in the critical segments of the workforce receive in return for their efforts? (This will often differ by segment.)

2. What balanced path or paths fit the enterprise situation and the value proposition? (Several enterprises pursue two paths simultaneously.)

3. What are the primary sources of extra energy that the enterprise can readily tap? (More than one source is needed over time.)

4. Which alignment approaches and mechanisms can produce the necessary balance between (or simultaneous improvement in) enterprise performance and worker fulfillment? (It is important to be distinctive in a few rather than to be dabbling in all.)

Shaping the Employee Value Proposition

An employee value proposition postulates why individual employees should engage themselves both rationally and emotionally in the enterprise effort. It describes clearly what an employee can expect to give and get from being a member of a particular workforce. This simple idea goes to the very heart of what creates a truly higher-performing workforce— the balancing of enterprise performance requirements with individual fulfillment needs. More specifically, it is the balancing of both performance and fulfillment at a higher level for both.

An employee value proposition parallels the widely understood and accepted idea of a customer value proposition. Any successful business can articulate succinctly how its products or services offer value to a customer. It can show that the benefits received plus the price charged add up to a good deal. Similarly, an organization seeking a peak-performance workforce should be able to succinctly describe to employees both the fulfillment offered (benefits) and the performance required (price).

Perhaps J. Willard Marriott's famous statement illustrates it best: "If you take care of my guests, I will take care of you." At KFC, the statement might be "Those who provide the Colonel's value to our customers will be warmly recognized and celebrated in ways that are both satisfying and fun." The Marines might put it this way: "Those who adhere to the Corps' fundamental values (honor, courage, and commitment) will become part of a unique family that ensures its members are always proud of who they are and what they do." These simple statements convey a deep, emotional meaning to members of the workforce in each case.

Employee value propositions, however, are seldom explicitly articulated even in peak-performance workforces. There are no big ad campaigns that make them highly visible to the public. In conducting the hundreds of interviews for this book, rarely would interviewees cite the employee value proposition where they worked. Instead, we asked them to simply describe the gives-and-gets of being a member of the workforce. It was usually a telling question. When the interviewee was clearly a higher-performing worker in a superior workforce, he or she quickly and clearly described what was expected of him or her (i.e., worker performance) as well as what was received in return (i.e., fulfillment).

Where there was no peak-performance workforce, the interviewee often struggled to give a clear answer, which was invariably prefaced with "I suppose" or "maybe" or "I guess." In still other cases, the value proposition articulated was understandable to both employer and employee, but it had no higher-performance component. For example, one woman described the "gives" of her job by saying, "I put in my forty hours and do what I'm told." As for the "gets," she replied, "My boss doesn't yell at me." All in all, she considered this to be a better value proposition than her previous job—where her boss did yell at her all the time.

An organization's employee value proposition is closely related to its potential balanced path or paths in a very complementary way. The proposition is focused on the individual and speaks directly to what he or she can expect to give and get in working for the enterprise. It describes what is offered to an employee and communicates why a person should work there versus somewhere else. Unfortunately, most companies today have embraced the need for a new employment contract (which recognizes the inevitability of unforeseen cutbacks), but appear to be giving away elements that heretofore produced workforce commitment. As Peter Cappelli explains in his *The New Deal at Work: Managing the Market-Driven Workforce:*

> *By dismantling the internal arrangements for managing employees, the new deal erodes mechanisms that bind employees to the employer. By encouraging employees to look to the market, the new deal makes it easier for them to*

leave. . . . By making employees more mobile, the new deal forces employers to pay trained workers a wage equal to their value in the market or see them walk.[1]

The balanced path is focused on the organization as a whole, speaking to "the kind of place this is" and "what it's like to work here." It describes how the organization goes about delivering on its employee value proposition(s). As illustrated throughout the book, the balanced path epitomizes an integrated organizational approach that combines alignment approaches, mechanisms, and energy sources. In defining your employee value proposition and choosing your path or paths, you are in effect defining your higher-performing workforce strategy.

Pursuing a Balanced Path or Paths

The choice of paths was not something that the companies we surveyed thought about directly—since we developed the concept during the research. Yet, the companies that had enabled a peak-performance workforce made clear choices. Sometimes the choice evolved naturally out of their history, such as Southwest Airlines' "choice" to be *the* low-cost airline, or Hambrecht & Quist's "choice" to serve the entrepreneurs of Silicon Valley. In other cases, a seminal event or difficult struggle led to or reinforced a company's choice, such as KFC's return to the Colonel in the aftermath of several mergers and the Marines' return to their warrior spirit in the aftermath of the Vietnam war. And sometimes the choice was simply that of unusual visionary leaders, such as Bernie Marcus and Arthur Blank at The Home Depot or Richard W. Vague and John C. Tolleson at First USA.

The choice of paths is clearly more judgmental than analytical. The choice requires making an initial determination of what seems to fit the circumstances and then verifying that fit with as many facts as can be obtained. The analysis described earlier certainly helps, and it may even change the early judgments. It is not wise, however, to try to be overly prescriptive. As a company's leaders work to determine which path or paths match existing conditions, they should find ways to tap into the workers' natural convictions about the appropriate path to take. A company is better served by initially choosing a path emotionally credible to many than by choosing one credible to only a few because of logical analysis.

A very important aspect of choosing paths is to consider the natural combinations that might fit your situation. For example, the Recognition and Celebration path is always best as a support path and often particularly complements the Process and Metrics path. The Mission, Values, and Pride path matches well with the Individual Achievement path. The Entrepreneurial Spirit path often works well on its own. There are no inviolate combinations, however, and many combinations can work if the performance and fulfillment circumstances call for them. It appears unwise, however, to attempt more than two paths at the same time.

Sources of Energy

Most companies leave the sources of energy to chance—and, therefore, often overlook or fail to take advantage of readily available sources. What organizations like the Marines, 3M, and Marriott have done with their history is possible for many other companies as well. Even relatively young enterprises like The Home Depot and Southwest Airlines get incredible mileage out of their seemingly short history.

Of course, you cannot create a legacy that does not exist, nor can you rely on a colorful leader like Bernie Marcus or Herb Kelleher if you do not have one. You can, however, get more serious about bringing customers and competitors to life at the workforce level. And you can build increasing levels of pride among the workers as their achievements accumulate.

What's more important, an enterprise should not rely on any single energy source. Growth inevitably runs its course, magnetic leaders fade away, competitors and customers change over time, and even rich legacies can erode. Consequently, the mere existence of a source of extra energy is not enough. Conscious, consistent, and determined efforts must be made to draw that energy into the organization to make it meaningful to the employees and to find mechanisms to both reinforce the energy and align it with the aspirations of the enterprise.

The following kinds of questions are often useful in identifying and accessing sources of extra energy for your workforce:

✦ What do workers remember best about the company's history? What stories are passed along in informal gatherings? Who and where are the heroes?

+ What are workers most proud of when they reflect upon their job and their work? How often do they achieve beyond what they themselves thought possible?

+ Where are the most respected leaders in the organization, and what differentiates them from the norm? Who and where are the role models?

+ What kinds of symbols are displayed in company facilities?

+ What kinds of awards and recognition are given to what kinds of people? How are these regarded by both the recipients and the nonrecipients?

+ How much direct contact is encouraged between customers and members of the workforce?

+ How is internal and external competitive spirit fostered throughout the workforce?

Complementary Alignment Approaches

Being distinctive with respect to a handful of alignment approaches demands choice. We all know that we cannot be all things to all people, yet many companies have overloaded their system in trying to do just that. The list of good personnel practices is virtually endless and consumes volumes. Well-meaning professionals make strong cases for everything from empowerment to diversity programs. Recruitment, training, compensation, and rapid advancement all matter—but the only thing that consistently differentiates the higher-performing workforce is choosing where to be distinctive and being disciplined about sustaining that distinctiveness over time.

The choice of which alignment approaches to emphasize starts with an assessment of your current practices in each of the several possible approaches you could pursue. Where are you doing a good job now, and where could you become truly distinctive in the eyes of the workforce? Few can match the Marines' core values, the Colonel's dozen, or SWA's discipline in turning its planes around. The mechanisms that support this kind of distinctiveness are many, and no two companies achieve distinctiveness in the same way on even a single approach. All the enterprises that we studied, however, had chosen a few alignment approaches and devised a handful of complementary mechanisms to ensure the long-term consistency of workforce behaviors and awards.

The approaches selected, of course, should complement one another and be consistent with the sources of energy that a company can access. That does not mean that each path has a prescribed set of alignment approaches, although certainly some fit better with each path (as summarized in table 2-2 in chapter 2). The purpose of the path concept is to provide a basis for both selecting and integrating the complementary alignment approaches. And where more than one path is to be pursued, it is important to choose approaches that can support both paths. It is also important to find mechanisms that can serve "double duty" in complementary approaches.

In selecting a few approaches for distinctive execution, the following questions can often be helpful:

+ What kinds of both regular and special communications are best received by your employees? What characterizes the most energizing of those communications?

+ Which formal management processes have the most influence on workforce behavior and generate the most enthusiastic workforce participation?

+ Which informal networks (e.g., communication, advice, and information) are the most effective throughout the workforce?

+ What employee programs, events, and celebrations are most highly regarded, and why?

+ To what extent are leadership opportunities cultivated broadly without being conditional upon formal position or title in the organization?

+ To what extent are members of the workforce familiar with the overall purpose of enterprise policies and programs? How enthusiastic are they about these efforts?

+ How well known are both company and individual performance achievements? Can employees differentiate the relative importance of various achievements?

Chasing a Moving Target

It would be great if an enterprise could decide on a balanced path, pick a few distinctive alignment approaches, get the right mechanisms in place, and "let 'er run." Of course, it doesn't work that way. Not only is the competitive arena for most companies one of constant change, but the relative effectiveness of both approaches and mechanisms changes over time. In addition, the achievement bars (both performance and fulfillment) are regularly and relentlessly being raised. Furthermore, workforce groups seem to be energized by different things at different points in time.

The answer to this constant turmoil remains the same, however. Keep closely to the basics, be relentlessly selective, and pursue distinctiveness at all costs. Staying in close touch with the performance realities of the marketplace and the fulfillment realities of the workforce is hard work, but it is not impossible—even in light of the constantly changing landscape. And once you have determined and mastered your pathway, it becomes much easier to keep that path clear and open than "clearing a path" was at the outset.

RECOGNIZING WHAT WILL BE DIFFERENT

Clearly, life will be different for enterprises that decide to pursue a higher-performing workforce—regardless of the path or paths chosen. The demands on leaders at all levels will be much greater, and the standards placed on frontline managers and employees will be much higher. Nor will all of the emotions generated be positive. Nevertheless, the carrot is worth the effort.

Greater Demands on Leadership

Obviously, a peak-performance workforce requires greater and different leadership throughout the organization. The change in leadership is necessary—even if the person at the top is not incredibly magnetic and distributing leadership all the way to the front line is not one of the chosen themes.

Of course, nothing affects workers more than their immediate boss. He or she is the person who most affects their life and determines their perspective on the company. If the supervisor is abusive, unhelpful, un-reliable, or simply unavailable, the workers are unlikely to "do more" unless extraordinarily self-motivated and self-enabled. Whatever the company may be doing to pursue a balanced path, develop distinctive alignment approaches, and tap unique sources of energy, it will mean little, however, to a worker with a bad boss.

Conversely, a great boss amplifies anything the organization does to develop a peak-performance workforce. Hence, having consistently bet-ter frontline managers is essential, regardless of the path followed. They are the gatekeepers, bottlenecks, and amplifiers (positive or negative) of any higher-performing workforce effort. Taking action to recognize the good bosses and to deal promptly with the bad ones sends positive sig-nals throughout the organization.

Clearly, a different emphasis and perspective is required for the lead-ership of a peak-performance workforce at all levels. The focus must go well beyond leveraging one's own time. It is more about working with and developing people than decision making and more about creating positive attitudes and energizing environments than providing better direction and broader control. Although rational leadership is part of developing a peak-performance workforce strategy, a great deal of *emo-tional leadership* is required to make it happen. Emotional leadership is personal, caring, and highly interactive. It must tap sources of emo-tional energy.

This sort of leadership was evident within all the cases. One of the better illustrations came from comments of the Marriott employees we interviewed. They often cited an obvious oxymoron—great bosses—as an important part of what enabled and motivated them to do more. They included not only their current bosses, but also a series of great bosses over the years. Marriott operates with a fairly traditional hierar-chy and regularly promotes and changes supervisors and managers. Yet the company seems to have created a critical mass of "emotionally as-tute managers" who leave a lasting and positive impression on those who work for them. One Marriott employee captured the essence of a great boss in the following comment about the general manager of the Salt Lake City Marriott:

Robert is down-to-earth; he talks to you as a person, not an employee. He's a true gentleman—he treats everyone well, not just the senior managers. He makes you want to please him and make the hotel better for him. You can't "fake" this kind of concern for people.

Marriott employees also mentioned other types of emotional leadership by managers beyond their demonstrations of genuine concern for workers. The managers tell lots of stories about customer service experiences, they personally model the right guest service and associate behaviors, and they are willing to get their hands dirty and do the work themselves when someone needs to be shown how or needs extra help.

Higher Standards for Managers and Employees

Along with a higher-performing workforce must come *higher-performing management*. Beyond making greater demands on leadership, such workforces also require differences in the way businesses are managed. Managers of higher-performing workforces face many challenges. Although similar challenges may exist in other companies, they are less critical management concerns than they are in peak-performance workforce situations.

Jan Carlzon (of Scandinavian Airlines System) popularized the notion of "moments of truth" in his book of the same title.[2] He was speaking of defining moments in customer service. The concept is equally applicable to employees. Managers of higher-performing workforces look for moments when something can be done for employees that will earn their best efforts and loyalty for years—even if it means making a decision contrary to usual business practice. As we saw in chapter 7, Sandy Olson of Marriott made such a decision years ago, when she shut down the hotel laundry for an entire day so that her staff could attend the funeral of their co-worker's mother. Thong Lee, the man whose mother had died, never forgot the gesture, which gave rise to his lifelong loyalty to Marriott. Such incidents not only create enduring dedication from the employees affected, they also create the folklore through which others learn of the company's commitment to its workforce.

Sometimes, everything a company has done to develop workforce performance becomes seriously undermined. Even within the companies with peak-performance workforces, trying events can still force leaders to make tough trade-offs. For example, at KFC, Chuck Rawley, the chief operating officer, had to describe plans to sell off several outlets and lay off managers at a two-day event focused on the theme "The RGM is No. 1." Similarly, Marriott (like most hotels) overbooks rooms based on probabilistic calculations that sometimes cause front-desk associates to turn away valued customers.

These kinds of trade-offs are not unusual. In companies without peak-performance workforces, such actions may not have much effect on the workforce—they were expecting no different or no better. In companies with higher-performing workforces, however, the impact can be very negative. Any time that the company is perceived to fall short on the promise of its balanced path, it will be held to a higher level of accountability than a regular company. When tough decisions must be made, management must make extraordinary efforts to explain and justify the decisions.

Even within well-developed higher-performing workforces, certain inevitable tensions remain as the unavoidable results of competing interests. Sometimes the tensions are between performance requirements and fulfillment needs. Such tensions are "rubs" within the organization that are generally recognized by workers and management alike. They are also issues for which there is no obvious or easy answer.

For example, at the Hill's Pet Nutrition plant workers are very committed to their team-based work system. It creates a positive work environment, provides new opportunities, and helps add variety to the production work. At the same time, many workers feel a lack of individual recognition and the effect of teammates who don't always pull their load.

Tensions such as these are classics in management literature. In higher-performing workforces, however, managers really wrestle with and agonize over these tensions much more extensively. They look for incremental improvements and try to keep a fair balance between the competing interests. In so doing, they are simply establishing essential parts of their management responsibility for maintaining a truly higher-performing workforce.

Finding and following your path(s) to a higher-performing workforce can be both fearsome and demanding. The challenge is not for every enterprise, even those that aspire to outperform the competition—provided average workforce performance does not hinder higher-enterprise performance. Moreover, a true peak-performance workforce is a moving target: each level attained also opens up the potential for reaching a higher level, and the dynamics of a competitive marketplace constantly push would-be market leaders to "better their previous best."

Even the possibility of segmenting your workforce does not make the task any less demanding. Although concentrating on certain segments reduces the scope of the effort, a rapidly changing marketplace invariably causes the enterprise to pursue different market segments, which can mean getting higher performance out of different workforce segments. This is one reason why we saw several of our case examples in pursuit of different paths at different times in their history.

Despite the changes, difficulties, and inevitable setbacks along the path, however, those who stay the course and successfully climb their particular mountain swear by the benefits of an emotionally committed, peak-performance workforce. To those tempted to undertake the challenge, therefore, we echo the words of Rita Bailey at Southwest Airlines:

Go for it—but do it your way!

✦ APPENDIX

Table A-1   PARTICIPANT COMPANIES AND ORGANIZATIONS

Participant	Description	Balanced Path(s) Pursued
Avon Products, Inc.	• Leading global beauty products company; case explored manufacturing operations in Chicago and Puerto Rico	• Process and Metrics • Mission, Values, and Pride
BMC Software	• Provider of mainframe and open-systems software products	• Entrepreneurial Spirit
CompuCom, Inc.	• Leading value-added reseller and on-site computer service provider	• Entrepreneurial Spirit
First USA Inc.	• Rapid-growing "mono-line" credit card issuer	• Individual Achievement
Hambrecht & Quist	• Innovative investment bank; key financier of entrepreneurs in Silicon Valley	• Entrepreneurial Spirit
Hill's Pet Nutrition	• Supplier of fast-growing Science Diet dog and cat food products	• Process and Metrics • Mission, Values, and Pride
The Home Depot	• World's largest home improvement retailer	• Individual Achievement • Entrepreneurial Spirit • Mission, Values, and Pride

Table A-1   PARTICIPANT COMPANIES AND ORGANIZATIONS
(*Continued*)

Participant	Description	Balanced Path(s) Pursued
i2 Technologies	• State-of-the-art provider of logistic supply chain management software	• Entrepreneurial Spirit
Johnson Controls *Automotive Systems Group*	• Number one manufacturer of auto seats and components	• Process and Metrics
KFC	• Number one fast food chicken restaurant in the world	• Process and Metrics • Reward and Celebration
LCI	• High-growth telecommunications company	• Entrepreneurial Spirit
MACtel Cellular Systems	• Start-up cellular service provider in Anchorage, Alaska	• Entrepreneurial Spirit
Marriott International	• Premier-performing hotel chain in several different lodging segments	• Mission, Values, and Pride • Process and Metrics • Reward and Celebration
McKinsey & Company, Inc.	• Leading international consulting firm serving large, multinational enterprises	• Individual Achievement • Mission, Values, and Pride
NASA *Johnson Space Center*	• Coordinating agency of all U.S. manned space flights	• Mission, Values, and Pride
Perot Systems	• Fast-growing systems/information technology consultant	• Mission, Values, and Pride • Individual Achievement

Table A-1   PARTICIPANT COMPANIES AND ORGANIZATIONS
(*Continued*)

Participant	Description	Balanced Path(s) Pursued
Sea-Land Service	• Created "piggybacking" concept of containerized shipping	• Process and Metrics • Mission, Values, and Pride
Southwest Airlines	• Number one–performing airline in the world	• Mission, Values, and Pride • Reward and Celebration • Individual Achievement
Texas Instruments *DSP Group*	• Top maker of digital signal processing (DSP) chips	• Entrepreneurial Spirit
3M *(Specialty Chemicals)*	• Leading office products and chemical producer with long history of innovation	• Mission, Values, and Pride
U.S. Marine Corps	• Highly trained and disciplined branch of armed services; unique relative to other branches of military	• Mission, Values, and Pride
Vail Resorts *Ski School*	• Largest ski resort company in North	• Entrepreneurial Spirit

Table A-2   OUTSIDE-IN CASES

Participant	Description	Balanced Path(s) Pursued
Champion, International[a]	• Leading international paper company; pioneer in self-directed work teams	• Mission, Values, and Pride
General Electric[a]	• Diversified industrial, technological, and financial leader	• Process and Metrics • Mission, Values, and Pride
Hewlett-Packard[a]	• Leading manufacturer of computer paraphernalia	• Mission, Values, and Pride • Individual Achievement
Toyota[b]	• Global automotive leader in quality and reliability	• Process and Metrics • Mission, Values, and Pride
U.S. Navy Seals[b]	• Special attack force of the U.S. Navy, specializing in covert underwater operations	• Mission, Values, and Pride

[a]Based on earlier research conducted by the author for The Wisdom of Teams: Creating the High-Performance Organization (Jon R. Katzenbach and Douglas K. Smith, Boston, Harvard Business School Press, 1993) and Real Change Leaders: How You Can Create Growth and High Performance at Your Company (Jon R. Katzenbach and the RCL Team, New York, Times Business, 1995).
[b]Based on internal unpublished McKinsey research efforts in which the author participated.

Table A-3   COMPARATIVE PERFORMANCE INDICATORS

Company	Description[a]	Evidence of Higher-Performance Workforce[b]

Avon Products, Inc.	• World's leading direct seller of beauty and related products
	
	• Markets to women in more than 130 countries through 2.6 million independent sales representatives
	
	• Company Financial Performance
	
	<table><tr><td></td><td>CAGR Sales</td><td>CAGR Pretax</td><td>ROE Five-Year Average</td></tr><tr><td>1988–1993</td><td>0.06</td><td>0.13</td><td>59.46</td></tr><tr><td>1993–1998</td><td>0.05</td><td>0.02</td><td>119.29</td></tr></table>
		• Morton Grove is lead facility on new technology products; also the Avon training center for international visitors
		
		• 1995–1997 Global Micro Merit recipient for achievement of zero microbiological rejects on production of world-leading 15,000 annual daylots.
		
		• OSHA recordable incident rate reduced 59% the past 4 years
		
		• Lost workdays cases down 56% the past 4 years
		
		• Recycling awards and accomplishments:
		   Presidential Award in 1996 for Environmental Achievement (Gold Awards in 1994–1995)
		   $400,000 savings in recycling credits and cost avoidance
		   53% of total facility waste is recycled

BMC Software	• Provider of mainframe and open-systems software applications
	
	• Company Financial Performance
	
	<table><tr><td></td><td>CAGR Sales</td><td>CAGR Pretax</td><td>ROE Five-Year Average</td></tr><tr><td>1989–1994</td><td>0.37</td><td>0.39</td><td>31.56</td></tr><tr><td>1994–1999</td><td>0.35</td><td>0.39</td><td>25.96</td></tr></table>
		• Highest employee productivity (gross profit per employee) in the industry over three-year period (1993–1995)
		   BMC: $275,000
		   Microsoft: $265,000
		   Peer average: $110,000
		
		• Market share leader in its category

[a]Financial data are from Standard and Poor's Compustat Services. Sales and pretax income are in millions of dollars. ROE is percentage (ratio).
[b]All facts and figures, if not specifically noted, are from the time period of the research (1996–1998). All financial data are from annual reports for the years indicated.

Table A-3   COMPARATIVE PERFORMANCE INDICATORS   *(Continued)*

Company	Description[a]	Evidence of Higher-Performance Workforce[b]
CompuCom, Inc.	• Number one value-added reseller and on-site computer service provider • Company Financial Performance 		*CAGR Sales*	*CAGR Pretax*	*ROE Five-Year Average* | 1988–1993	0.45	0.48	13.60 | 1993–1998	0.17	–0.49	15.28		• Best consistent profitability record among peers • Highest gross profit per sales rep CompuCom: $1,000,000 Peers: $200,000
First USA	• High-growth "monoline" credit card issuer and innovator • Division of BankOne • Company Financial Performance 		*CAGR Sales*	*CAGR Pretax*	*ROE Five-Year Average*	 1991–1996	0.36	1.36	16.02		• Grown to be the fourth largest credit card issuer in fifteen years • Record of product innovation with the development of over one thousand "affinity"-card-issuing relationships • Continued innovation through the workforce's ability to generate and rapidly yet rigorously test hundreds of new product ideas each year • Recognized in the industry for attracting a very strong management team

Hambrecht & Quist

- Independent investment bank serving the "new economy"
- Company Financial Performance

	CAGR Sales	CAGR Pretax	ROE Five-Year Average
1995–1998	0.19	−0.01	28.10

- Ranked first for number of technology IPOs from 1995 to 1997
- Ranked first in aftermarket IPO performance in 1996; second in 1997
- Professional staff productivity typically twice that of big investment banks (half the staff to do the same-sized deal)
- Professional staff turnover of 12% in 1996 and 15% in 1997 versus Wall Street benchmark of close to 20%

Hill's Pet Nutrition
Richmond plant

- Supplier of innovative, fast-growing Science Diet dog and cat food products
- Division of Colgate
  Comparative financial data not available
- Created greenfield high-commitment work system at newly built plant in Richmond, Indiana, and transferred practices to other three plants. Over a five-year period, during which the number of product items doubled and volume increased by 70%, manufacturing performance improved on multiple dimensions, e.g.:
  Productivity increased by 52%
  Through-put up 32%
  Safety incidents down 65%
  Changeover time down 72%
- Richmond plant operates on par with others in terms of cost but operates far more flexibly (greater variety of products, shorter runs, faster changeovers)

Table A-3 COMPARATIVE PERFORMANCE INDICATORS *(Continued)*

Company	Description[a]	Evidence of Higher-Performance Workforce[b]
The Home Depot	• Largest home center retailer in North America, employing over 120,000 people • Company Financial Performance 	*CAGR Sales*	*CAGR Pretax*	*ROE Five-Year Average*
1989–1994	0.36	0.36	18.76
1994–1999	0.27	0.29	16.51		• Company's growth and overall success widely attributed to the motivation, involvement, and teamwork of employees at the store level • Posted record earnings for eleventh straight year in 1996 • Ten-year average annual total return to investors (1986–1996) of 40.2% versus industry average of 8%
i2 Technologies	• State-of-the-art provider of logistics supply chain management software; recently has expanded into electronic-commerce support • Company Financial Performance 	*CAGR Sales*	*CAGR Pretax*	*ROE Five-Year Average*
1995–1998	1.41	0.87	18.09		• Stellar growth in an otherwise mature market (enterprise resource planning software) through consistent record of product innovations • Driven by a clear, compelling, and widely held goal of saving $50 billion for their customers by the year 2000 • Low turnover in key software development groups (about 2% in 1995–1996)

Johnson Controls
Automotive Systems Group

- World's largest supplier of automotive seating
- Leading worldwide market share (34% in 1996)
- Company Financial Performance

	CAGR Sales	CAGR Pretax	ROE Five-Year Average
1988–1993	0.15	0.06	10.02
1993–1998	0.15	0.20	14.07

- Employee-focused, process-based organization extending from manufacturing plants to new product development teams providing integrated seating and interior systems for auto manufacturers
- High employee involvement (e.g., problem solving, best-practice development, process improvement) has led to industry-recognized high performance:

  Shingo Prize (sponsored by National Association of Manufacturers) in 1996 for outstanding performance in quality, productivity, delivery, materials flow, inventory management, customer satisfaction and safety

  Pace Award (sponsored by Automotive News and Ernst & Young) in 1995 for industry leadership in innovation

- Just-in-time manufacturing processes have cut inventory to key customers from 30–35 to 2 days or less

KFC

- Fast-food pioneer with long history of quality food and hospitality
- Division of Tricon
- Unit of RJR Nabisco and PepsiCo during relevant period

  Comparative financial data not available as subsidiary

- Focus on employees was key to performance turnaround (around 1994, sales were flat or falling, and store margin had been dropping)

  Sales up 8% in 1995 and 7% in 1996 in flat industry

  Operating profits up 52% in 1996

  Restaurant manager turnover reduced from 27% to 17%

- Awarded Golden Chain (by *Nation's Restaurant News*) in 1996 for refocusing on customer service

Table A-3 COMPARATIVE PERFORMANCE INDICATORS *(Continued)*

Company	Description[a]	Evidence of Higher-Performance Workforce[b]
MACtel Cellular Systems	• Cellular service provider in Anchorage, Alaska • Privately held division of IAU	• Strong community orientation; intense focus on customer service • Market share leader (55%) in region of service • Lower customer churn (2%) than industry average (6%)

Marriott International *(lodging)*	• Hotel operator with over 135,000 hourly workers and over 229,000 rooms under a broad portfolio of brands (ranging from Fairfield Inns to Ritz-Carlton)
	• Company Financial Performance
	
	                                                  ROE
	        CAGR CAGR Five-Year
	        Sales Pretax Average
	1993–1998 0.01 0.18 22.45
		• Development of Pathways to Independence program to bring welfare recipients into the workforce (with 80% of graduates staying on the job for a year or more)
		• Ten percent occupancy premium over competitors, resulting from brand strength and consistently positive guest experiences
		• Cited by *Business Week* (1996) as one of the ten most family-friendly employers

NASA *Johnson Space Center*	• Coordinator of all U.S. manned space flights	• Groundbreaking, one-of-a-kind work • Significantly better success record than European or Japanese space agencies

- Recent emphasis on "more, better, faster" has resulted in both increased productivity and innovation
  - Shortened procurement times (three versus twelve months)
  - Lowering costs per event (e.g., 25% cost reduction in a shuttle mission)
  - Totally new approaches to space exploration (e.g., the smaller is better approach of the Mars *Pathfinder* spacecraft and its *Sojourner* rover)[c]

Perot Systems

- Fast-growing, entrepreneurial systems/information technology consultant
- Company Financial Performance

	CAGR Sales	CAGR Pretax	ROE Five-Year Average
1996–1998	0.29	0.38	22.91

- Heavy emphasis on values; ability to harness individuals' entrepreneurial drive
- Rapid growth in a highly competitive market; went public in February 1999

Sea-Land Service

- World's largest (by volume) container shipping company, serving 120 ports worldwide
- Turnaround of Hong Kong terminal operations through employee involvement in problem solving and operations innovation. From 1994 to 1997:
  - Overall terminal throughput increased 200%
  - Employment dropped 12%
  - Costs per container lift (basic unit of production) dropped 32%
  - Container lifts per hour rose 212%

[c]The Mars *Pathfinder* spacecraft was a project of the Jet Propulsion Laboratory, not the Johnson Space Center.

Table A-3 COMPARATIVE PERFORMANCE INDICATORS (Continued)

Company	Description[a]	Evidence of Higher-Performance Workforce[b]

Southwest Airlines	• Leading low-cost airline
	• Profitable in every year since 1973; six consecutive years of record profits through 1997
	
	• Company Financial Performance
	
	                                  ROE
	        CAGR CAGR Five-Year
	        Sales Pretax Average
	1988–1993 0.22 0.25 9.96
	1993–1998 0.13 0.22 14.73
		• Annual employee turnover of just 7%
		• 105,000 applicants for 3,000 positions in 1997
		• Best safety record in industry
		• Second lowest cost per average seat-mile in the industry
		• Serves 2,400 customers per employee, with nearest competitor at 1,200 per employee
		• Planes fly 11.5 hours per day, versus industry average of 8.6 hours

Texas Instruments
DSP Group
	• Top maker of digital signal processing chips
	
	• Company Financial Performance
	
	                                  ROE
	        CAGR CAGR Five-Year
	        Sales Pretax Average
	1988–1993 0.06 0.06 5.38
	1993–1998 0.00 −0.02 13.20
		• TI engineers championed and created the digital signal processor (DSP) market that proved to be a major growth engine for TI (and a business retained through recent divestitures)
		• Continued excellent record of new product introductions and first to market with leading-edge technology
		• Clear, growing market leadership in fast-growing DSP market
		    1994: TI 45%; nearest competitor 26%
		    1995: TI 42%; nearest competitor 27%
		• Revenue per employee 44% higher than industry peers
		• Employee productivity improved 50% in two years, while peer group improved only 15%

3M

- Leading office products and chemical producer
- Company Financial Performance

	CAGR Sales	CAGR Pretax	ROE Five-Year Average
1988–1993	0.06	0.01	20.32
1993–1998	0.01	−0.01	23.06

- Long history of successful product innovation and growth
- Cited in *Built to Last* as a visionary company
- Awarded 1995 National Medal of Technology for "nine decades of innovation"
- In 1996 new product sales rose 15%, products under four years old accounted for 29% of total sales, and sales per employee increased 10%

United States Marine Corps

- Highly trained and disciplined branch of armed services
- Intense pride and tradition generates collective energy, motivation, and discipline

Vail Resorts
Ski School

- Largest ski resort company in North America
- Comparative financial data privately held
- World's largest ski school, with about 1,400 instructors
- Guest participation (percentage taking lessons) of approximately 12%, the highest in the industry
- Highest customer satisfaction, highest number of repeat students, and largest number of personal requests for instructors of any resort in North America
- More instructors named on the list of one hundred top ski instructors than any other resort (*Skiing Magazine*)
- Turnover of just 8 to 10% per year for a seasonal job

Notes

Chapter 1

1. David Novak, former CEO of KFC, as quoted in the Louisville (Ky.) *Courier-Journal,* February 9, 1997.
2. Kevin Freiberg and Jackie Freiberg, *Nuts! Southwest Airlines' Crazy Recipe for Business and Personal Success* (Austin, Texas: Bard Press, 1996).

Chapter 2

1. Abraham H. Maslow, *Toward a Psychology of Being,* 2d ed. (Princeton, N.J.: D. Van Nostrand Company, 1968).
2. Peter M. Senge, *The Fifth Discipline* (New York: Doubleday Currency, 1990), first described the organization of the Hill's Pet Nutrition Company.

Chapter 3

1. Jon R. Katzenbach and the RCL Team, *Real Change Leaders: How You Can Create Growth and High Performance at Your Company* (New York: Times Business, Random House, 1995).
2. *United States Marine Corps,* <http://www.usmc.mil>.
3. James C. Collins and Jerry I. Porras, *Built to Last: Successful Habits of Visionary Companies* (New York: HarperBusiness, 1994).
4. "McKnight Principles," *3M Worldwide,* <http://www.3m.com/profile/looking/mcknight.html>.
5. *3M Worldwide,* <http://www.3m.com/index.html>.
6. Collins and Porras, *Built to Last.*
7. *3M Worldwide.*
8. "Who We Are," <http://www.3m.com> (June 19, 1997).
9. William Keenan, Jr., "Getting Customers into the A.C.T.," *Sales & Marketing Management* (Bill Communications, Inc.), February 1995, pp. 163–166.
10. Collins and Porras, *Built to Last,* p. 155.

11. "McKnight Principles."
12. "Who We Are."
13. De'Ann Weimer, "3M: The Head Is on the Boss," *Business Week,* March 15, 1999.

Chapter 4

1. Senge, *The Fifth Discipline.*

Chapter 5

1. "The Folks Who Brought You Apple," *Fortune,* January 12, 1981.
2. Thomas DeLong, "Hambrecht & Quist," Case 9-898-161 (Boston: Harvard Business School, 1998).

Chapter 6

1. Tom Peters, *The Circle of Innovation* (New York: Alfred A. Knopf, 1997), p. 97.
2. Collins and Porras, *Built to Last.*
3. David Maister, *Managing the Professional Service Firm* (New York: Free Press Paperbacks, Simon & Schuster, 1993).

Chapter 7

1. *Business Week,* November 1996, p. 111.
2. Ronald Henkoff, "Finding, Training, and Keeping the Best Service Workers," *Fortune,* October 3, 1994.

Chapter 8

1. Deborah Fine and Aeon, Inc., *Star Wars Chronicles* (San Francisco: Chronicle Books, 1997), p. 186.
2. Howard Gardner, *Leading Minds: An Anatomy of Leadership* (New York: Basic Books, 1995), pp. 8, 9.
3. Collins and Porras, *Built to Last.*
4. Freiberg and Freiberg, *Nuts!,* pp. 26–27.
5. Ibid., pp. 29–35.
6. Collins and Porras, p. 16.
7. Ibid.
8. *3M Today,* 13 (February 1996): 2.

Chapter 9

1. Peter Krass, *The Book of Business Wisdom* (New York: John Wiley & Sons, 1997), p. 31.
2. Peter Carbonara, "Hire for Attitude, Train for Skill," *Fast Company,* August–September 1996, p. 74.
3. Ibid., p. 27.

4. Freiberg and Freiberg, *Nuts!,* p. 85.
5. Ibid., p. 103.

Chapter 10

1. Peter Cappelli, *The New Deal at Work: Managing the Market-Driven Workforce* (Boston: Harvard Business School Press, 1999), p. 48.
2. Jan Carlzon, *Moments of Truth* (New York: HarperCollins, 1989).

Index

About the Author

JON R. KATZENBACH is the Senior Partner of Katzenbach Partners LLC, a professional firm in New York City that specializes in leadership, team, and workforce performance. For over three decades he was a principal and director with McKinsey & Company, Inc., where he served as a leader in that firm's organization and change practice. Mr. Katzenbach has written numerous articles and books on leadership and team and workforce performance, including *Teams at the Top*, *Real Change Leaders*, and the bestselling *The Wisdom of Teams*, which he coauthored with Douglas K. Smith. He and his wife, Linda, live in Hobe Sound, Florida, and East Hampton, New York.